If you want to understand India, make the world a better place, and fall in love, then this is a book for you.
James Carleton
journalist, ABC

This book reads like smooth silk. It gives a vivid account of the conditions of Tamil villagers, the status of rural women and the hurdles in the development process. It is a well-crafted book written straight from the heart of a person who loves India and has been an inalienable part of India. It should be read by Indians and non-Indians alike.
Professor T. Krishnan Nair
Chennai

A journey of love, idealism, challenges, rich with the pungent spices of India. The story of the Australian country girl who marries her Indian idealist renews your faith in humanity. It's a beautiful read that opens your mind and senses to new ideas embracing inclusion.
Susanne Gervay OAM
multi-award winning author, head of the Society of Children's Book Writers and Illustrators, co-president, Society of Women Writers NSW

Anne Benjamin's book transcends the limits of the memoir to become a definitive insight on the intersections of two cultures, Australian and Indian, while retaining the warmth and intimacy of the personal narrative.
Dr Meenakshi Bharat
president, International Federation of Modern Languages and Literatures, executive member, Indian Association for the Study of Australia

Saffron and Silk

An Australian in India

ANNE BENJAMIN

David Lovell Publishing
Melbourne Australia

Published in 2016 by

David Lovell Publishing
PO Box 44, Kew East
Victoria 3102 Australia
tel/fax +61 3 9859 0000
publisher@davidlovellpublishing.com

© Copyright 2016 Anne Benjamin
This work is copyright. Apart from any fair dealing for the purposes of private study, research, criticism or review, as permitted under the Copyright Act, no part may be reproduced by any process without written permission. Inquiries should be addressed to the publisher.

Front cover: fabric image by Krishna Somya, courtesy iStock
Design by David Lovell Publishing
Typeset in 12/16 Baskerville
This edition printed through Ingram Spark

National Library of Australia Cataloguing-in-Publication data
Benjamin, Anne, 1946- author.
Saffron and silk : an Australian in India / Anne Benjamin.
   ISBN: 9781863551571 (paperback)
  Benjamin, Anne, 1946- . Australians – India – Biography.
  Women – Australia – Biography.
  Foreign spouses – India – Biography.
  Intercountry marriage.
  India – Social life and customs.
  India – Politics and government.
954.035

Contents

The stranger	1
Indian bride	12
Settling in	20
All in a day's work	32
Finding my place	46
Getting around	57
Days of fire	67
Taking sides with the poor	82
In the mango field	95
Whorls of belief	111
Linking my worlds	123
Not like this	131
Meetings	139
Motherhood	150
View from the balcony	164
A skein of silk	175
Family matters	185
Returning	196
India again	208
The map	223

Acknowledgements

No book is created in isolation. This book began with a WEA writing course offered by Pearlie McNeill in 2006. Pearlie set an assignment that triggered an avalanche of memories. My family gave me reason to turn those memories into something larger than one short story and it was their belief in me that kept me going. I appreciate their willingness to act as sounding-boards on too many occasions to be counted. As always, my sister in writing, Carmel Summers, encouraged and responded to my early effort. My friend, Dr Rugmini Venkatraman, not only advised me on language, but in our early-morning walks briefs me on culture, history and customs. I owe an enormous debt to Mr S. Muthiah, well-known and highly-respected in Chennai, who generously offered to proof the first edition of the book and commented thoroughly on the details. A true scholar and gentleman. While I have relished all this advice, any errors of fact or insensitivity of opinion are mine and mine alone. Finally, I am indebted to David Lovell, friend and publisher, who in enthusiastically taking on this project gave me a birthday present I had only dreamed of.

To Susai
Mariam, Shanthi and Mathew

The stranger

'BUT HE'S A STRANGER', my mother lamented when I announced my intention to marry. I suspect that this might be the cry of every mother when her daughter announces her intentions to marry anyone but the boy-next-door.

In this case, Mum had a point. Neither she nor Dad had met the man in question. In fact, he had never set foot in Australia.

Three months later, I stood with my new husband in the light of early evening beneath an arch in the gardens of the Hotel Ashoka in the South Indian city of Chennai as we welcomed guests to our wedding reception. It was, in fact, one of four receptions, but then when you marry an Indian, especially the one I had married, you don't do things by halves. He (my husband of three weeks) stood beside me, tall and devastatingly handsome, with his thick black hair and full jet beard. He was wearing a long cream silk shirt – a *jibba* – that reached mid-thigh over a cream silk cloth (called a *vaishti*) that was wound around his waist and hung down to the leather sandals – or *chappals* – on his feet. I too, wore cream silk, a sari, and like his clothing it was embroidered with gold. Around our necks, we wore huge floral garlands like pink and red-petalled elephant trunks. The fragrant and heavy rose and jasmine weighed heavily and damp against the beautiful cream silk of my wedding sari. My hair, unmistakably ginger, was pulled back into a bun from which curls escaped in the humid evening air. A large red dot had been placed on my forehead. My eyes were edged with black kohl – the well-intentioned efforts of a young woman acquaintance to turn me into a real Indian bride – that, to me, seemed odd on my pale skin and left me looking somewhat startled. Which indeed, in many ways, I was.

We stood for some hours, greeting over three hundred people. Women in vibrant silk saris of peacock blue, blood red and bottle green, heavily decorated with jewellery glinting from their necks, ears and wrists. They posed for photographs with their menfolk and children and then passed into the enclosed garden where tables had been set for a banquet. Live music played and lights in the trees and shrubs added to the air of festivity. Guests brought gifts. Some honoured us by wrapping a ceremonial silk shawl around our shoulders. The local archbishop blessed us on his way to a table near the stage where Indian classical dancers were performing. My husband greeted each guest by name and introduced me. I smiled and nodded, acknowledging them with my hands pressed together before me, as if in prayer, and inclining my head, *Vanakam*. If someone had asked me the names of those I had greeted, I would have struggled to name just one of them.

All this happened in May 1984. My husband, whom for simplicity's sake I'll call 'Benjamin', had lived his life in the south Indian state of Tamil Nadu although his family came from the state of Kerala on the western coast of South India. I had lived my life in the Hunter region of New South Wales and later in Sydney. We had been married in Sydney in late April. The wedding reception in Chennai (then still known as Madras) was the most formal of three celebrations that we enjoyed in India.

After the initial shock, my mother had shown her characteristic resilience. She appeared to accept the idea that her fifth child and middle daughter was forsaking her single status, her country and her academic position to marry and live in India all in one move. The closest my family had been to India was occasionally to buy one of those small cardboard tubes of pre-mixed 'Madras curry' powder used mostly to spice up egg sandwiches or sausages. I was soon to learn that no true Madrasi would ever dream of using anything so bland. This inconsequential link with India was about to be taken over by a re-orientation of my life.

My parents had married in 1934 and made their home in Singleton in the Hunter Valley. By the time I was born, we lived in a large, ever-expanding house on the banks of the Hunter and adjacent to Dad's garage and produce business. One of eight children, I grew up in the predictable and secure fifties and early sixties. My father was a public and generous player in town life, developing the local golf course, serving on the hospital board and as deputy mayor, as well as being active in supporting the local parish and convent. The floods of February 1955 devastated Dad's business and we moved down the valley to East Maitland where Dad began from scratch to develop a new business in real estate as well as wholesale produce.

My family should have known I might look further afield when choosing a husband, because after completing my schooling as a boarder back at the Catholic girls school in Singleton, I had joined a religious order in another part of the state with the intention of becoming a foreign missionary. I gave it my all, but after six years, and still only twenty-two, decided my calling lay elsewhere. India was certainly not on my mind, although, after gaining my teaching qualifications while completing a degree at the University of Newcastle, I did study Indian history in some depth. It was China that captured my attention at that stage. I taught a little, and then took off overseas for three years to the University of Notre Dame in Indiana, where I learnt a little about American football, discovered a lot about life and finished my doctoral studies in religious education. By 1983, I had been teaching for some years in Sydney at tertiary colleges that have now been incorporated into Australian Catholic University.

SAFFRON AND SILK

In 1983, I made two overseas trips and was planning a third. The first was to attend an education conference in Edmonton, Canada, where I presented a paper on curriculum publications that I'd authored. The second was to work for a short period with educators in Papua New Guinea. The planned trip was to China – an interest still alive from my student days. Benjamin also was registered for the conference in Edmonton. The day before he was to leave India, he had been out with friends at the American Consultate and overnight had become very ill. He had almost decided to cancel his flight. Providentially, as he describes it, he improved enough to fly. During one of the conference sessions, he raised his hand.

When he stood up to speak in that crowded auditorium, I sat up and listened. I can't remember the exact words he used. His interjection wasn't a question. More like a grenade. His voice rang out to challenge Euro-American assumptions in the conference discussion: 'There's another world, another perspective.' He knew how to capture authority in his tone and drama in a flourish of his arms. I was to watch him use this kind of intervention again later. But here, in that Canadian summer of 1983 on the university campus in Edmonton, I was seeing and hearing him for the first time. I approached him afterwards, because I too wanted justice for those who would never be powerbrokers.

Close up, he was handsome in a wild kind of way, long thick black beard matched by shoulder-length hair. He wore a forest green short caftan made from homespun cotton and the rich colour of his shirt set off the black of his hair. He was about my age, I guessed, probably somewhere in his mid-thirties, and he stood tall above me.

The conference participants divided into a majority – ruling – caucus of greying middle-aged middle-American women and a younger polyglot multi-hued mob of individuals from everywhere else. I became part of a small group from the polyglots that included another Australian, Filipino women, a Malaysian, a young Canadian couple, a man from Papua New Guinea, and, larger than life, the bottle-green Grenade who was from South India. Most of us in the group were from universities or schools – Mark from Papua New Guinea was later to become Vice-Chancellor of one of his country's universities. Unlike most of us, Benjamin offered non-formal education to young village people through an organisation which he had founded and directed.

The warmth of those few days in Edmonton drew people outdoors and me out of my self. Thin young men bared daisy-white chests in frenzied games with frisbees. Their skin marked them as locals who had peeled off the layers of protection needed for their long winters. Those of us more used to sunshine simply luxuriated in its gentleness. The evenings were still and balmy. One night, in a noisy barn, I found myself flapping my wings and shaking my tush in the 'chicken dance'. My partner, in a manner of speaking, was the handsome Benjamin. We entered the melee on the floor together but he danced as much with himself as with me. The music spun faster and faster. His movements totally ignored the norms, invading space in all directions. His arms and legs became more erratic, until the strings of his puppet-master snapped. We gave up. The dance, and the moment, was over. Out of breath and out of the constraints of familiar expectations, I allowed myself a little private imagining: had he and I (in this ungainly crazy moment) just discovered 'our' song?

Rather, would we even *have* a song? On the long flight back home, I permitted myself to wonder. Was this stranger the man I hadn't even known I was looking for? After all, in my mid-thirties, I was almost (but only almost) accustomed to being single. I found myself talking about him with people who were safely removed from my normal circle. I still had plans to travel to China over the coming Christmas, but even before I had flipped the calendar to December – surprising myself and without any explanation to my family – I was on my way to India to find answers to my wonderings.

I had prepared with excitement and in the way of an academic for my first visit to India by reading – history, travel and Salman

Rushdie. As I reached Singapore, I began to sense the difference between what I had known and what lay ahead and it was sensual and very unacademic. A wraith of humidity entwined itself around me as soon as I left the airport. The afternoon torrential downpours brought only temporary relief. In the seat beside me on the Air India flight into Chennai was an elderly white-haired British lady, on a pilgrimage to the western city of Puttaparthi where an Indian teacher and holy man, Sathya Sai Baba, had made his ashram. Her devotion was enthusiastic and child-like, as she showed me pictures that reminded me of the holy cards of angels and saints from my childhood. Hers showed a man with a fuzzy halo of dark hair, with a long orange shirt stretched across his chubby torso. More than this, it was the tiny plastic containers of lime pickle served by the airline which triggered for me the exotic reality of my journey.

Arriving near midnight, I entered the jostling chaos which is Chennai airport – families greeting each other with strident exhuberance, taxi drivers touting for fares, insistent luggage bearers, angry-sounding officials. I did not want to miss one detail of this aural and visual cacophony, and already my senses were overcharged. Benjamin was the only person I knew in India and he met me with a friend who owned a car. It was late November and the monsoon season was in full force. The short journey from the airport into the suburbs was fuzzy with mystery. As we drove, the rain streamed down around us obliterating everything else, so that my early impression of India was of water, mist and the hypnotic pendulum of rubber wipers.

Early the next morning, Benjamin took me to a rural area about an hour's drive from the city. We stopped at a camp, a few kilometres by dirt road from the nearest village. I saw young women and men talking in groups around two small thatched mud huts and a large meeting room whose walls and roof were made from woven coconut leaves.

My visit to this remote place was to be no romantic pastoral courtship. I had known that in advance, fortunately, and had willingly agreed to join him for the conclusion of a two-week training program that he had been conducting for young folk from the villages. So, for three days, I sat cross-legged on the sandy floor, while the palm-leaf shed was awash with idealism – and information – about environment, social justice, community organisation and development. Despite recurring pins and needles, I was entranced watching these young villagers debate with such vigour and conviction. They spoke predominantly in Tamil, an ancient language with no roots in any of the Anglo-Saxon or Romance languages with which I was in any way familiar.

I grasped the occasional English words that were thrown into the swirling tides of discussion, heaving myself up for respite from the sleep which kept pounding on my head and eyelids. As for Benjamin, he followed his voice into every space. His height and bearing commanded attention, as did his handsomeness and his ability to release smiles, laughter and nodding heads from his listeners. I sensed that it was the wave of his words that surged and withdrew and roared with the constancy of the sea that would become my ambience if I ever were to link myself with him.

Before breakfast each day we all spent time clearing rocks from the site and planting small trees, carrying water in buckets from the lake across the road. Our simple vegetarian food was cooked in large aluminium vessels over outdoor fires by lean dark men dressed in cotton shirts and *lungis*, wrap-around sarongs which they doubled up when they squatted over their pots. We ate our rice, *sambar* (lentil curry) and vegetable with our right hand (as is the custom) sitting cross-legged in the open with the food served on banana leaves placed directly on the ground. At night, I took a candle and went to sleep with the other women in one of the mud huts. The goats sheltered there during the day and the rain came through the thatched roof. It was best to forget the goat droppings that had been visible before darkness fell. The women and I danced a prone ballet all night, rolling around on the clay floor, as we tried to dodge the dripping water and fit our hips into the ruts in the hard ground that the checked homespun cotton sheets on which we slept failed to soften. There were no toilets or bathing facilities so I did as rural women do and went out to the fields in the translucent ultramarine of pre-dawn to do my business. In the morning, my face was spotty with mosquito bites.

When I left India after two months, I had seen enough. I had an armoury of reasons why I should not pursue my interest in this man any further: highly educated certainly, but he was hardly what my parents would call 'secure'. He was passionate, more like fierce, in his work for social justice in his country, with a radical anger not far beneath the surface of his energy and charm. He was so absorbed in his work that he lacked any sense of time, on one occasion returning on his 'Bullet' motor bike to where he had left me in the city only when it was dark, two hours after the agreed time. He spoke with admiration of my handwriting more than of my person, and of my willingness to attend the training camp more than of my study, experience and whatever other qualities I had. He was neither patient nor predictable. He was neither romantic nor intuitive. And he was as extraverted as I was introverted. A few months later, Benjamin came to Australia, and as we stepped out together once again on the floor, we made a stunning bridal couple.

Benjamin had arrived two weeks before the wedding, and family and friends had taken him into the fold. How could they not? He was handsome and charming – I am, of course, totally objective about this. I was more amazed than offended when one 'educated' Australian blurted about my intended, 'But is he clean, Anne?' Others had suggested the relationship would not last and counselled me not to sell my house and to keep my options open. Mum kept to herself unsettling fears about Dad. As I made plans for the wedding and departure overseas, she struggled to cope with the dementia which was beginning to erode Dad's normal cheerfulness.

Many people made our wedding memorable. I had chosen the chapel of the Teachers' College where I taught for the ceremony. Benjamin had invited to the wedding Sydney-based relatives of some of his friends in Chennai and one of these, Shantha Alexander, 'tied' my sari for me – a cream and gold silk sari which Benjamin had brought with him just a few weeks before the wedding. I wore yellow roses in my hair to match the ones I carried. He wore the same cream silk *vaishti* and *jibba* he was to wear for the Chennai reception. My sister Maureen, with flowers in her dark hair, looked stunning in a dark green sari as my bridesmaid. The groomsman was a friend from Sri Lanka; my niece and the daughter of another of Benjamin's connections were flowergirls. My sister Margaret and some friends provided music. A bishop and five priests presided.

Benjamin and I walked together up the aisle – asking my father to 'give me away' made little sense to me. We welcomed our guests, made our vows and, nuptial Mass concluded, in a gesture towards Hindu marriage ceremony, walked hand-in-hand four times around the altar on which fire – in this case, candles – burned. We symbolically touched a stone to represent the difficulties we would overcome together and recited a mantra that had been sent to us as a blessing by a Hindu friend. Not that Benjamin was Hindu. His family was as Catholic as my own, but his friend had sent the blessing at the last minute and our chief celebrant kindly accommodated our request to include it. Friends and family generously helped cater for the occasion, one friend making a mountain of choux pastry as the wedding cake. The gardens of the college at Castle Hill shone their autumn best.

We then spent a few days at Port Stephens, catching fish that were too small to eat, and, later, less than a week after the wedding, I left my small house with its leafy wooded garden in the northern suburbs of Sydney to its new owners and I was flying to Singapore en route to Chennai.

When Benjamin and I had discussed marriage, he had made it clear that he wanted to continue his work in India. I had just completed a large curriculum project and, apart from my ongoing teaching, had no pending commitments that would hold me in Australia. So, it made sense that, after marriage, we would live in India. So now I was returning with my husband to *his* country. For the occasion, I had decided to wear a simple cotton sari with reddish floral sprigs on a light ground. In other respects the flight from Singapore into Chennai had been similar to my earlier one the year before: check-in counters where passengers lined up with all sorts of massive cartons, mostly holding enormous televisions bought at Singapore prices at a time when India had exorbitant custom duties. Many of the box-burdened passengers were scruffy villagers wearing the checked cotton sarong scrunched around their waists known as *lungi*, or the white version of the wrap-around, the *vaishti*. They had been paid by someone with money to cart the stuff back and to avoid the duty. As the plane eased down before landing at Chennai, chaos broke out as these villagers began standing up to gather their gear and flustered stewards and stewardesses pleaded with them to stay seated.

With his confident bearing, local know-how and some good-humoured bantering, Benjamin eased our passage through the she-mozzle of customs and immigration. He had also alerted a good friend of his who was a high-ranking customs official in what is known as the Indian Revenue Service (IRS) that we would be arriving. We emerged without complications.

As we left, one of the officials in white trousers and epauletted white shirt handling our documents was a grey-haired man, well into his fifties. He was a traditional Hindu Tamil, gold rings on his fingers and ash on his forehead.

'You are wearing a sari, Madam?' There was no need to answer. He looked me up and down. 'You wear the sari well. Very nice.' He smiled. I smiled back. There was not much else to do.

'And you are going to live in Chennai? Very good. Very good.' He was clearly touched by my decision to marry and live in India. He looked directly at me with something that was possibly admiration, nodding his head from side to side in the Tamil way which can mean, 'Yes', 'No', 'Maybe', 'Oh' or 'Really!'

The Stranger

'My name is Narayanswamy.' He pointed to the badge on his shirt. 'I will be your father in India. I will look after you.' He smiled broadly and nodded his head vigorously. 'I am your father. If you need anything, any time, I will help you.' His possessiveness was both good natured and confusing. 'Do you need any money?'

'No, No. Thank you. Thank you.' Hands up emphasising. '*Vanakam*.' My sandalled feet had not yet hit the Chennai dust and I had acquired another father as well as a father-in-law.

Benjamin shepherded me out towards the crowds milling at the terminal entrance. Family were there to meet us. His brother and his sisters honoured us by placing garlands made from shaved sandalwood around our necks, a fragrant and gracious welcome. Then we were driven to the north side of the city, reaching his father's home around two in the morning. There, my father-in-law and his wife, Benjamin's step-mother, were waiting to receive us. We sat in the front room while we were served with cake, which we first shared, putting a piece in each other's mouth, ritualising a blessing for a sweet life ahead.

Indian bride

BENJAMIN HAD ARRANGED for the reception at the Ashoka Hotel to take place a few weeks after our arrival. In some ways, I was a stranger to my own wedding celebrations in Chennai, just as he had been at the Sydney events. I am sure many of his friends were curious to see the 'foreigner' whom he had married. I was a little anxious about measuring up. My personal preparations for the reception began in the office where Benjamin worked. I was given a makeover by Sujatha, the young accountant. Enthusiastically, she tried to convert my Anglo-Irish pallor into traditional Indian beauty, rather challenging given my complexion and short red curly hair. Even though it was with misgiving, I let her do it.

It was not a large wedding reception by Indian standards, but it accentuated the simplicity of our Sydney event. How cheated my husband must have felt at our relaxed gathering of eighty or so family and friends. In Sydney, the guests were all close, intimates. In Chennai, they included family and friends, and many work colleagues: village workers, our own office staff and government officials. I felt warmth and kindness from those who came to share in our celebration. Yet, in truth, it was an event in which I was largely a passive observer rather than an active participant. It signalled some of the surrender of control that I would have to make, at least initially, in my move from my own to my husband's environment.

The other two Indian receptions took place out in the country. We had hired a car and had driven north to Benjamin's home village, Kannigairpair. The car slowed as we approached a small village called Palavakkam, and at a rickety corner tea shop, where workers paused, leaning back against the counter to sip their tea, we turned right off the main road. The car continued on past paddy fields until we came to a large flat lake on our left. Across the road facing the lake was about an acre of land that Benjamin had named *Cheyalnagar*, or 'Action Place'. This was where I had spent time on my first visit a few months previously. Benjamin had developed it as a base for leadership training programs for young women and men from the local villages and also to model what reforestation could achieve. On the bare land he had built two small red clay huts thatched with palm fronds and a larger shed built from casuarina poles and thatched walls and roof.

The reception at Cheyalnagar was thoroughly enjoyable with about fifty young men in creased shirts with rolled-up sleeves, slacks and leather *chappals* on their feet, and a few young women in simple cotton saris. We sat in a circle on mats spread on the hardened clay and some of the girls served us tea in small steel cups. Six wiry men in the cotton *lungis* performed a traditional dance with long sticks that was a bit like a battle drama. The local leader, a serious dark young man called Durairaj, who was coordinator of the rural development program, spoke some nice words in Tamil and presented us with a large stainless steel water pot. I found the steel vessel practical and attractive.

That evening, there was another reception back in Kannigaipair. It was an event for the whole community, involving a meal for about three thousand people, with free movies screened in the outdoors. In the course of the evening, lit by portable fluorescent tube lights, which seem to be a feature of large Indian outdoor functions, there were speeches delivered from high up on a tented podium. The speakers were the District Head of Adult Education, Benjamin and others, including local elders and Benjamin's former teachers. In preparation for this event, I had been instructed to keep out of sight and so had relaxed during the day with a book on a string cot or stretcher in the shade of the small coconut grove on the family's two-acre holdings. Villagers lined up in shifts throughout the evening to take their place sitting cross-legged on the ground for the wedding feast, served on banana leaves. I was largely irrelevant to the event. So, having appeared on the podium for the speeches and been duly scrutinised by the villagers curious to see the outsider whom the Doctor's son had married, the bride left the reception and went to bed – alone. It was two in the morning and the line of villagers was still waiting to be fed.

I lived in India for a little over three years. During this time, Benjamin and I began our married life and had our first child. I worked with him in a non-government organisation committed to development of the poor and disadvantaged. Through that work, I was privileged to be immersed in depths of India way beyond the experiences of the usual tourist or expatriate living abroad. My contact with other foreigners was slight and in the dealings I did have with the foreign community I felt peripheral. We lived within the local Indian community and the fellowship of those who work for the well-being of those who are most disadvantaged. At times, along the journey, I wondered how we would survive together, but then, I imagine, I was not alone in that.

I began these stories to try to make sense for myself of the rich Indian experience which has been mine since 1984. I needed to understand if for no other reason, than to understand the man who is my husband, because while he is now an Australian citizen, intensely involved in the life of this country, he has never – and will never – let go of his Indian identity. Some of my stories tell of oppression, violence and poverty. I do not apologise for that, although I am sensitive about

Indian bride

narrating such things about a country to which I came as a guest. I include them because they are part of my life that is now inextricably linked with India. There are also stories of beauty and fun and goodness. Both elements are part of the whole story. As I have attempted to make sense of my experiences, I have become more entwined with this country of my husband, family, friends and passion.

Whenever anyone visits or settles in another country and culture, one brings the limitations of one's own perspective and history. In my case, I missed large parts of the conversations going on around me because I was not fluent in Tamil. Especially in the early days, because I was not cued in to the Indian variant of English, and because the locals were not tuned-in to the Aussie variant of English, I failed to communicate readily. These are the superficial obstacles shaping my perspective. Far more profound and complex are the cultural intricacies. Living within the local community, I developed some understandings and considerable comfort and familiarity. I would never profess, however, to have more than a stranger's perspective on that enormously complex world which is India, or even on that part of South India in which I lived. In this I understand one of India's founding fathers, Jawaharlal Nehru, when he warned, 'To endeavour to understand and describe India today would be the task of a brave man – to say anything about tomorrow's India would verge on rashness.'[1] Always, I am looking and listening through a window which is only ever partially open to me.

I come to this task with respect for the complexity and richness of India; admiration for the determined women and men, many of them Benjamin's colleagues, who have shown their commitment to justice and development over decades; and seeking a little more understanding of my husband, whose vision is generous, who embodies renewable energy in his passions, and who constantly challenged and challenges my home-town worldview. I hope to communicate my

---

[1] Jawajarlal Nehru, quoted in Gupte (1985), *Vengeance: India after the Assassination of Indira Gandhi*, New York, W. W. Norton & Co., p. 40.

experience in a way that contributes something towards greater understanding of India and its people.

The state of Tamil Nadu, of which Chennai is the capital, boasts a civilisation dating back more than 2500 years and was home to some of the great classical Tamil kingdoms. The Tamil people proudly promote their language as one of the oldest surviving classical languages with extant literature said to date from between 600 BCE and 300 BCE.[2] After the East India Company established a settlement in 1639 in what was to become modern Chennai, the company manipulated the rivalries between local rulers to expand its own sphere of influence. Early in the nineteenth century, most of southern India was consolidated by the East India Company into the Madras Presidency. With Indian Independence in 1947, the Madras Presidency became Madras State. The state later split along linguistic lines and some areas became part of Andhra Pradesh to the north, Karnataka and Kerala to the west. In 1968, Madras State was renamed Tamil Nadu, 'land of Tamil'. In 1984, Chennai, still known as Madras, was a city of around four million; by 2012, there were more than 6.4 million people in a state population of over 72 million.

Now, here I was, in 1984, a foreign Indian wife about to make her home in this ancient country. Almost immediately after our return from Sydney, we left for a few days away in the southern Tamil Nadu city of Tiruchirappalli, otherwise known as Trichy. We caught the overnight train from Chennai and arrived in the large town early the next day. Benjamin had work needing his attention. I was keen to see as much of India as I could while it gave him the excuse to introduce his bride to some of his colleagues.

The marketplace was busy and colourful, but dry and dusty. Car, lorries, bullock carts, buses and bicycles all surged through the bazaars. Roadways wandered without apparent purpose, detouring

---

[2] I will use the terms 'Common Era', or CE, for the time after Christ (otherwise, *Anno Domini* – AD), and 'Before the Common Era', or BCE, for the period Before Christ (BC).

Indian bride

around buildings and landforms. Outside one of the shops, a large vessel of water was available for drinking with a common cup provided. I watched Benjamin scoop a cup of water and pour it into his mouth, the cup never touching his lips. When I tried, I ended up with water all down my chin and chest. This very Indian skill continues to elude me. Trichy, which is on the Cauvery River, is dominated by a massive rock jutting out over the old city. The city dates back to the times of the classical Tamil kingdoms and it is easy to see how the great protuberance of the rock formed a natural citadel. On the dome of the rock sits the Rock Fort and Rock Fort Temple. In between visits to organisations, we met with families who were friends of Benjamin. I enjoyed their kindliness but still was feeling my way. Before catching the train back to Chennai, we stopped briefly at St Joseph's, a Jesuit tertiary college established in 1844. There, over the refinements of tea, an elderly Belgian Jesuit, noting the obvious, that I was not the more-usual twenty-something bride, impudently asked me my age.

'Old enough to have learnt a little', I replied, surprised by the words that fell out of my mouth, 'and young enough to know I have much to learn.' I decided I could use this answer for many more years.

Locals laughingly describe Chennai as having three seasons: hot, hotter and hottest. They are not joking. Arriving back in Chennai in May, I was in time to experience the beginning of the hottest season.

A few weeks later, I tried one Sunday afternoon to begin to describe for my family and friends back in Australia what had been my experience so far: beginning with the sights, the sounds and the routines of life in Chennai. I quickly lost myself in the street smells of incense and freshly-ground coffee; I became entangled in the density of social-religious-political relationships; and I grew confused by all the colours of silk and the cacophony of sound. On that first attempt, I gave up.

India overwhelmed me. Her colours are the stuff of fantasy,

shining in the fabrics and costumes of women, even the poorest. Wild lavish purples and reds and oranges swirl together on one sari, with emeralds and magical midnight blues. India, now as then, bombards my eyes and ears; she gets up my nostrils and under my fingernails and adds her special *masala* – spice mixture – to my taste buds. I become mindful of my skin in a new way: its sweatiness, saltiness, clothes clinging, dust between my toes in my sandals. Back in 1984, I began to understand for the first time the gospel story about washing feet. I craved a cool drink to wash away the dryness and discovered, instead, the hospitality of sweet, strong, scalding tea. I learnt that soda water with lime is a drink made in heaven.

Once we were travelling to visit a village. It was one of those days when my skin yearned for moisture. We stopped by a well and I scooped cool water over my face. The memory of that sensation is still with me. So too the luxury of scooping cup after cup of cold water from a bucket and pouring it over my head and body.

When I mentioned to friends in Australia the power of the smells I had found in India, their smile chided me that, of course, there would be smells: what did I expect of such a thronged place? How could I share with them the layers of my experience? I recall mornings when I travelled in the city. We would cross over the notoriously stinking Buckingham Canal as we made our way in and out of curved streets and main roads. The impression of my morning ride, once the pungent canal was behind us, was of the homely aroma of scalding milk and of coffee from the many roadside stalls; I recall the wisps of sweetly-fragranced jasmine trailing us as we passed the women flower sellers sitting close on the roadway and the elegantly-clad women wearing the white flowers in their freshly-groomed plaits; the ever-present background of sandalwood incense, burning in small shrines, in shop fronts, and before the icon (of whichever saint of whichever faith) that the autorickshaw driver had chosen for his own.

It was the sounds, though, more than the smells, which assaulted me at first in India. I must have carried some subconscious romanticised image of a country totally immersed in the spiritual, like one never-ending Quakers' meeting. In reality, India is cacophonous and frenetic, and its spirituality, like any enduring spirituality, is embedded in the minutiae of everyday life. On many occasions in the first months, my companions appeared to speak to each other in a language which I could not recognise. I would then realise, with a shock, that they had in fact slipped into English – an English as incomprehensible to me as their Tamil, and as incomprehensible, I discovered, as my Australian accent was to them. Over the weeks, I puzzled about the angry sounds from telephone conversations. Could they all be arguing all the time? Tamil, I discovered, is a language with many hard sounds, and the guttural explosions were compounded by a delinquent and contrary telephone system.

Settling in

OUR FIRST HOME was a room above the office where Benjamin worked. With postgraduate qualifications from the highly-regarded Madras School of Social Work, Benjamin had worked in organisations dedicated to social justice and development. In 1974, he had established an organisation and had devoted himself to that. Since 1977, the organisation had been known as the Centre for Human Development and Social Change, referred to in shorthand as CHDSC or simply, 'the Centre'.

The Centre was housed in a pleasant residential suburb called Shastri Nagar near Adyar on the south side of Chennai. The ocean was a few kilometres away. Many of the neighbours were also friends of my husband's. A few doors up was our surrogate mother and her family, Dr Elsa Benjamin, always welcoming. Next to the devout Christian Elsa lived a handsome young Muslim couple, Tanveer and Tahzeen. In time, we celebrated with them the births and then the growing energy of their two young boys. A little further down and across the street were the Johnsons, whose relatives had helped pin my wedding sari for our Sydney wedding, and who were to become the kind of friends where you feel part of the family. A few houses on from them lived artist Gowri Nayak and her elderly father. With such friends in the vicinity of the first office, where Benjamin and I could

Settling in

enjoy good company and conversation over sweet *chai*, I began to feel less a stranger.

The finest feature of my new home was the flat roof, and the crowning glory of the roof was the bathroom – a separate structure on the far side of the roof. Access during the wet season was, well, wet. The rest of the time (which was most of the time), this was a spacious haven for the wonderful revival offered by a cold bath using bucket and dipper. We both have fond memories of that bathroom.

In the weeks that followed, we enjoyed great hospitality, not just in Chennai, but in other cities and villages we visited where Benjamin had friends and professional colleagues. I watched and assessed what was acceptable and what was not. Invariably accompanied by insistent hospitality, this round of visits largely deferred us from confronting the reality of my total ignorance about India, let alone South Indian food and how we would address this problem.

The kitchen in the office was a miserable place. Our first experience of a cook was a fierce dark woman called Kasiamma, from the nearby slum. I refused to unpack any kitchen goods for this kitchen in protest over its darkness and dirtiness. My goal became to bring a little more light and a little less grime into that dim place. After an initial burst of cleaning frenzy, I acknowledged the futility and thereafter did as little as possible there, reheating food, boiling water and frying eggs occasionally. I hated it intensely. We ate our meals at the table which during the day served as a meeting place for the Centre.

Kasiamma fitted well into it. Short, sharp and tough, she came twice a day and cooked some basic lentils and rice which we re-heated in the evening. Apart from suggesting the occasional purchase of fish, I made no decisions about meals and enjoyed them not one bit. Even tea we sent out for, more often than not, as we had to use our day's supply of milk quickly before it curdled. A real Indian wife would have used the morning's boiled milk to make curd or yoghurt. Fortunately, we enjoyed many people's hospitality during those first months. And when we received invitations to weddings, we looked forward with basic – I mean, *basic* – anticipation to the prospect of a good meal.

Not long after my arrival, Kasiamma invited me to her home. On the agreed afternoon, I wandered down 4th Cross Street and made my way past clay-and-thatch dwellings to the row where she lived. I walked past a large open well, the drinking supply for the colony. Its surface was green with scum. Kasiamma's place was a single room made from the same rough red bricks I had seen from the street. She opened the wooden door and, ducking my head, I entered into dimness. The only light came from the small doorway we had entered and gradually I could make out that the room was about two by three metres. It was bare except for a rolled-up mat and a few items in one corner. A neighbour carried in a chair and Kasiamma motioned me to sit, *Utkaar*. It was not the time to be precious about being the only person sitting down while your hostess and her neighbours looked on, and we made reasonably futile, but mutually well-intentioned, attempts to mime a conversation. I was intensely conscious of my mother and her unfailing graciousness. Kasiamma brought me a cup of water. I thought of the well I had passed. I thought of some of the more extreme phobias of people I knew in Australia about health and health risks. A cup of water. Nothing more. Nothing less. I drank the water and handed Kasiamma the cup.

Back in the office, I was spared in my monolingual ignorance the full blast of Kasiamma's fiery language. Her tone and stance said it all. She was picturesque – squat and solid. For me she embodied elements of the legendary heroine Kannagi, whose statue is one of those lining the great sweep of ocean along the Marina Promenade in Chennai. Kannagi is the inspiration for a stern moral epic poem, *Silappatikaram*, possibly written in the fifth century CE. This is one of the most famous works within the Tamil literary tradition going back thousands of years. There are several versions of this celebration of Tamil culture, wifely loyalty and justice. I have adapted the following from the various versions I have read.

Settling in

Kovalan, the son of a wealthy merchant, married Kannagi, the lovely daughter of another merchant. They lived together happily, until Kovalan met a beautiful courtesan called Madhavi. He fell in love with her and spent all his wealth on her. The lovers quarrelled. Repentant and penniless, the faithless husband returned to Kannagi, who had been patiently waiting for him.

Kovalan and Kannagi decided to make a fresh start and moved to the great city of Madurai. Their only asset was a pair of silver anklets filled with precious rubies. Kannagi gave them to Kovalan who took one of them to the market to sell to raise some money. But, as happened, a jeweller who had stolen silver anklets belonging to the Queen saw Kovalan trying to sell Kannagi's anklet in the market, and cunningly decided to set Kovalan up as a scapegoat. He informed the King that he had caught the thief. Guards seized Kovalan, and, there and then, without a trial, the King had him killed.

Kannagi rushed to the King's palace, filled with rage at the King for denying justice to Kovalan. She carried her second anklet and forced her way forward past the guards and pushed herself before the King.

'What jewels are there in the Queen's anklets?' she demanded of him.

'Pearls', he replied.

Kannagi hurled her anklet to the ground before the King so that it broke to reveal the rubies. Her husband's innocence was proved. The King and the Queen, realising their blunder, fell down dead as dispensing justice was the first requisite for kings in those days. Still filled with contempt for the injustice, Kannagi tore out her left breast and flung it on the city, cursing it. She started a fire that spread through Madurai, destroying it.

The statue of Kannagi on the beachfront in Chennai that I saw each time we rode past depicts her gripping the anklet tightly in one hand as she angrily demands justice of the King.

Over the coming years, I was to meet many women in India who embodied Kannagi's determination to wrest justice from those in power, especially justice for other women. In her confrontations with Benjamin, Kasiamma, our first cook, embodied the fire of Kannagi, even if the issues were no more profound than the quality of her cooking. She and Benjamin clashed from time to time over domestic trivia, and, having insufficient language to intervene, I left them to it. They had their last spar some time in July. Now we had to fend for ourselves. Despite my abhorrence of the kitchen, we somehow managed.

About this time, the goods I had shipped from Australia arrived. In Sydney, I had packed with care and excitement. My things were at the Port, so Benjamin and I set off, passport and receipts in hand. We located my trunks. They were in a vast shed, open on one side to the yard that led towards Beach Road; the other side open to the wharves. The concrete floor beneath our *chappals* was gritty with a fine black mineral dust, blown in from the ships. We waited. Under the iron roof of the shed, the day was hot and oppressive even so close to the water. Eventually, officials came. They ordered me to open the two metal boxes and proceeded to toss my things out on to the floor. Pale green sheets, a gift from my work colleagues, fell out. Fine cotton nighties, undies, shirts. Despite my dismay, I felt sufficiently threatened in front of such officialdom not to object. This was not a time for banter or Australian humour. Better to have my goods than to lose them for being indiscreet. It was not clear what the men were looking for, and it crossed my mind that they might have simply been curious. When they were done, we moved to the next stage, signing off wads of documentation.

Our time had run out. The office had closed for the day. So, we dusted off the linen, re-packed the trunk, locked it and returned to the Centre. The next day, we began stage two. It was beginning to remind me of a heroic contest, in which players are set up against terrifying creatures and have a limited time to get to the end point. There were, in all, seven signatures that we had to obtain, and, although Benjamin

Settling in

disputes there were so many, I still recall the big bundle of papers. The signatories were in different places all around the Port. From one end to the other, we raced; up a set of steep metal stairs at one end, then across the road to the Customs House for another golden signature. The clock struck! Once again, we had failed to complete the course. Back home we went for the second time, my trunks still waiting release. Fortunately, we didn't have to start from the beginning each day, so that on our third visit to the Port, we made it. We finished. We collected my goods and took them home.

With the familiarity of some of my own things around me, I now felt as though I was beginning to settle in. I had my books, linen and a few kitchen items. It was a good time for us to find our own home. After a long search, we found a spacious flat on the middle floor of a large house not far from the office, but fate determined that some more weeks were to pass before we moved in.

28 July 1984. The middle of the night. Six thousand, eight hundred athletes from 140 nations parade into Los Angeles Coliseum Stadium and past President Ronald Regan in the traditional Olympic Games opening ceremony parade. Benjamin and I are watching the drama unfold on television. We are not at home in the office at Shastri Nagar and at this stage we don't own a television. We are sitting in a nearby doctor's surgery. Benjamin is groaning in pain and bleeding heavily from one foot. I am stoically nursing grazes, shock and anxiety about him.

Benjamin had just completed a series of twenty-five meetings around the country, travelling with one of the many visitors who came to the Centre during the course of my first year in India. The Centre had arranged seminars with some of these visitors and visits to the rural centre for others; they included academics from USA, Canada, Zimbabwe and the World Bank; government officials from Delhi and Tamil Nadu; academics from Indian social science institutions and others involved in non-government organisations in India. During July, we had organised a major series of workshops at the request of French-Canadian, Raymond Cournoyer, who was a member of the religious congregation of Holy Cross Brothers, and who had many years' experience in education and social development in India, Bangladesh and other Asian countries.

Raymond's vision of a virtual Asian Development University, which would permit those involved in social development work to draw time and support to reflect analytically on their experience, was a brilliant concept, although it was not to be realised at that time. Raymond had asked Benjamin to assist him in testing support for this idea in India. They had travelled in a wide circle across cities in the north of the country and concluded their series of meetings in the southern states of Karnataka, Kerala, Andhra Pradesh and Tamil Nadu. Since they had travelled for most of July, leaving me alone at home, I was very pleased to see Benjamin again when they had returned. I also enjoyed the idiosyncratic and fascinating conversation that Raymond always brought with him.

To celebrate the satisfying end of their joint project, we enjoyed a meal at a local restaurant. Then, we accompanied Raymond in a taxi to the airport for his flight back to Singapore. We were relaxed and in good spirits. For some reason the flight was cancelled and passengers were to be accommodated overnight in a city hotel. So, we set off back from the airport, Raymond travelling towards the city in a cab, while Benjamin and I made our way in an autorickshaw towards the office and home.

Our driver was a young man called Vasu who had previously worked with Benjamin in the Centre. He had moved on and had recently found a job as an auto-rickshaw driver. By way of encouragement, Benjamin had hired him to take us back home. Vasu appeared outside the airport, full of smiles, beside the shining new black and yellow vehicle. It was small and three-wheeled, with a soft vinyl top fitted tightly over a thin metal frame. The sides were open, which

Settling in

provided good ventilation when the traffic moved, but offered little other protection.

We climbed in and followed Raymond's taxi along Guindy Road, knowing that soon the car would continue straight while we were to curve a little to the right. As the Ambassador taxi approached the divergence, Vasu accelerated. With a screeching of the two-stroke engine, he ducked out, attempting to pass the taxi from the left. The intersection was now very close. The heavy Ambassador and the little rickshaw were set on intersecting parabolas. Vasu made a bold attempt and further gunned the little autorickshaw. We sailed past the taxi. In those seconds, the stunned face of Raymond floated beside us. Vasu swerved back to the right to miss the concrete slabs lining the road but it was too much. The rickshaw began to tilt dangerously to the left and Benjamin's leg fell out the opening and hit a rock. I slid on top of him. Then our driver lost control and the whole thing capsized. As the vehicle slid along the roadway on its side, Benjamin's foot was trapped underneath. Sparks flew as the metal of the vehicle scraped against the hard surface.

I came out of the accident with minor injuries. Benjamin's left ankle was badly broken and he had a deep wound on his foot. Vasu, who had clung to the steering handle, was uninjured. The brand new rickshaw was heavily damaged.

The accident left Benjamin incapacitated. The stairs in the office were an unnecessary complication so for four long weeks he was confined downstairs. Each night, I brought down our sleeping mats to the front room of the office, pushed back the cane chairs to make some space and made our bed on the floor there. With the comings and goings of office staff at all hours, it was hardly conducive to intimacy.

Finally, early in August we shifted to our new residence in Indira Nagar. Sujatha, the young woman who worked in the Centre as accountant and who had done my makeup for the wedding reception, had suggested an auspicious day based on the Hindu calendar for us to move in. We went with some of our office colleagues to the new house and heated milk in a saucepan till it boiled over, symbolising the blessings wished for us in our new home. For devout and mainstream Hindus, life revolves around piety and devotion that in one sense is very familiar to the Irish-based piety of my youth. It is something I can understand and relate to, even if the expressions are different.

The house was bright and airy and offered us plenty of space. We had beds, sofa, a table and chairs manufactured in a training centre for needy boys. The workshop was run by a friend of Benjamin's, a cheerful, competent social worker called Nambudiri, and getting to know him and his wife Kamala added further to my sense of belonging. The furniture was plain but solid teakwood.

Our lives fell into a routine of a kind. I would rise in time each morning to collect our allocated ration of two sachets of milk at 6.15 from the booth across the road. Benjamin and I both worked at the Centre six days a week and there was no annual leave. While I enjoyed the work, I always found going to work on Saturday a serious cultural challenge to my Australian upbringing.

A small vegetable shop was built into the wall of the compound where we lived, with the counter facing into the street and a small living area behind for the shopkeeper Elumalai and his wife. All day long, servant women wandered up for gossip and the few tomatoes, onions, ladies fingers (okra) or eggs they needed for that day's meal. We also purchased our vegetables there, the convenience of a shop on our doorstep too good to pass by. We purchased our basic cereals loose, so that the wheat had to be cleaned of stalks and then taken to be milled and ground. It would come back as flour in our metal canister hot from the milling.

Electricity and phone bills were paid in person rather than by cheque and we renewed our milk cards at Booth Number 105 on the fourth of each month. Gas came in red cylinders which needed to be ordered and received. I washed most of our clothes in a bucket, but we also had an old twin tub machine, which took two hours to complete

Settling in

a load. Many of the domestic complications circled around the water supply, which was limited and unpredictable.

The water supply was an issue for all of Chennai. Like many houses in the city, ours had a well. It also had an underground tank which received water from the Municipal Corporation. In an effort to ration supplies, the Corporation released water into tanks such as ours for about an hour each morning. The water was then pumped from the tank to a reservoir on the roof of the three-storied house from where it could flow down through the plumbing at the turn of a tap. The Corporation supply of water was inconsistent especially towards the end of my stay in India in 1987 when Chennai faced a serious water shortage. However, the complications we experienced also had a human character.

Our landlord at the time had two wives. Downstairs Wife and her two children lived on the ground floor of the house; Upstairs Wife and her two children on the second floor. We lived in between. Adding to the idiosyncrasy of our living arrangements, the already-fickle water supply trickled or dried up according to the shifting relationship between the two wives. Downstairs Wife, first in time and in legal standing, controlled the motor which pumped the water from the Corporation-supplied storage tank to another tank on the roof. Upstairs Wife determined when, and if, she would turn the tap which released the water back down to the households.

When war flared between the two, each woman took up her particular weapon against the other. We were mere observers, but like innocent bystanders in many conflicts we suffered collateral damage. There were days when our daily supply of water came in the morning. There were days when the water came at 8.30 in the evening. There were days when the water came at 11.00 pm just when we were dozing off. There were days when one of the women would go out for the whole day, or occasionally more, without warning us or making provision for 'tap-turning'. And whenever the water came, there would be a mad helter-skelter from tap to tap in our kitchen and bathrooms to catch the few measured drops Upstairs Wife had deigned to provide before closing the valve. The water that we collected and stored in drums and buckets for all our household needs then needed to be boiled for consumption purposes. Water management became a big part of my life.

There were many times in my first year – years – in India when I was frustrated. This was true at work, where I was restricted by my lack of language. I felt it much more in domestic matters, where I initially felt inept in shopping, in dealing with all sorts of door-to-door vendors, in negotiating over prices and even in the basic everyday matters of cooking a different food style with different apparatus. I was not used to grinding and drying spices and didn't know where to start. At this stage, too, Indian food was less fashionable back home so access to cook books in English was limited.

A full year after my move to Chennai we took delivery of our first refrigerator. It was delivered and installed, I recall, around 8.00 pm on a Saturday evening. It had cost us over 9000 rupees. This purchase was a big one for us on the salaries we earned in a non-government organisation and I suspect Benjamin decided to buy it more for me than for himself. Between us we earned 1700 rupees a month: 900 rupees went towards our rent and so we lived, as many others around us did, storing enough perishable food for a day at a time. Where time permits, this is a simple and practicable approach.

Benjamin and I shared some disasters in our joint efforts to unravel the mysteries of sustaining ourselves. On one memorable afternoon, we attempted to prepare *idiyappam* ('string hoppers') that are steamed noodle-like cakes made from forcing a rice mixture through tiny holes. We squeezed what we considered the right mix of flours through the tiny pin-dot holes of the brass sieve. We steamed them for what we thought was the right length of time. Alas, what had been such an apparently effortless task for so many others resulted for us in gelatinous dumplings with the consistency of wet cement. We turned off the gas, scraped our sad effort into the bin, and found solace in walking to a friend's place where we were comforted with hot sweet tea and *tiffin* – the afternoon snack (more like a light meal) which comes in a wide variety of tasty morsels. We have not attempted *idiyappam* since.

All in a day's work

THE OFFICE HAD BECOME too cramped for the activity of the Centre and the landlord wanted the building for his medical practice. Desks were crammed into what would have been the main living room of a house. Men and women edged around them and there was inadequate storage for all the bundles of paper. Above this congestion was the ongoing whirr of the overhead fans and the shouting which seemed to characterise local phone calls. So, late in February 1985, we loaded our files and accounts, our journals and books, our tables, chairs and filing cabinets, our duplicator and manual typewriters, and all the necessary paraphernalia of an office on to a series of bullock carts and three-wheeled cycle carts for new premises just a kilometre away.

The pattern of my life then became something like this ...

Benjamin leaves early for work on his Bullet, a 350cc Royal Enfield motorbike which is our family car. It has a distinctive throb which announces him well before his arrival. I take my time to do some household chores, leaving home about 8.30. The walk to the new office from our home in Indira Nagar takes about twenty

All in a day's work

minutes. Along 1st Main Road, I seek the shade of trees where I can, keeping to the edge of the thin crust of bitumen to avoid the rubbish dropped over the compound wall of the large homes of the well-established citizens of the area.

I am cheered as I pass by the vibrant red and yellow hibiscus flowers of our immediate neighbour. Next door, at a large brown house, with a deep upper balcony set back in an inviting cocoon of shade and privacy, a servant is emptying slops onto speckled green and gold crotons in the garden that runs from the gate along a driveway. Across the road, on the left, the home of the Vice-Chancellor, the driver in crushed khakis and *chappals* gives the heavy black Ambassador car a polish which it doesn't need.

By the time I reach the intersection and cross Main Road near the small bakery on the corner, the collar of my yellow cotton shirt is already damp. The hem of my long skirt is dusty. This section of street is unsealed and deep gutters run along each side. Here the street is quieter and more suburban. '*Vanakam*', I greet the elderly Mr Nayak, father of our friend Gowrie, as he takes his morning walk. Two schoolboys, in white-ish shirts and baggy khaki shorts, dangle flat feet from the end of their bare skinny legs seemingly intent to stir up as much dust as possible.

'What time is it, Madam?' they ask. 'Who will win the cricket? Do you speak English?' By the time I try to work out an answer in Tamil, counting in my head from one to nine (very slowly), they are gone. I laugh and move on. Soon, I pass a small thatched school, which is a source of daily bewilderment to me. 'A, e, i, o, u ... A, e, i, o, u ... A, e, i, o, u.' Yes, they're at it again. On it goes, over and over, the chant of three-year-olds, learning the vowels of a foreign language for which they have no immediate need.

From the school, I shortly come to busy M. G. Road. (In a land of long names, initials are frequent. In this case, they refer to Mahatma Gandhi.) I turn left and think cool thoughts of where M. G. Road meets the ocean a kilometre or so away beyond the many small shops and restaurants. I cross near the wooden tea stand on the opposite corner that marks the entrance to Subramanian Colony. This street is unsealed. I pass the slum with its red clay dwellings and thatched roofs, hard clay floors, smoky interiors and marvel again how each new day children emerge looking polished and shiny for school – hair oiled, tightly plaited or slicked down, uniforms clean and ironed. I sense the investment their parents are making in the promise offered by an education. I think what a responsibility this places on all teachers: to deliver on this promise.

A large curry leaf tree flourishes in a vacant lot next to the low white rendered building on the right which is the Centre's office. Because there are fewer houses here and more room for cattle to wander, I watch more carefully where I place my feet on the corrugated ruts. I take note of some unusual activity at the Muslim house across from the office as I turn in through the gate. A young goat is being carried in through the gate and it is making a squealing fuss.

'Good morning, Madam.' A slim young man in slacks and synthetic shirt greets me. He is turning his cycle around at the same time as he mounts it. Manimaran, general administrative assistant, is, as usual, on his way to some errand.

'Morning, Manimaran. What is the goat for?' I ask him, nodding with my head towards the opposite house.

'Id, Madam', he replies, his smile broadening as he steadies the bike. *'Biriyani.'* Biriyani is a rich festival dish of spiced rice which can also include lamb, mutton or chicken. While it is a speciality for Muslims, it is also used by Hindus and Christians for weddings and other festive occasions.

I shake dust from my sandals on the step before entering the grilled porch. In the main room, elderly Joshua, proper as ever, stands to greet me from his desk. Joshua's Master's degree is from England. He is one of the program officers, bringing a background in social work as well as administration which helps keep the work of the Centre on track. Joshua is a Malayalee (from the Indian state of

Kerala) so speaks that language as well as English and Tamil. He also reads and writes Tamil.

Sujatha, the accountant, is not in yet. She has a Telugu background, that is, her engineer father and mother are from the neighbouring state of Andhra Pradesh. Educated in Chennai, Sujatha speaks Tamil, English and Hindi, as well as her mother tongue, Telugu. However, she reads and writes only English and Hindi. She is somewhat distracted these days as her parents have announced her coming marriage. She knows the young man well and they have grown up together as neighbours and playmates. She had assured me when the news was first broken, that the process of choosing a husband did allow for her to say no, had she wanted. In this case, she was very happy about the choice and these days she is often looking a bit weary when she comes to work, tired from days of shopping for saris.

Benjamin has come and left.

'They are busy across the road', I comment to Joshua. 'Manimaran said the goat was for Id. I thought we had celebrated Id back in June.'

'That was Id after Ramadan', Joshua explained. 'Now it is Peru Naal Id. This happens at the end of the Mecca pilgrimage. The kid goat celebrates Abraham's willingness to sacrifice his son.'

'Poor goat.' I guess it didn't have a chance to say no, I think to myself. I know about Abraham and Isaac, but am still sorting out the different Islamic festivals.

The other two program officers, Janaki and Lakshmi, are both qualified in social work and are charming and good fun to work with. Both speak Tamil, English and Hindi fluently, while Lakshmi reads and writes English and Tamil and Janaki reads and writes English and Hindi. Benjamin speaks English, Tamil, Malayalam and Telugu and fudges in Hindi, Japanese, German, French and Italian when required; he reads and writes English and Tamil. It is the first time I have realised the distinction between speaking, reading and writing skills. The multiplicity of languages complicates our work in getting documents written. I am thinking of a Seminar for Women that I am planning where we will need a Tamil translator for some key speakers and Lakshmi to write the Tamil report while I will write the English report.

I continue on to the library. It is stuffy. I turn the switch for the overhead fan, relieved to find that the power is on. I toss my hat on a battered filing cabinet beside my desk and hang my cloth bag on the back of the plain wooden chair. One by one, I open the glass windows behind their hard metal security grill. The air improves immediately. I take a cloth from one of the grey metal book shelves and dust the overnight grit from the varnished desk top.

A cool hand wash in the small bathroom opening off the library completes the ritual. I pull out my chair and sit down, take some used paper, turning it over to the clean side. *Centre for Human Development and Social Change, Annual Report 1984*, I write and wonder where to go next. The task in hand, the annual report for the previous year, is offering me lots of distractions as I muse back over the previous months, my first in the Centre and in India.

My role in the Centre was research coordinator and coordinator of women's programs. My starting salary for a six-day working week that spilled into seven was Rs.600 (then around $AUD60) per month. Benjamin, as director of the Centre, was paid at this time Rs.800 per month, a little less than that paid by local banks to the unskilled *peons* who stood outside the bank opening the door for customers as they came and left. It was not the usual career move.

Lacking local knowledge, language and any particular experience in social development, I was conscious of being a liability rather than an asset to the Centre (and Benjamin) in the beginning. In addition, we approached things very differently: for a start I brought a sense of time sharply divided into slots, such as meal times, work times, leisure, personal, professional; my employer-husband's sense of time had no such arbitrary divisions – Sunday is as good as Monday for working, and 6.00 am or 10.00 pm is as good as 9.00 am. At the same time, he seemed quite satisfied for me simply to sit in on meetings while I was eager to be *doing something* more specific. A disadvantage of this approach is its passivity, that, in the oppressive Chennai heat, in the midst of conversations which (before my ears attuned to Indian English) might as well have been in Swahili, could too easily turn into torpor. I battled many times with eyelids of stone in those early weeks, more embarrasssingly so when I did so in the office of some government official. Small consolation that, even when I shut my eyes 'just for a minute', as far as I am aware, I didn't snore. I was frustrated with this: How could I use my mind? How could I feel productive? How to keep awake? It probably did not impress my boss either.

Benjamin, admirably punctilious about keeping detailed financial and adminstrative records for government and the Centre's own purposes, thrived on activity and interaction, which did not always leave him time to execute what my mother had drilled into me as 'a place for everything and everything in its place'. So to make myself feel more useful and because it suited my own style of working, I used my 'idle' moments in the Centre to focus on some aspect of the organisation which I could subvert towards what I saw as a little more administrative good order. I tried to tidy it up. It was a meagre contribution to human development and social change in India.

Benjamin describes the Centre which he had established in 1975 as *a small inter-disciplinary social science institute concerned with micro-development problems in South India*. What that meant in practice was that we worked, in particular, with non-government organisations (NGOs) from across the state and beyond, offering them leadership training, advice and other support. Our Centre's work with these other NGOs was on the basis of principles which were self-evident, seductively idealistic and radical: the inalienable right of every woman and man to participate in decisions affecting their lives; an understanding of development to include the totality of persons and society; and the radical transformation of social structures to ensure all persons have equitable access to society's resources.

At times, there were up to a dozen staff working in the Centre's city office with others employed in the Centre's rural program. When he was in, Benjamin directed the action. He had a bell on his desk – which I chose to ignore – which he used to summon Manimaran, his administrative assistant, to deliver or collect mail, meet an overseas visitor, fetch tea, or the phone, water, rent or electricity might need to be paid; and it was Manimaran who went to Central Station to queue for train tickets. Workers arrived from the rural area to report on activities or to collect money to pay bills. Visitors from smaller non-government organisations came to seek advice on a range of matters. I gradually sorted out how these various staff members fitted in and what they did.

The Centre placed a particular value on educating young adults in understanding poverty and the socio-political-economic-cultural entanglements of development so that they could become leaders in freeing their communities from them. I agreed with Benjamin that this approach was important for long-term change, but it is much harder and more elusive than offering healthcare, or training young people in carpentry, or women in hygiene and childcare, or even in planting trees. Sometimes, when I struggled to see how we were making any headway, I longed wistfully to do something more concrete and measurable. It was the staff in the rural area who did most of that.

The Centre's rural program in 1984 was conducted in about thirty villages in an area 60 kilometres north-west of Chennai. The base for the rural program was Cheyalnagar, the plot of land where we had been entertained by the rural youth not long after our wedding and where I had spent three monsoonal days and nights the previous year. The rural program was supervised by a slight, dark-skinned, earnest young man called Durairaj. He was modest and quiet and Benjamin valued his judgement. A team of eight full-time people worked with him. One was a stocky man, Ekambaram, who had joined the Centre at the same time as Durairaj in December 1983. He seemed older than Durairaj, who was about twenty-five or six. What Ekambaram lacked in formal education he more than made up for in his fiery commitment to the poor in his village.

I was surprised as I read back over our activities for the year to realise what we had actually achieved, for in the midst of it all it was sometimes hard to see the outcomes, embedded as they were in the hands-on messy business of getting things done.

As part of the Centre's Community Organisation program, Durairaj and his team worked with local communities, identifying their needs and issues so as to help them find their own solutions. In particular, they encouraged village women to to get involved in the community around issues relating to health, childcare and sanitation. I recalled a young woman I had met in one of our training programs. She had come from a village in Tamil Nadu where girl infants were often killed at birth, to remove the burden of providing dowries for their marriages. Even though this young woman had completed a university degree, she had no awareness of the facts of reproduction and birth control. Other issues included questions about fair trading at ration shops, proper roads and water supply. Durairaj and Ekambaram also held weekly sessions during the year with about twenty young women and men to build them up as leaders within their villages. Many of the Centre's staff were, like Ekambaram, known as 'Untouchables', being of the lowest castes and today called 'Dalits'.

The Centre also conducted an adult education program with funds from the Government of India. During 1984, we ran thirty adult education centres in the villages with over 900 learners. In a follow-up program, nearly 750 of the original 934 returned to take part. Our approach to adult education was to build up functional literacy and numeracy skills using material that was about the villagers' lives: the social, political and cultural issues affecting their poverty. We also wanted to make them more aware of their entitlements and of the government services available to them. In anticipation of 1985, the government had sanctioned the Centre to run sixty adult education centres, so Benjamin asked Durairaj to recruit and train additional animators. One of the new staff members Durairaj had taken on was a young man called Dorai, who stood out from his colleagues because of his sturdy build and fair complexion.

In our Centre's files, I was amazed to discover, we had details of more than 500 non-government organisations in Tamil Nadu alone; they ranged in size from a handful of idealistic young men and women to sophisticated organisations employing hundreds. Some had been in existence for ten or twenty years; others came and faded for want of resources or organisational know-how. The larger ones generally relied on funding from within India or from international donor agencies. The groups' focus depended largely on the conviction, and sometimes idiosyncrasy, of their founders, and their scope was diverse.

Ekambaram, for example, had set up his own organisation in a village where he tried to raise the awareness of the unskilled farm labourers and their rights for fair pay and conditions. He had previously completed some of our Development Training Programs, and by working part-time with our Centre, he was able to support himself in a simple way. Mostly, members of these small organisations, like Ekambaram, lived very frugally amongst the villagers, and so they were close to their problems and the imbalances in society – inadequate pay, police harrassment, persecution of those of low caste, the corruption of government officials, the grinding cycle of malnutrition, illiteracy, poverty and hopelessness, especially for women who, when pregnant, worked in the fields right up till childbirth and returned to work a few days later.

The Centre's training programs were directed at the leaders of such voluntary, not-for-profit, grassroots movements and organisations. In 1984, fifty-six young people had completed four programs in Development Studies, each of fifteen days' duration. The content was substantial. It included analysis of the Indian social situation, Indian history, analysis of different approaches to development and constraints to Indian and world development. Two courses were conducted in English and two were conducted in Tamil. The courses were led by Benjamin and the Centre staff and always involved significant external speakers – specialists, academics, activists and senior bureacracts. The Centre had offered these young rural people a meaty program that was intended to enrich the philosophical foundation for their generous efforts with the poor in their own contexts. Many came from poverty, and, in turn, helped others.

One day a few months previously, Durairaj had come to the office in Thiruvanmiyur to tell Benjamin that a violent storm had destroyed the casuarina pole and coconut leaf shed at Cheyalnagar which had been constructed late in 1983. A second shed had been erected to house our rural training programs. This new shed withstood a cyclonic battering in November, but like the two mud and thatched huts on the site needed constant maintenance. We had begun to raise funds for a permanent brick and cement training shed and a well. In the meantime, however, I had been successful in convincing my employer (as only a wife can) that the building of a rudimentary latrine and bath house for women attending programs was essential. I was pleased with this outcome, but I would have been better pleased had I been consulted in its design since the first version was a rectangular space with palm-frond walls in the middle of an open space at some distance behind the mud huts. The male minds at work had given no thought, it appeared, to place it in a more discreet or convenient location. At least it was less likely to attract snakes in the open area.

Not surprisingly, our training programs also focused on the environment. Environmental action was urgently needed in a situation where there was inadequate drinking water, no sanitation, unhygienic housing, serious deforestation and gross industrial pollution. Along the road which runs in front of Cheyalnagar, the women, who already walked up to seven kilometres every day to fetch kindling for their cooking fires, needed to walk further each day as the forests dwindled.

Other programs offered practical training to small voluntary groups, such as book-keeping and accountancy and management of their legal reporting accountabilities. Another stream of work was associated with the Centre's support for smaller organisations through advice and consultancy. The word 'consultancy' was used loosely as no fee was ever charged for this service. During 1984, about ten requests a week came through the mail or telephone or through visits. Young men with shabby clothes, dusty sandals and bright faces came and sat with Benjamin as he counselled them in his own inimitable way and Manimaran provided them with cups of tea.

There were two organisations in particular that we supported through Benjamin's mentoring of their leaders, one dedicated to Development Communication, which took mobile audio-visual resources and street theatre to the villages as informal education, and a rural-based organisation, Society for Rural Action for Development, led by Benjamin's older brother, Alphonse. The organisations carried evocative names like Depressed People's Development Association or acronyms like SEEDS or AWARE. They would have liked us to give them funding, but unfortunately we had little ourselves and that was on a project-to-project basis. Sometimes, we would develop a project proposal, send it off to a donor agency in Europe, Australia, Japan or North America, and then wait for up to two years for a rejection. Sometimes it was longer.

I made a number of trips with Benjamin during 1984. Early in June we had travelled to the north western state of Maharashtra, to a place called Puntamba on the Godavari River. The village of Puntamba is about 300 kilometres north of Mumbai and I have a memory of long stretches of lush sugar cane growing beside the tracks as we made our train journey. We were attending a conference organised by the Program for Social Action (PSA), a group of Christian organisations involved in work similar to ours. While our Centre was deliberately non-denominational and secular, Benjamin had many friends in the PSA network. The Indigenous population (*Adivasis*, as they prefer to be called) in the Puntamba area had been oppressed

All in a day's work

over centuries even while they provided the labour for the sugar crops and factories. The large sugar cane industry continued to be controlled by the wealthy and by politicians. Puntamba was an appropriate site for the meeting.

My fellow participants brought colour and passion to our encounters over the three days. Most of them had worked over many years, with few resources, in a long-term struggle to get fairer conditions for the poor. There was a white-haired theologian whose extensive writings on liberation and the Gospel had inspired many in the minority Christian churches. When he spoke, his word carried authority and conviction. There were feisty young men who had challenged the powerful in their local areas. When it came to the more formal side of the conference, I was sensitive about my outsider status and settled into an observer role.

In between the sessions, I enjoyed conversations with other participants, such as Xavier Dias who worked with tribals in the northern state of Bihar. Xavier had travelled to the conference from Bihar with Anthony Murmu, a shortish man, perhaps in his early fifties. Murmu had a moon-like face with hair thinning across the dome of his head. He was obviously respected. Benjamin, in this as in so many matters my personal Wikipedia, told me that Murmu was an *Adivasi*, a tribal, from the north of India. A Christian, he had been ordained as a Jesuit priest and then had stood down from the priesthood to enter the national parliament in 1977. People at the conference still addressed him as 'Father' Murmu, and while he carried his authority in a quiet way, he was cheerful and unassuming. The meeting concluded and we dispersed. Anthony Murmu was to die just six months later.

Late in October 1984, my sister Carmel came through Chennai with her husband on her way back to Australia after a stint working for IBM in the USA. She brought with her for the Centre our first computer, a Morrow. Immediately my life was transformed. Our secretaries still pounded away on manual typewriters, every document being carefully inserted with about three layers of carbon copies. Our advanced technology included one electric typewriter, golf-ball type, at this stage. I would proof the letters or reports or project proposals, reluctant to find the inevitable errors occurring, especially when, for all the secretaries, English was their second language. Besides, we operated on a shoe-string budget and used our clean paper sparingly. I was the primary writer in the Centre, and with the computer I moved overnight from the straitjacket of carbon-paper to being able to edit – yes, edit, not just correct – the quality of what we wrote.

Nonetheless, as I quickly learned, there were special techniques needed even with this wonderful computer. Power supply in Chennai was never constant, especially in the summer. To save energy, there were regular power cuts at certain times of the day. There were also unpredictable cuts and brown-outs. Too many times I was caught out. Furiously typing away in the study at home completing a report or research project, enjoying the satisfying task of creating my own work rather than correcting others', when ... the fan would sigh into a slowing whirr, and at the same time the screen would fade before my eyes into one last flashing icon in the middle before it blacked out. I never quite perfected the technique of writing in ten-minute snatches before a quick save.

And so, as I sit at my desk and prepare a report that reviews a year in the life of the Centre and my first months in India, the afternoon begins to cool. The report more or less finished, I enjoy the softening light as shadows begin to bless the late afternoon. Women come out to collect water from the pump in the street; others squat over pots outside their thatched huts preparing the evening meal. Children from the nearby settlement bubble up as they do each day at this time to resume their chasing of bicycle tyres up and down our dusty street, manipulating them between slow-moving buffaloes and the women drawing water at the pump. A little girl comes with her father to dig worms from the vacant plot next door. A flower seller passes leaving a trail of jasmine fragrance. A goddess of ten years poses Shiva-like on the neighbour's wall. Three boys take turns to conquer a half-sized bicycle. Then the goddess is called to crouch patiently while her hair is combed and searched for lice. A barefoot boy of about twelve with a grubby white shirt hanging over loose-legged shorts sells sweets from a large green glass dome on his push cart. I am tempted to try some.

I hear Benjamin's Bullet before he turns the corner and comes down the road. He has been out all day. He cruises to a stop outside the office. I imagine him sniffing the *biriyani* wafting from across the street. It is time to take a break. It is time to sit in the front breezeway and enjoy some hot, too-sweet, too-strong tea with my husband.

Finding my place

MY MOTHER WAS NOT the only one who needed to adjust to the idea of a stranger. Although Benjamin's family had met me the previous year when I had spent about six weeks in India, his father, step-mother and family still had to get used to the idea of Benjamin bringing a foreign wife to Chennai. He had grown up with stories about the dangers of western alliances and had shared with me tales his family elders had recounted.

My memory of one story goes along these lines. A businessman in south-western India married an English woman. They settled in the state of Kerala. All went well for the first year, and then the wife began to ask her husband to supply her with items from the life she had left behind in England. In particular, she longed for imported soap and perfumes to use in her bath. He gave her these luxuries while his business was going well. Then his business went into decline and he explained the cost of these indulgences was beyond him. Still she persisted. When her husband finally told her that he simply could not afford to give her what she wanted, she became petulant and cross. One day, he returned from work to find that she had left him.

In another story, there was a South Indian gold merchant who had married an English woman. The merchant dealt in gold objects, especially jewellery, which he sent to England. He used the gold to

Finding my place

obtain a large mortgage from a bank in England. Unfortunately, his wife discovered that the 'gold' being sent to England was really brass dipped in gold. Not long after, she persuaded her husband to let her return to England for a brief holiday. On arrival, she promptly informed the bank of his deception. The bank – not surprisingly – stopped the loans and moved against the man to repay all outstanding monies. His business –and no doubt their marriage – never recovered.

Despite this background briefing, Benjamin had gone ahead with the marriage.

Not long after our arrival in Chennai, we went to the village where my husband had grown up. Kannigairpair, a village about 30 kilometres north of Chennai, is his 'native place', an important identifier. 'What is your native place?' men and women would often ask each other on meeting for the first time. *Place* served to set boundaries around people, helped them to be understood; it was part of who they were. In Australia, I would probably have defined my native place as Singleton or Maitland or Newcastle even though I had lived for five years in Sydney. Newly arrived in India, I redefined my native place far less precisely as 'Australia' or 'Sydney'.

In this context, names are important. My husband's full name is Kakkaseri Mathew Susai Benjamin, also known as K. M. S. Benjamin or, after he settled in Australia and needed a 'first' and 'second' name, Susai Benjamin. In India, he was addressed as Benjamin or Mr Benjamin and by his friends, simply as Benji. His father's name was K. J. Mathew, addressed as Doctor Mathew. His brother, K. M. Alphonse, was addressed as Alphonse or Mr Alphonse. In this system, brothers and sisters, and even husbands and wives, need not automatically have the same last name, although the common family name was there for those in the know. The shared initial 'K' in my husband's family's case indicated that they originated from a small town in Trissur District in the state of Kerala. Before our wedding,

Benjamin and I had a brief long-distance telephone discussion in which we considered what name I should take after marriage. There were a number of options, but I settled for Mrs Anne K. Benjamin.

As did many families in Chennai, Benjamin's family identified as 'Malayalee', that is, coming from Kerala, even though he was born in the state of Tamil Nadu. There are strong links of history, culture and language between the modern states of Kerala and Tamil Nadu, with the Malayalam language of the west coast deriving from the ancient Tamil. Indians have strong attachments to their particular state or region of origin and the richnesses of culture, language and custom that are distinctive to it: for each one, theirs is the heart of India. For Indians from the state of Kerala, Malayalees, this is especially so. Malayalees delight in their openness to new ideas and their capacity to succeed at anything (and everything). Wherever you go on earth, they boast, Malayalees are there. And, they add, when Neil Armstrong landed on the moon in 1969, he was greeted by a Malayalee with a cup of traditional *chai*, or spicy tea.

Kerala, the home of the ancient kingdom of Chera, land of the coconut, has long been characterised by tolerance and freedom. It is claimed that India's first mosque, first synagogue and first Christian church were all located there. My husband's family proudly claim links back to the Apostle Thomas. Tradition tells that Thomas, sent to evangelise the Parthians, Medes and Persians, ultimately came to the Malabar coastal area of modern Kerala as early as 52 CE. Benjamin shared with me the legend about Thomas that his father had told him. In those days, Hindu Brahmins would bathe in the tank, or artificial lake, outside the temple before entering into the holy place to purify themselves before their prayer. One morning, Thomas came across a group of Brahmins who were throwing water up in the air.

'Why are you doing that?' he asked.

'We are making an offering to the gods', they replied.

'Then why is your offering coming back down?' Thomas persisted.

Finding my place

The Brahmins shrugged, possibly getting a bit impatient with the inquisitive foreigner, 'It always does.'

'Then are the gods rejecting your prayers?' Thomas chided. And as he did, he knelt in an attitude of prayer, threw water from the tank, and it continued to rise. The legend concludes that a number of Hindus were converted on that day. Others ran away thinking that Thomas possessed unnatural powers that they could not explain and were unwilling to accept.

Fairly early in our relationship, Benjamin described himself to me as a descendant from those Thomas Christians whose lineage derives from those Brahmins converted by the Apostle. In the gospels, Thomas is portrayed as a person of impetuousness, scepticism, pessimism and also as being a twin. My husband could claim all but the last attribute.

We have Malayalee friends in Sydney who still continue the tradition of Thomas Christians, and are known today as Syro-Malabar Catholics or Marthoma Christians. Down through the centuries, these Christians have followed the liturgy of the Eastern Syrian Church while maintaining their Indian culture, whereas another group of Kerala Christians adopted the Latin rites of the Roman Church – under pressure from the Portuguese and the Jesuits when they settled in Kerala in the early sixteenth century.

Benjamin told me bits and pieces of his father's story as we rode the bus to and from Kannigairpair village on numerous occasions. Gradually, I fitted the jigsaw together. His father had been born in the village of Mattom, near Trissur in the princely state of Malabar in 1903 at a time when, still under British rule, the Malabar region in northern Kerala formed part of the Madras Presidency, or the Madras Province. Nationalism was emerging in India. Political awareness was strong in these predominantly Malayalam-speaking areas on the south-west coast of India.

In the early 1930s Mathew married a young woman called Mariamma. My father-in-law was a man who made his own mould.

His father had arranged for him to teach in the local Catholic school, but Mathew's individuality did not fit well within the life of a parochial school teacher and he wanted to leave, as soon as he could, to become a doctor. Mariamma had brought only a small dowry into the marriage, but she was an only child and there were expectations of a large inheritance of jewels. With the early death of her mother, this situation changed: Mariamma's father remarried and three more children were born into the family. Her inheritance was further jeopardised when her father died from a sudden heart attack.

Mathew left teaching and set up a medical shop. People who came to buy medicines often asked the young man about their minor ailments. When they recovered from their ulcers or wounds, more people started to come seeking his practical medical advice, for which, at this time, he held no licence. The local doctor began to lose some of his patients and was not pleased with the reputation that Mathew was developing. He threatened Mathew that he would report him to the police for practising medicine without any qualifications and registration.

Recognising the gifts that the young man displayed, a family friend who was a lawyer advised Mathew to go to Madras and study medicine. There was a major obstacle: he had no money. Mathew was without income with a young family to support. He turned to relatives for money but they either could not or would not help. In desperation, he sold up his medical shop in Kerala and made his way east across the province to Madras city to take up studies at the Kilpauk Medical College of the University of Madras.

In a strange city and without employment, he sought support from an uncle. Rather ironically, young Mathew who had abandoned a teaching career, sought patronage from a man who had made teaching his life for twenty-three years. In 1937, this relative, Professor C. J. Varkey, had been elected to the Madras Legislative Assembly. Prior to the election, Mathew had actively campaigned on his uncle's behalf in Kerala, and he no doubt hoped this would stand him in good stead in his need for somewhere to stay during his studies. It started out well enough. Mathew moved into the Varkey household which was conveniently located also in Kilpauk. After some weeks, however, Professor Varkey's wife asked her husband how long his nephew was going to stay at their house. Unfortunately, Mathew overheard their conversation. The young man had his pride. The next day he left the house and found a room somewhere else. It must have been basic accommodation because he studied at night under street lights. In his studies, Mathew combined both western and traditional medicine. This was to become the hallmark of his special skills and gifts as a doctor.

Doctor Mathew had established a surgery and dispensary in the bazaar in Kannigairpair, a village north of Chennai about twenty kilometres south of the state border with Andhra Pradesh. His practice was quite remarkable. He always viewed each patient as an individual, rather than considering just symptoms. His dedication and his ability to diagnose patients brought him many grateful supporters. One night Mathew had gone to take medicine to a patient. While he was returning, a huge storm deluged the area. The only way home was across a river near where it merged into the ocean. The storm had swollen the waters till they raced along topping the normal banks. Undeterred, and being somewhat foolhardy as well as determined, Mathew strode into the waters, holding his precious medical bag aloft. The waters raged around his waist, then his armpits, but he struggled on, straining his body forward to resist the forces. In the darkness, he lost his sense of direction until he saw another man ahead of him. This fellow was partly drunk but Mathew followed him and reached safety. He survived this ordeal and brought the medicines home safe and dry.

When Independence came in 1947, Mathew was forty-four years old. He and Mariamma already had six of their eight children. Two children had already died, and during this year their twelve-year-old son also died, from pneumonia. The pain of losing another child must have carried a double edge for the doctor who was so available to heal so many others in the village and its region.

Normally, in his practice, the Doctor drove a small cart, his bag beside him, with a driver in front urging on the horse or bullock to pull the cart. He made these trips mostly in the afternoon or evening and often at night for emergencies, and Benjamin grew up with a great respect and admiration for his father's medical skills. Later the pony and cart were replaced by a motorcycle and then a car. Then, showing the same energy and focus that characterised him as a rebellious young man, each Monday, for many years, Doctor Mathew rode his bicycle to the city, bought his medical supplies and cycled back – a journey of sixty kilometres in one afternoon.

The household comprised Mathew and Mariam, their children, Mathew's mother and two servants from Kerala. Mathew had built a home that reflected his own personality. There was an elaborate flower garden, goats, fowls, a cow, and a grove of coconut palms, mango and other fruit trees. Benjamin was the last of their eight children.

The local village school is just outside the house gate, located at the end of a dusty road which leads from the main road and abuts fields beside a large lake. It was here that Benjamin completed his primary schooling, with Tamil being the medium of instruction. For his secondary education, he joined his brother Alphonse as a boarder at San Thome High School in Santhome in the city. Over five years as a boarder, he developed a lasting appreciation for the Brothers of St Gabriel. He then gained admission to Loyola College, a Jesuit institution affiliated to the University of Madras.

Benjamin's mother, Mariamma, died in April 1968, towards the end of his first year in Loyola College. In 1970, consistent with his lifelong independence of thought, Doctor Mathew took the reasonably uncommon step of marrying a second time. The family called her *Kochamma*, or 'little mother', a Malayalee term of respect and endearment for a step-mother, and as with many relationships, this endearment was used rather than a personal name. Kochamma was also from Kerala, and had served as a nurse in the Indian army, going as far afield as the border with Pakistan. She had strong well-defined features in an open face and spoke her mind firmly. I liked her. I wondered about the strength of character that this would demand of a young single Indian woman in the middle of the twentieth century. It was after this that Doctor Mathew left the family home in Kannigairpair to live in the northern suburbs of Chennai at Ram Nagar.

In 1984, at 81, Doctor Mathew was still serving the villagers. By then, his car had been replaced by a brown three-wheeled auto-rickshaw, a personal version of the thousands of yellow-and-black low-cost taxis which populate Chennai, with their distinctive putt-putt two-stroke motors. Each day, Doctor Mathew would rise early, say his prayers, eat lightly and set off with his driver on the forty-five minute journey from Ram Nagar to Kannigairpair. He opened the dispensary from around 5.30-6.00 am, allowing patients to visit him on their way to work in the fields. His fee was between two and ten rupees which in 1984 equated to about ten to thirty Australian cents. At the end of the morning, he would return home to Ram Nagar, eat a light lunch, rest a while and spend the evening pottering in his garden and tending to his poultry, fish tank and a few cows before more prayers and retiring to bed early at 9.00 pm.

This was just a small part of the story into which I was entering when Benjamin brought me to Kannigairpair early in May 1984. His only brother and his wife, Elsey, still lived in the home in which the family had grown up. The farmhouse had its own idiosyncrasies but it has always held great emotional ties for my husband. He loved to sit in the front covered-porch, meeting with people, giving instructions to staff from the rural branch of the Centre and planning the future. A special attraction of his village home was the water. I always drank this water directly from the well, with no boiling and no fear of contamination. When bathing, it had a softness I have never experienced elsewhere.

Our visits to Kannigairpair were reasonably frequent. Benjamin and Alphonse shared interests in community development. Alphonse, the elder, was the quieter brother. His wife, Elsey, bubbled with fun.

Benjamin's eldest sister, Jubilee, had entered a convent and, in 1984, was principal in a school attended largely by the children of impoverished fisherfolk on Chennai's north side. His sister Gracey lived with her family in the same part of Chennai. To reach their place, we would ride past the long lines of fishermen's huts through the salty air along the Bay of Bengal waterfront. In 2004, this area would be one of those affected by the Asian tsunami. On the way to Gracey's we would sometimes stop to visit Benjamin's other sister, Angela, and her family, who lived in her husband's family home. On Sundays, we would often visit Doctor Mathew and Kochamma for lunch in Ram Nagar.

Benjamin's family welcomed me. If any of them wondered 'Would she last?' they never showed it. What they offered was kindness and generosity and a great deal of good humour. At the time, I thought I was, more or less, the only person whose poverty in language complicated communication with her in-laws. The limitations were mostly mine. My various Indian relatives spoke English, in varying degrees. It was my struggle with Tamil and Malayalam that was the barrier.

My unease in not being able to communicate better with my own family in-laws has limited our relationship. When you can only communicate simplistically, it doesn't lead to much depth. You can laugh together at some things, but the subtleties are cut out. And there is always scope for misunderstanding. Back in Australia, I discovered that many other families work within the same limitations of unshared languages, even within Indian marriages: a Tamil married to a Hindi-speaking wife; a Malayalam-speaking woman from Kerala married to a Bengali-speaking husband. It would have been helpful to have been more aware of this twenty years ago.

In the 1980's, 'cocktails', as Benjamin called us, were less

Finding my place

obvious, both in Australia and India. Having met many couples since, I realised that this was a visibility factor, and now 'mixed marriages' are more evident. Yet, at the time, Benjamin and I felt that there were not many marriages like ours around. In another sense, I often feel that there is *no* other marriage like ours around.

And, so, our life together started developing its own story and rhythm. In my imagination, I am once again on the balcony fronting 1st Main Road, Indira Nagar, waiting for a breeze to make its whimsical way from the nearby ocean.

Dusk makes a sudden departure as evening pushes her way down over the city. Faint tapping eases into my consciousness. Tap-tap. Silence. Tap-tap-tap. The sound is getting closer. A hoarse cry. In India, there are many such chants, as merchants trade up and down streets, selling vegetables, cashews, oranges, knife-sharpening, vessels. But this is evening, darkness has come and it is not the time for traders. I wait on the front balcony to see who, or what, will emerge from the shadows.

Tap-tap. Tap-tap-tap. Through the branches of a large hibiscus sprawling across the dividing wall, a cluster of white shapes moves through the darkness on the roadway. It pauses before our neighbour's gate, Tap-tap. Tap-tap. The shapes turn, leave the shadow of the hibiscus and merge into a person, who continues a slow shuffle towards me.

As he pauses under the light at our gate, I see an old man, frail and sinewy. A thick thatch of straight silvery hair crowns a bony skull. His sunken mouth suggests toothlessless and light reflects off silver stubble of several days on his cheeks and chin. He is wrapped in a large once-white shawl reaching down low, and from under a checked cotton *lungi* tied around his waist two skinny shins emerge. He is barefoot and carries in one hand a long stick. This is his staff of office, which he taps as he makes his rounds.

The night watchman. Employee of the neighbourhood's gentry.

A reminder of the English variant who sang rather than tapped, 'It's three o'clock in the mawrning, and aw-wl's well.' A legacy from the British and colonialism.

The watchman turns away. Tap, tap, tap. He moves in his measured way on hardened feet around the corner as he does at the same time every night. Tap, tap. Tap, tap.

Protected by this toothless warrior, we rest secure.

Getting around

I HAVE ALWAYS ENJOYED TRAVEL. I continued to enjoy it, even when the trip was a short one around Chennai or simply out to Benjamin's home village or to our rural centre. There was plenty of travel and it was good to feel enough at home in India to make some excursions on my own. I found them endlessly fascinating.

Not having the luxury of a car and driver, we usually travelled around the city on Benjamin's Bullet motor bike. I suspect few people knew Chennai's streets then as well as Benjamin and his Bullet. When I wore a sari, I sat side-saddle, hoping the metres of cloth would not unravel in the wind. We joined thousands of others commuting around the city on two-wheelers, which in many cases carried up to four or five family members.

With the eyes of a newcomer, I noticed things that often meant nothing to Benjamin. One day I was amused by a small hand-painted sign by the side of one of the main roads in the city: *Do not sound horn*. Heavy lorries lumbered past. Motorcycles roared. City buses belched black smoke with a grating chunder of mechanics. Garish trucks of the local government corporation blared past, and I could see their tailgates, decoratively emblazoned: *Sound horn*. Was this a case of lawmakers being above the law or the great inconsistencies which seem to blight bureaucracies everywhere?

If I needed to travel alone around the city, I normally took an autorickshaw. Yellow and black autorickshaws cost, at that time, much less and were much faster than traditional taxi cabs. With their capacity to weave in and out of traffic, they are the baby tigers of India and an essential element in the Chennai streetscape. If they are the baby tigers, their drivers are full-grown claws-unsheathed adults. On one occasion I had negotiated my way safely back home. I had already been initiated into one of the most sustained wars in human history – that between passengers and drivers in Chennai autorickshaws.

Lesson one: On entering the auto, and only after you are seated, indicate that you wish them to use the meter. This could provoke a short or long discussion, depending on your patience and the good humour of the driver. Often in the 1980s – and this is now almost universally the case – the meter will not work, so, depending on the weather, your energy, and the supply of autos in the area, you either climb out and find another one or settle for a reasonable fare. Once established, you indicate where you wish to go. Often, you need to give directions. *Po* ('Go') got us under way; *ingae* ('here') announced we had arrived; *aamaa* gave assent we were on the right path; *illai* said 'no' and was useful in a range of situations; those wonderful corruptions of *righta* and *lefta* were my standbys, but when it came to riding in an autorickshaw, my favourite was *mella*, 'slowly'. Usually it was more like *mella, mella, mella*, with rising panic as the vehicle raced through intersections and around other vehicles.

Lesson two: Do not attempt to pay until you are safely deposited at your destination. Then pay by the meter (a reasonably dull affair) or enter into more argy-bargy about paying by the meter (which is now impossible to do).

On this particular day, I had come by a known route and I was well aware of the normal fare. The driver still persisted in overcharging. So I paid the correct amount and went inside. The irate driver followed me to the door and after I had closed it from the inside he slid across the padlock on the outside of the house, locking me in.

Getting around

Benjamin was away at the time. I was not too perturbed; and the next morning a neighbour released me.

When we visited Kannigairpair village, we usually travelled by bus. We would catch an autorickshaw from our home across to the rural bus terminal (locally known by one of those uniquely Indian-English words, mofussil) at a place called Basin Bridge. There we would scramble to get a seat on the bus and travel for about forty minutes to the village. As we walked from the bazaar to the family home, there were always locals who would want to speak to Benjamin. After some initial interest during my first visits, I think I ceased to hold much curiosity for them.

The villagers' conversations with Benjamin reflected the old hierarchies. Merchants and traders, many of whom belonged to a Chetty caste, often in crisp white shirts worn loose over white *veshti*, were confident of their status; middle-aged women folk who had known Benjamin all his life were friendly and smiling, not pausing to talk much, but shaking their heads from side to side. Some of them would call out from their doorstep as he passed. The labourers, in their checked *lungis* wrapped around their waist and tucked up to free their skinny legs for ease of movement, might touch their heads with one hand in greeting, as they puffed on a thin cigarette hanging from their lips.

When we visited the family home in Kannigairpair, I always enjoyed watching the children as they kicked the dust on their way to and from school. The school was next door to Doctor Mathew's home, so the children all needed to pass by the gate. Often we would be sitting in the shade of the front porch, reading or meeting with people or simply enjoying some hot tea. This was the school in which Benjamin had received his entire primary school education. There were two simple brick structures. In one, the older primary classes met, the only furniture being a teacher's table and chair and blackboard; the larger one was a classroom for the senior students up to Year 10, largely girls in fresh navy and white uniforms, hair neatly tied in braids and be-ribboned. One end of this room was partitioned off with a series of large wooden presses, their backs turned to the classroom, and opening into a smaller part of the room which served as a teachers' space. I asked if I could look at the resources inside the cupboard and discovered maps, a plastic skull and a small collection of well-worn texts.

The teacher-in-charge was a man in his late forties or fifties. He was enthusiastic and talked to me about his love of literature and poetry. He was teaching the older primary classes from his chair at the front of the room while other teachers worked with the smaller children outside, where they sat on sand in the shade of the building. There were no displays in the room. The classroom interaction was typical of what I had observed generally in Indian schools at that time – teacher-talk, student chanting of rote learning and reading of text books by older students. Around this time, the state of Tamil Nadu was performing above the national rate of literacy in both urban and rural areas, with a high proportion of children staying on between Grade I and Grade IV. So, despite very meagre resources and very basic facilities, village schools, such as the one in my husband's village, were serving children with some effectiveness. Not all children were as well served. Benjamin had complained to me that in many rural schools teachers simply did not show up. This was borne out twenty years later when a national sample conducted by the World Bank indicated that during unannounced visits to primary schools right across India, a quarter of public sector teachers were absent, and only about half were teaching.[3]

I worked for sixteen years in a school system of seventy-five schools and around 42,000 children in Sydney and we had our share of complications and challenges. What my mind finds dazzling to comprehend is the scale of the education system in India within which the little village school in Kannigairpair operated: a system which, in

---

[3] M. Kremer et al, 2004, 'Teacher Absence in India: A Snapshot', in *Journal of the European Economic Association* (resubmitted version, 27 November 2004).

Getting around

2006, schooled nearly 140 million primary-aged children. For India, a further challenge is the additional seven million children between the ages of five and ten years who are not in school; most of these, over six million, are girls.

When Benjamin and I needed to go long distances, our limited resources made lower-class ticket trains or buses the only feasible choice. For me, this was an advantage. Trains in India are a microcosm of India itself. In the time since the first train chuffed and whistled its way out of Mumbai in 1853 on an inaugural thirty-four kilometre journey, Indian railways have sprawled tentacles 63,000 kilometres across the country. By the end of 1984, I had already travelled with Benjamin to Trichy, to Bangalore, to Mumbai and then on to Puntamba where I had met Xavier and Anthony Murmu, and to the remote village colony in the hills of Andhra Pradesh. Later, we travelled to Dindigul and on to the mountains of Kodaikanal, where we stayed with some Australian friends.

We visited Bangalore regularly. Our time there was always busy with meetings but also gave us the encouragement that comes from sharing time with colleagues. We both enjoyed these opportunities to catch up with a few very good friends who shared our interests and work. Bangalore is about 360 kilometres west of Chennai in the state of Karnataka. The delightfully fresh air was a welcome break from the constant humidity of coastal Chennai, reminding me a little of Sydney winters. We would leave Chennai in the evening on the Bangalore Mail, sleeping comfortably on our second-class wooden berths until the train pulled into Cantonment Station around dawn.

On one such occasion, we arrived and stepped out into that particular crystal light which comes with early mornings in India. There was a magic freshness. Our arrival coincided with the cry of the imam from the local mosque, and his call to prayer was answered by the more mundane summons of roosters and crows, whose raucousness matched the crazed crackle of the mosque's amplifiers. These sounds were magnified and highlighted in this moment before the normal bedlam of the city day had broken out. We took a cycle rickshaw from the station to our hotel, where we would bathe and breakfast before a day of visits. The rickshaw rider was thin and elderly. He had his brown woollen shawl pulled closely around bony shoulders against the chill. As the old man wheezed his way up an incline, Benjamin jumped out and told him to stop. He slipped onto the bicycle seat and, with the driver walking beside us, drove me to the top of the hill.

On another one of our travels, we stayed in the home of a friend who was a very successful businessman. Here, India showed me another face: the same hospitality, but this time in elegant and spacious comfort. The bare feet of the housemaid made only a soft swishing sound on the marble floor, as she brought a freshly cooked breakfast of delicious *appam*, a kind of fermented-rice pancake. Through the window, I watched the driver polishing the car at the front door in readiness to take our host to his chicken hatchery on the outskirts of the city while our host and hostess chatted about their daughter and her life in the USA.

We would conduct our business so that we still had time for more informal visits. In particular, we enjoyed long friendships with the James family and with their involvement in a school for needy hearing-impaired children; Hemchandra, who was involved in peace activism; and Corinne, a radical feminist passionate about improving the lot of women. Siddartha was a long-term friend who had developed an organisation called Pipal Tree, a centre for dialogue outside Bangalore. He had founded it in response to growing religious intolerance, a conviction that human spiritual values must include solidarity with the poor and oppressed, and a search for forms of spirituality which would defy the notion of religion as being divisive. The name comes from the famous Bodhi tree in Bihar in north India under which the young Siddartha Gautama found enlightenment sometime around the fifth century before Christ. In 1987, Pipal Tree in Bangalore based its work on the sense of spirituality which is the core of

Getting around

all religions with no caste or class association and drew its inspiration from Vivekananda, Christ, Buddha and Gandhi.

On one of our visits to Bangalore, we hired a car and driver for a day's trip to a village in the neighbouring state of Andhra Pradesh. Our goal was a commune-farm project just beyond the village of Penukonda. On the map as the crow flies, Penukonda is just 122 kilometres due north of Bangalore, which is the capital of Karnataka state, and the drive there and back seemed quite reasonable. Our driver found his way without much difficulty in about two hours. We visited the community, met with the leaders, and sat with the young people who were its members to enjoy a simple lunch in an open area covered by woven palms. Our car left the farm and drove the few kilometres back to the narrow sealed bitumen which passed through Penukonda. As we approached the dwellings which made up the village, khaki-clad police stepped out from the side of the road and erected a barricade. The car stopped. Police said nothing to us, but spoke to the driver in Kannada – the language of Karnataka state – and took the driver away. Benjamin and I sat in the car and waited. After a short while, the police returned and asked us to get out of the car and to take our things. We complied. We then learned that the car had been trading as a hire car without a proper licence to do so. The police seized the car and driver and we were left standing by the side of the road.

We did not have a lot of options, so we waited until a local bus came along and began the journey back to our hotel in Bangalore. We changed buses a couple of times on a serpentine journey around the hills and country areas of Karnataka. The sun had set before we finally arrived back at our hotel in the city about six hours later.

It was during such travels that I was made more aware of the liability that, as a foreigner, I presented to Benjamin. We had little money and so we needed to manage it carefully. Benjamin was very mindful that some folk tended to assume that foreign woman equals wealth, and so, if he had a purchase, a taxi-hire or accommodation to negotiate, he would often tell me make myself scarce until the business was done. Over time, I began to weary of this game, and even began to think that, while I might do it very differently, I was capable of doing some negotiating of my own. Sometimes, it could be fun, and some years later I wrote the following *tanka* after an encounter with a particularly smooth shopkeeper.

> shawl bazaar vendor
> attends me like his mother
> silken persuasion
> with padded stealth
> the tiger strikes[4]

It was not all hard work. Benjamin and I enjoyed these trips, even if they were primarily about work. They took us away from the public eye of the office and offered us a chance to see places through each others' eyes: his were the eyes of a son of India, one with an encyclopedic capacity for facts and a loving impatience with the injustice, corruption and inefficiency within his country, as well as the eyes of a former occasional tourist guide (a necessity when the organisation had not been able to pay him sufficiently); mine, the eyes of the ignorant, curious about absolutely everything and amazed by so much of it. He tended to view things through a lens of political relationships, while I looked more to the personal and interpersonal.

Some of those we met were friends from when Benjamin had studied at Loyola College, affiliated with the University of Madras. There he had been associated with a student group known as the All India Catholic University Federation (AICUF). Involvement with AICUF had given him the opportunity to develop his leadership skills and to follow his altrusim. Some of his friends had also completed the same course as he at the Madras School of Social Work. This post-graduate school, which functioned autonomously but later became affili-

---

[4] *Year of the Tiger: A Eucalypt Challenge*, 2010.

ated with the University of Madras, has produced strong advocates for social justice. In some cases, the ties between professors and students have survived distance and time to still be alive and important thirty years later. Something idealistic and inspiring had transpired in these educational experiences.

On one occasion, however, we made a trip with the sole purpose of having a holiday. A good-humoured gentle man called Jaykaran, brother of our friend and neighbour, Dr Elsa Benjamin, invited us to spend a few days in a comfortable guest house on the edge of the ocean at Tuticorin, the Anglo-Dutch name for Thoothukudi, a historic port city about 550 kilometres south-west of Chennai. We seemed to have the large company retreat to ourselves, except for an array of employees who looked after the place and provided our meals. It was a nicely-timed break for us. White sands edged down gradually to the sea and as we walked the broad expanse, strong winds blew the sand across our feet and into the tufts of silvery grass above the beach.

Tuticorin is another of those Indian cities with layers of history and civilisations in its foundations. The people up and down the coast around the city are known as Paravars, or, as they prefer, Bharathars, one of the oldest Indian castes, and one associated with the powerful Pandyan Kingdom. This ancient kingdom is said to have thrived as early as the sixth century BCE and survived in various forms into the fifteenth century CE. The Pandyans controlled the pearl fishing along the south coast of India in the waters between India and Sri Lanka which might have been the inspiration for Bizet to set his opera, *The Pearl Fishers*, just across the water in ancient Ceylon.

Facing east into the Bay of Bengal (Gulf of Mannar), and a mere two hundred kilometres across the Palk Straits from Sri Lanka, Thoothukudi is only a two-hour drive from the southern tip of India at Kanyakumari. A chain of low islands and reefs is all that separates India from Sri Lanka at this point. The harbour offers a strategic location which was exploited by the Indigenous locals, the Paravars, and then in turn by the Portuguese in 1548 and the Dutch about a century later, until they in turn conceded it to the British in 1825. A lighthouse shining out onto the Strait has guided fisher folk and pearl divers since the 1840s, but the port is claimed to be one of the oldest in the world. It continues to be a major port and a large centre for salt pans and ship building.

During our brief stay, we went to the shipyards. The dinosaur rib-cage of a partially-completed vessel lay open to the sky on the sand. The frame towered above us when we stepped inside. Craftsmen clambered barefoot over the huge skeleton as they moulded timber into arcing walls which would smooth the passage of the traditional country fishing dhow before the wind. With a little imagination, we might have been watching workmen of one of the great Pandyan kings preparing a vessel to carry spices to Egypt, to Greece or Rome. It might even have been the vessel which carried an embassy to Augustus Caesar about 29 BCE.

Unfortunately, I was suffering a stomach upset during this visit which took a little from my enjoyment of the fine meals presented. However, it was an opportunity for Benjamin to bring out the remedy which has become the stand-by for such ailments in our family: rice soup or *kanjee*. *Boil rice in plenty of water till it is over-cooked. Do not drain the water. Add salt and take as a soup.* A cure for anything intestinal is guaranteed. *Kanjee* can also be dressed up – if constitutions permit – with pickles, yoghurt or vegetables.

We travelled to Tuticorin, as we did for most of our longer trips, in second class sleeping berths on overnight trains, maximising our working time both in Chennai and in the place we were visiting and minimising accommodation costs. Waking up in a crowded carriage with well-used toilet facilities after a broken overnight sleep has some drawbacks, but for me they were always worth the sheer magic of arriving in a new place in the freshness of dawn. Sometimes, it was nearly quiet. Often, it was cool. Always, the morning sky was transparent with light.

Days of fire

ON A SUNDAY AFTERNOON some time in 2001, the Valhalla theatre in Balmain, Sydney, screened *My Mother India*,[5] a documentary directed and written by Safina Oberoi. Daughter of a Sikh father and Australian-born mother, Safina's documentary is based on her family's experiences in Delhi in the aftermath of the assassination of Indira Gandhi in 1984. Afterwards, she invited comments from the audience. Rising, I began to speak, and found I wanted nothing more than to sob my heart out. It was then I realised how deeply a few days late in 1984 had scratched themselves into my soul as an ugly drama was played out in India, especially in its capital.

When my younger sister Carmel and her husband Ian had said they would come through Chennai in the last few days in October 1984, I could hardly wait for their visit. Benjamin and I were there with a car to greet them at the airport. Over the next few days we visited Benjamin's brother Alphonse and his wife Elsey in the family home in Kannigairpair village; we visited Doctor Mathew and Kochamma and took photos in their garden; we visited other family members and friends, and generally enjoyed a few days of wonderful chatter.

---

[5] Safina Oberoi (2001), *My Mother India*, Chili Films, Sydney.

The computer that Carmel and Ian had brought with them from the USA for us had become entangled in customs at Mumbai, so they came on to Chennai without it. Benjamin was due to fly to Bangladesh for an Asian-Pacific Workshop organised by the Commonwealth Secretariat in London. Always a great 'fixer', before he left, he arranged for Manimaran to travel by train to Mumbai, sort out the customs issues and then have the computer flown back to Chennai. Then, we would pay the duty owing – some tens of thousands of rupees, I vaguely recall – and take delivery of this wonderful gift. The train journey to Mumbai takes about twenty hours and so we didn't expect to see Manimaran for at least two days.

All went to plan. Benjamin had flown to Bangladesh. On Wednesday 31 October, we were waiting at home for Manimaran's return so we could go to a bank in the city, withdraw the necessary cash, and then drive back to the airport to collect the computer. Carmel and Ian's time in India was running out and we were anxious that everything would be completed on time. I didn't want to discourage them, but having now been in India about six months, I knew how easy it was for plans to go awry.

At around 11.00 am, Carmel and I were talking in the living room. Ian, who was standing on the front balcony, called to us. There was noise and commotion in the street. Men and women huddled, arms waving. People were shouting. All-India Radio had just broadcast news: at 9.40 am the Prime Minister, Indira Gandhi, had been shot. Two of her Sikh security guards had fired on her as she walked across the garden from her residence to her office in No 1, Safdarjung Rd, New Delhi. The radio announcers were explicit, identifying the guards as Sikh, that is, the turban-wearing followers of the Sikh religion originating in the fertile north-western state of Punjab. The news had an immediate impact even in Chennai.

We realised, without fully comprehending how right we were, that, if we were to secure the computer in time for Carmel and Ian to leave India as scheduled, we would have to continue on with our plan. We sensed the unrest that was unfolding across the city. At 1.30 pm, Radio Australia announced that Mrs Gandhi was dead. She had died at 10.50 am, about an hour after the shooting. Her chances of surviving the thirty-two bullets fired into her body at close range had been non-existent. For the rest of the afternoon, All-India Radio continued to broadcast its story that the Prime Minister was fighting for her life in the All-India Institute of Medical Sciences (AIIMS) in New Delhi.

Unfortunately the bank we needed was in the centre of Chennai. Would Manimaran return in time? I paced to the kitchen window, rubbing my forehead against the vertical wooden dowels which acted as a security screen. Then back to the front veranda to peer through the glazed windows lining the front wall. I rang the Centre. The staff had heard the news. No, Manimaran was not there. I asked one of the office staff to take his bicycle down to the taxi rank on the main road to get us a cab. After about fifteen minutes, a taxi came. It was at the door. The driver was walking between the car and our door with impatience. If he left, we might not easily get another vehicle. We went down and waited at the car. Finally, an autorickshaw putt-putted around the corner. Manimaran jumped out as the vehicle stopped. He had done what he had been asked and had returned, but only just. He had flown into Chennai – his first flight – on the last plane that would fly into the city for a number of days.

I had already discovered, with some surprise, a strong strand of sentiment in many South Indians. In an extreme example, a local man had recently doused himself with kerosene and ignited himself, apparently as a sacrificial prayer, when the Chief Minister of Tamil Nadu, the faded film giant, Marudur Gopalan Ramachandran, MGR, was ill. Now, two thousand kilometres from Delhi, I had underestimated the impact that the attack on the Prime Minister would have in Chennai. I simply failed to comprehend it. Chennai stopped in its tracks. Public transport halted. Bus loads of people were left in the streets as drivers and conductors got out and walked away. Thousands of workers left their place of work. Life in India stopped. It was a violent and vicious death. The people of India were bewildered.

The streets became crammed with people finding their way home. Into this chaos we drove, three foreigners, Manimaran and the young accountant, Sujatha. The car edged through agitated pedestrians as we made our way slowly to Mount Road and the Bank of America. The crowds blocking the streets were emotional. Somehow Carmel and Ian got into the bank and withdrew the cash. We tried to leave. The driver was unhappy. If he were to accidentally knock someone, his life could be in danger. People surrounded the car in front of us and tried to take it over. They closed in on us, clamouring to get into the car, or to get us out. Tense and uncertain, we kept the windows closed and the doors locked.

'*Po. Po.*' *Go*. Manimaran urged the driver.

'Don't stop. Don't stop', Ian was saying, over and over.

Sujatha was rummaging in her brown vinyl handbag. She took out her lipstick and opened it. Carmel and I watched.

Jai Hind – Long live India – the young woman scrawled on the windscreen. The patriotic greeting appeared to work. Indira Gandhi's father, the great Jawaharlal Nehru, had used this same greeting at the conclusion of his speech after the assassination of Mahatma Gandhi. The crowd eased a little.

'*Po. Po. Mella.*' *Carefully*. Sujatha and Manimaran kept encouraging the driver. '*Ipo.*' *Now*.

'Just go.' I added my own feeble effort, more a wish than an instruction. The car eased through the crowd, gradually gathering some speed. Between Sujatha's and Manimaran's efforts, and a very nervous driver, we made our way back along Guindy Road towards the airport. Here the crowds were thinner, but we were still shaken by the incident in the city. It was not a day to relax.

For some reason, the customs officers at the airport were still at their desks. I saw Mr Narayansamy, and was glad that he had taken a protective liking to me.

Days of fire

'My daughter, my daughter', he greeted me, eagerly shepherding us through the bureaucratic labyrinth, going out of his way to assist us and facilitate the process. As Carmel recalls, we went up from floor to floor in the customs building, from office to office, and with each higher floor, the desks and the offices became larger. Finally, we paid the customs duty, took possession of the computer and respectfully farewelled my customs 'godfather'. We were beginning to realise that we had been lucky to have managed this episode so uneventfully, and quickly made our way back home.

In the security of our Indira Nagar flat, we focused on the television, watching the numbing repetition of the day's events: people milling around outside the hospital in Delhi, medicos huddled, the Prime Minister's home in New Delhi, her bloodied garden.

Finally, at 6.00 pm, hours after the whole world had known the grim truth, All-India Radio officially announced to India's people that Mrs Gandhi was dead.

By then, a small group within and close to the Congress Party had decided on a successor. At 6.40 pm, President Giani Zail Singh ratified their nomination and Rajiv Gandhi, elder son of the former Prime Minister, was sworn in as the seventh person to become Prime Minister of India. Giani Zail Singh was a courtly turbaned gentleman, who always wore a red rose in the buttonhole of his long fitted jacket. He had been in Yemen when he heard the news of Mrs Gandhi's shooting and had returned in time to go to the hospital and to ask Rajiv to accept the role. Just before midnight, we watched and listened as the new Prime Minister addressed the nation. Rajiv's wife, Italian-born Sonia Gandhi, was there, as she also had been there in the garden immediately after the shooting. She had heard the shots from the house and had run to her mother-in-law. She had then cradled the shattered body in the car on its way to the All-India Institute of Medical Sciences.

Rajiv Gandhi was a fresh-faced young man. Until the death of his younger brother Sanjay, his aspirations had seemed confined to being a pilot with Indian Airlines. I watched him speak that night, first in English and then in Hindi, urging the nation to honour his mother's memory.

'Nothing would hurt the soul of our beloved Indira Gandhi more than the occurrence of violence in any part of the country', he counselled. 'Indira Gandhi is no more, but her soul lives. India lives. India is immortal. The spirit of India is immortal. I know that the nation will recognise its responsibilities.'

He was forty years old and had been in Parliament only two years. It was a brave and dignified performance.

Carmel and Ian left India the next day or so, somehow managing to make their way to the airport. Their visit had been all too short and disrupted in a way beyond our imagining. I was pleased for their sakes to see them leave without further complications, but it was a strange time for me as I made my way back to the house alone. Benjamin's absence was palpable in every room.

I spent the next few days in our apartment, watching grainy images in black and white of thousands filing past the catafalque in Teen Murti House, where Mrs Gandhi's body lay in state. In between this mournful parade, programs replayed moments from Indira Gandhi's public life.

She had been born in 1917, the daughter of Kamala and Jawaharlal Nehru, India's first prime minister, and the granddaughter of Motilal Nehru, another nationalist leader. She had grown up within the Freedom Movement. She associated with Mahatma Gandhi and the other key players. It was not surprising that, after her father's death, she too would enter politics. Through her marriage to Feroze Gandhi, a Parsi from Mumbai, Indira Priyadarshini Nehru had fortuitously acquired a name which was honoured in Indian history at least as much as her father's. Feroze Gandhi was no relation of Mahatma Gandhi. In 1984, Indira Gandhi was in the fourth year of her fourth term as Prime Minister, the first three in succession from January 1966 to March 1977.

Commentators recalled the milestones of her leadership with sombre deference. My work at the Centre had left me a little less reverential. I recalled the controversial episode in her political life, when, following a High Court decision in 1975 convicting her of electoral abuses, and in the face of mounting protests, she had persuaded the then-President to declare a State of Emergency. During the next twenty-one months, elections were postponed, political opposition was squashed and civil rights suspended while the Prime Minister ruled by decree to 'modernise' India. Memorable among these were draconian measures engineered largely by her younger son, Sanjay, to clear the Delhi slums and introduce family planning. In these processes, a quarter of a million people – many, as happened, from Muslim areas – were forcibly resettled, leaving thousands of people homeless. Sterilisations were performed under duress.

One of my favourite authors is the Indian-born Canadian, Rohinton Mistry, and one of his books, the disturbingly beautiful *A Fine Balance*, incorporates these events, grinding to the final tragedy. Salman Rushdie, in his monumental novel *Midnight's Children*, also bitterly satirises the same period. When Emergency was finally suspended and elections called in 1977, not only did Congress lose, but both Indira and Sanjay lost their seats.

Sanjay, Indira's heir-apparent, had insisted on flying a commercial airliner with passengers without a valid licence and flying stunt planes and executing dangerous aerobatics over the capital, Delhi. In June 1980, while he was attempting to exit from a complex loop in a single-engine two-seater plane over his office, Sanjay lost control and crashed. After his death, Mrs Gandhi had turned her attention towards her elder son, Rajiv.

Initially, when the crowds gathered outside the hospital in Delhi where Mrs Gandhi had been taken, there was shock and distress but no sign of tension. At around four in the afternoon, this changed. About thirty young men approached the area, almost in formation. First, they set fire to a scooter so that it blocked the traffic. They took weapons from a truck which had arrived with them. They then proceeded to drag Sikhs out of nearby buses, pulling off their turbans, setting them on fire and beating the men.[6] At the same time, false rumours began to be broadcast in the city that Sikhs were poisoning the city water supply, rejoicing over Mrs Gandhi's death and murdering trainloads of Hindus. These were the first indications of the nightmare that was to follow.

I sat in our living room in Indira Nagar watching the relentless images on the television, hour after hour. Mrs Gandhi's body lay in state in Teen Murti House, the gaunt beak profiled on the bier, the distinctive white patch at the front of her black hair. The camera panned the long lines of mourning public and notables, local and international, moving slowly around the corpse; moving out to the long lines of faithful waiting patiently outside for their turn to pay their respects. Over and over, Doorharshan, the national TV channel, replayed the scene from the garden, the hedge beside where she last stood, the Sikh guards who shot her so savagely, grave-faced Congress Party members. Then, as the day of the funeral approached, the arrival of foreign heads of state and dignitaries, more black cars and sombre faces being greeted by the President, the new Prime Minister and other government leaders. Hour after hour, Doordarshan screened national mourning. It was morbid and fascinating.

Behind this projection of national grief, other more macabre images were beginning to appear. In Chennai, there were reports of an occasional incident, but from the national capital came news of passengers killed on trains; a sense of a city running amok, of order breaking down. In the images and confusion in the press and on the TV screen, I saw Congress leaders amongst the mobs bent on a vendetta.

Over the next four days, more than two thousand Sikhs were

---

[6] Journalist Dev Dutt, quoted in Pranay Gupte (1985), *Vengeance: India after the Assassination of Indira Gandhi*, W. W. Norton & Co., New York.

killed in Delhi alone. The chilling fact is that the violence was targeted. Sikh households and shops were attacked, their owners burned and murdered, while non-Sikh dwellings next door were left untouched. The action was led by certain members of the Congress Party, and the police failed to protect the populace.

I sought out some of the first-hand records of what happened during those days. Payal Singh, a Sikh journalist who happened to be in a group of Sikhs travelling by train to Delhi for a wedding at the time, was in the midst of her journey before she learned of Mrs Gandhi's death. Two hours from Delhi, on 1 November, their train was attacked. Payal Singh wrote of the hours she and her companions spent while a mob went from coach to coach in search of Sikhs. The brutality of the assault was horrifying. The travellers were told that the police could not control the mob and had walked away. Women suggested that the male Sikhs would be safer if they went to the ladies' compartment. When the train reached Delhi, no security arrangements had been made at the station. When Payal Singh left the station with other women, they saw the bloodied bodies of Sikhs being unloaded from the train.[7]

The full extent of the barbarity that had occurred only became public in the weeks that followed. A journal, *Manushi*, documented what had happened during those days, based on the eyewitness reports of Madhu Kishwar and Ruth Vanita who visited the most affected areas in Delhi. Working in the Centre with Benjamin, I had responsibilty for the Centre's library and I knew this journal; I admired its tenacious work for the rights of women and read each issue eagerly. Madhu and her colleagues organised a peace march which was shut down by the police. They visited the refuge camps and spoke to victims. They testified before some of the numerous commissions and committees of inquiry established by the Administration. And they detailed their findings in affidavits and published a series

---

[7] Payal Singh Mohanka (2005), 'That Horror 21 Years Ago', *The Round Table*, vol. 94, issue 382, October, pp. 589-598.

of powerful articles in a number of magazines.[8] These were women whose scholarship and balanced commitment to justice I had come to respect.

Why did Mrs Gandhi's trusted guards shoot her? Why did they shoot her and then immediately surrender themselves, standing passively until, some time later, they were taken into custody? How was it that, without trial or authority, the assailants were shot by those holding them, resulting in the death of one of them?

The story, like most stories in India, is complex, involving political lust, religion, displacement of the poor, graft and ineptitude. It includes Mrs Gandhi's resistance of fierce action by some Sikhs regarding Punjab. This had been going on over a number of years with violent attacks by certain elements within the Sikh activists. There had been terrorism in Punjab, the traditional home state of Sikhs. The drive by some for a separate Khalistan had dominated the newspapers for the months since my arrival in India. Most feared of all was Janail Singh Bhindranwale, who had incited violence against Hindus and Sikhs alike in Punjab. Bhindranwale had set up his headquarters in the Sikh holy of holies, the sacred Golden Temple in Amritsar. It was a provocative move in a deadly political game.

In June 1984, Mrs Gandhi had lost patience. She had ordered the Indian army to attack the Golden Temple in what was known as Operation Blue Star. I did not ever visit Amritsar, but it is an ancient and venerable site in the Punjab. The Golden Temple dates back at least to 1588. In its heart, the Harmandir Sahib, the holy of holies, the Sikh holy book, the Guru Granth Sahib, is honoured. The temple is surrounded by a pool whose waters are considered holy. Like Sikh temples (*Gurdwaras*) around the world, anyone is welcome. The

---

[8] See *Manushi*, no. 25, Nov-Dec. 1984; *Manushi*, no. 26, Jan-Feb. 1985; Madhu Kishwar, 'Affidavit of Nanavati Commission', http://www.carnage84.com/affidavits/nanavati/promi/madhukishwar.htm, accessed April 2009.

only requirement is that visitors act with respect within the holy place which is the temple and that women and men cover their heads. The four entrances to the temple signify the importance of this kind of acceptance and openness. I have experienced this a number of times in Australia and have enjoyed the hospitality of the community meal at a *langar*, or community kitchen. The situation in 1984 was fraught: a holy place in the control of terrorists. I understood it as being akin (given similar terrible circumstances) to the Italian army attacking the Vatican.

The Golden Temple complex suffered a great deal of damage. All in all, 600 people died, including Bhindranwale, as well as hundreds of innocent pilgrims – men, women and children – as well as some who lived close by the temple. While the Sikh terrorists' demands for a separate Punjabi (Khalistan) nation were not supported by the majority of India's 14 million Sikhs, the army's attack on the Golden Temple and its desecration outraged all Sikhs.

Another factor behind the eruption of Delhi into violence went straight back to the time of Emergency and creation of colonies of aggrieved and hungry citizens whose thuggery could be bought by political parties with a few rupees, cheap drink and the promiscuous thrill of being active players in national events.

Another day passed. Still I watched as the tributes to Mrs Gandhi and the blood letting continued. On the third day, in the evening of Friday 2 November, when many foreign dignitaries had arrived in the capital in preparation for the state funeral, Prime Minister Rajiv Gandhi made a public appeal for peace. He stated that he would not allow violence.

In later months and years as prime minister, Rajiv Gandhi came across as charming and very persuasive. I recall a TV interview some time later where he went live on air with a group of children and permitted them to question him about anything, which is a rash thing for any politician to do. His media presence was gracious and even modest. However, I cannot forget my outrage and impotence, sitting alone in our living room in Chennai, when whoever was in charge in Delhi (and I assumed that had to include Rajiv Gandhi, the administration and the police) permitted three days to pass before taking action to try to control the national obscenity that had been unleashed. Rajiv's appeal released the political will for appropriate action. The violence began to ebb. And then, with one directive, the army appeared in force and the killing and burning ceased. There seemed to be something chillingly deliberate in that delay.

It was too late. The damage had been done. Rajni Kothari, another highly-respected political scientist, whom I knew from the Centre's library, described one of the camps where survivors were taken. He writes of women and children 'huddled together with shock and grief inscribed on every part of their beings'. The only males in the camp were younger than ten, and even they were rare. Family groups had been reduced to widows, girls and infants.[9]

Less than three weeks after the murder of over three thousand Indians in the wake of his mother's own murder, Rajiv Gandhi was to make this public and now infamous comment:

> Some riots took place in the country following the murder of Indiraji. We know the people were very angry and for a few days it seemed that India had been shaken. But, when a mighty tree falls, it is only natural that the earth around it does shake a little.

His comment added salt to the pain of the nation, especially to the thousands of traumatised widows and children huddled in fear for their lives. I lamented how little I knew about so many things. This episode put faces and tears to what I had learnt in history lectures at Newcastle Uni, but for many Sikh families it brought back the pain of forty years, when, with the Partition of India and the creation of Pakistan at the time of Indian Independence in 1947, much of Pakistan was carved out of choice farmland in Punjab. Millions of people from what was previously Punjab migrated eastwards so as to live within the new borders of India, leaving behind their hereditary homeland

[9] ibid.

and possessions. About half of them were Sikhs. Against this tide, four million Muslims were making their way westwards towards their new home in Pakistan. In the clashes that occurred in that brittle time, it is reported that over two million people died, many of them Sikhs. In the wake of the pogrom in 1984, many Sikh widows made the decision to leave Delhi and once more migrated in search of a home.

The next day, 3 November, I watched on television as the funeral procession for Mrs Gandhi left her residence. At four o'clock, Rajiv lit her funeral pyre at *Shakti Sthal* – the 'place of strength and power'. Her ashes were later strewn over the Himalaya and various Indian state capitals.

In the midst of my distress about what I had seen through the media, the women at *Manushi* continued to write. I eagerly opened each edition of their magazine and was heartened by their reports of another side to these events. For example, in Delhi, a Hindu man, Prabhu Dayal, rescued the women folk of his Sikh employer, only to lose his own life in the process. Hindus hid Sikhs inside their homes, factories and other premises during these days, resisting attempts by outsiders to raid their compounds; they assisted male Sikhs to escape by persuading them to remove their turbans and cut their traditional long hair and beards (an offensive action for a male Sikh) and by giving them bicycles or transporting them to safer areas; Hindus protected and saved at least one Gurdwara and other Sikh property from being burnt down; Delhi University teachers and students kept vigil around the entry point to where Sikhs lived; and Hindus gave shelter to Sikh neighbours even though it meant their own property was destroyed.

There have been nine formal inquiries following these events of 1984. There has been little justice for the victims. Twenty-one years after the massacres, the final report was submitted to the Congress-led government on 9 February 2005. It was not placed before the Indian Parliament until 8 August. This report, which indicted prominent Congress leaders, was vigorously condemned because it failed to deal with those it named. Three of those indicted were still members of the Congress-led government.

Protests forced some belated action. A few days after the final report was tabled in Parliament, Prime Minister, Manmohan Singh, a Sikh, apologised for the 1984 riots, stating:

> I bow my head in shame that such a thing took place ... I have no hesitation in apologising to the Sikh community. I apologise not only to the Sikh community but to the whole Indian nation because what took place in 1984 is the negation of the concept of nationhood enshrined in our Constitution.

The irony of the apology coming from a Sikh has always bemused me.

The assassination of Indira Ghandi was cruel and unjust. Even harder to live with were the four days that followed her murder. How am I to make sense of these events of 1984? The outrage against the Sikhs haunts me. I have hesitated to write this story, but I have done so because I marvel at India's resilience and because the evil of these days still disturbs me – as it should. The events of those days should have left such a deep scar that all humanity should vow that they will never happen again.

Yet they have happened again in India – in Gujarat, in Ayodhya, in Mumbai. They have happened again in Rwanda, in the Middle East, in Serbia and Croatia, in USA, Bali, Spain, Sri Lanka and UK. Even in laid-back Sydney and Brisbane, after September 11, 2001, there were a few individuals who chose to attack local Islamic centres; in the discordant summer of 2006 in Sydney, riots between ethnic groups on Cronulla beach confronted us. That is why I record this story.

A small group of India's citizens bloodied India in 1984. It was also an abdication of leadership by those in authority, by those charged with protecting citizens, and by the citizens who did nothing. What is it that tips men and women over a line so that they forget the names of their neighbours and no longer recognise the same human features which make us all sisters and brothers? What is it that turns people just like us into 'them', 'the other', a faceless group? In the human family, very few of us are evil, and all of us are in some way broken. In projecting all blame onto a particular group of people we ignore the dark side of ourselves. We transfer our own faults and weaknesses, so that issues become black and white. In this way, the attacks upon the Sikhs were a denial of the brokenness in the total Indian situation.

What happened within a country can happen between nations, whenever we brand a whole nation or group of nations as evil. The assassination of Indira Gandhi was calculated. The appropriate response is to ask why. Congress needed to ask why the Prime Minister's personal security guards, two otherwise loyal young men with bright careers, should take the action they did. Likewise, we in Australia and other countries need to ask why extremists of any kind attack our people.

Recently I came across the reasons that Safina Oberoi has given for making her moving documentary.

> My family suffered no loss in 1984: our house remained standing, my father and my brother were not killed, my mother and I were safe. And yet we lost everything. Nothing ever looked the same again. For we had looked into the eyes of Mother India and we had seen the Dark Side.[10]

For me, I have looked into the eyes of the dark side of humanity, and I don't want to forget what I have seen.

---

[10] Safina Oberoi, Youtube, accessed May 2009.

Taking sides with the poor

WE HAD CHOSEN as the reading during our wedding the passage from Luke's Gospel where Jesus gives his 'maiden speech' for his public life, the 'I am come to bring good news to the poor' statement-of-intent regarding his mission. As I saw more of India, especially through our work in the Centre, I began to understand a little of what it meant to be poor. One such insight came during a visit to a village somewhere in the north of Tamil Nadu and southern Andhra Pradesh which was a centre for *beedi*-making. *Beedis* are local cigarettes which should convince the most inveterate smoker to give up. They are thin, dark and pungent.

We stopped in a village and entered a small thatched hut, typical of those I had seen in the dwellings clustered near the family home in Kannigairpair. It was dim inside the hut, with the stuffy smell of damp earth which evoked for me memories of the mud left in our Hunter Valley home by floods in February 1955. Two or three women sat cross-legged on the earth floor rolling *beedis*. Also with them was a little girl. She was small. Her face had the pinched narrow look that comes from consistent hunger, and her eyes shifted around, glassy and devoid of sparkle. She too was working the leaves and stuffing them to make cigarettes. I could only guess her age. She might have been eight. She might have been twelve. She should have been in school or outside playing, chasing other children, shouting and singing. She was rolling *beedis*. She had a quota to meet, just as the adult women did. I understood that she was paying off a debt that would trail off into a long future to cover the costs of a loan her family had taken.

This nameless little girl remains just one of millions of children trapped in bonded labour. The cheap labour of a child becomes much more profitable when it is tied to a debt that a family is unlikely ever to be able to repay. Later on, remembering this little girl, I read up about such children. One girl, it was reported, explained how her ten-year-old sister worked each day from 7.00 am till 9.00 at night as a bonded labourer. If she worked too slowly or talked to other children, the supervisor yelled at her and hit her; when she was too sick to go to work, he would come looking for her. This nine-year-old concluded:

> I don't care about school or playing. I don't care about any of that. All I want is to bring my sister home from the bonded labour man. For 600 rupees I can bring her home – that is our only chance to get her back. We don't have 600 rupees … we will never have 600 rupees.)[11]

(Six hundred rupees is the equivalent of approximately $AUD20. Sales of *beedis* in India each year are worth about 40 billion rupees.)

If she fitted the typical pattern of that place and time, the child I saw that day probably worked six and a half days a week; she would have been unpaid for the additional half day on Sunday, because that was a catch up day for work not completed on the other days. The debt incurred by her family could only have been repaid in full in one instalment, a near-impossibility since they had to borrow in the

---

[11] Human Rights Watch (1996), *The Small Hands of Slavery: Bonded Child Labor in India*, Human Rights Watch Children's Rights Project, Human Rights Watch/Asia, accessed September 2008.

first instance. In addition, the labour agent would have paid her only a proportion of her earnings, so that, even if her family had earned enough in a few weeks or months to pay off the debt, they would continue in bondage for years. She would eventually have married into poverty. She would be likely to have contracted tuberculosis or some other lung disease. She would probably have suffered back and leg ailments, problems with her small joints and damaged eyesight.

The practice of bonded child labour is, of course, illegal in India. Despite tougher legislation introduced by the Indian government in 2006, despite the long-term efforts of committed senior Indian bureaucrats and the valiant efforts of many non-government organisations, children continue to be exploited as bonded labourers in workplaces that are dangerous and dirty and expose them to all kinds of risk. In 2007, it was estimated that there were still millions of Indian children in bonded labour, among the highest in the world, in a range of industries, that included not only *beedi*-making but others such as making matches, glass-blowing, glass bangles, firecrackers, carpet weaving, agricultural tasks, domestic work, food industry, wayside stalls and restaurants.

In stark contrast to the little girl I saw hard at work is the idyllic image of the Indian poet from Bengal, Rabindranath Tagore. In *The Banyan Tree*, he conjures up a childhood which belongs by right to all children.

> O you shaggy-headed banyan tree standing on the bank of the pond,
> Have you forgotten the little child? ...
> Do you not remember how he sat at the window and wondered at the tangle of your roots? ...
> Sunlight danced on the ripples like restless tiny shuttles weaving golden tapestry.
> Two ducks swam by the weedy margin above their shadows, and the child would sit still and think.
> He longed to be the wind and blow through your resting branches,

to be your shadow and lengthen with the day on the water,
to be a bird and perch on your topmost twig, and to float
like those ducks amongst the weeds and shadows ...

I met the little nameless girl rolling *beedis* when we were visiting a small band of idealistic young people in the non-government organisation in her village. Because of their work, perhaps that child in the dingy hut was given another chance. Perhaps she eventually got to school and to play on the bank of the local pond. I would like to think so. Today, she would be thirty-something. Most likely, she has her own children. The odds suggest that her children are rolling *beedis* also.

Being poor is entangled with history, culture, politics and the family into which a child is born. I had been in India less than a month when I had first heard of communal violence. Towards the end of May 1984, violence had erupted in the textile centre of Bihwandi, an area to the north of Mumbai (then still known as Bombay). Chilling reports appeared in the papers of Hindus attacking Muslims, Muslims attacking Hindus. The assaults were vicious. Men and property were doused in kerosene and burnt. Two hundred people died.

In Australia, I had used the word 'communal' as a positive descriptor about people living or working in community. Now, I learnt a new meaning for this seemingly-harmless word. India prides itself on being a secular state. This is used, not in the sense of a state devoid of religious instinct (as used to describe some aspects of post-modern western societies), but to convey a respect for the rights and equality of all religions, giving official preference to none. Christopher Kremmer's explanation of India today as 'a secular society grafted onto a deeply spiritual society'[12] makes good sense to me. For centuries, India has balanced its cauldron of faiths and cultures with spectacular resilience, and while there have been wars and times of

---

[12] Christopher Kremmer (2006), *Inhaling the Mahatma*, HarperCollins, Australia.

trauma, the balance has always been regained. In this context, communalism is the feared cancer of India. It is a euphemism for violence and hatred spilling over between different religious or cultural groups.

I could never fully understand the complex intertwining of politics, history, jealousy and hatred that erupted into this bloodshed, but part of the story, at least, lies in the emergence of fundamentalist elements within Hinduism that have come to be known as *Hindutva*: India for Hindus.

From the beginning of modern India, Gandhi and other leaders had rejected the notion of one religion in India. Gandhi, in particular, had been catholic in his drawing on other religions for his inspiration. Despite his efforts, a nationalist ideology had started to emerge, even before Independence, that proclaimed India for Hindus and Pakistan for Muslims. This movement also attempted (and still attempts) to reduce the diversity within Hinduism to a monolith.

This took shape as early as 1925 in the organisation known as Rashtryia Swayamsevak Sangh (RSS) which became a parent organisation for many others within the movement. RSS emphasised a dictatorial model of organisation where volunteers were drilled both in fierce ideology and in physical readiness to fight. They worked for a 'Hindu Rashtra' (or Nation), India for Hindus. RSS opposition to Gandhi led to the Mahatma's assassination by one of the RSS-trained members, Nathuram Godse. The groups (of which there are many) preach a 'Hindu raj'.

In more recent times, this fundamentalist (some would say fascist) twisting of Hinduism has had political endorsement at the highest levels, especially when the Bharatiya Janata Party (Indian People's Party or BJP), in coalition with other parties, held power in national politics, between 1998 and 2004. This was a period associated with increased hostility directed against Indian Muslims and Christians. Few Australians would be unaware of the brutal murders of Australian missionary Graham Staines and his two young sons at the hands of Hindu extremists in January 1999 in the northern state of Orissa. The man convicted of leading the mob who burned them to death while they slept in their van had been active in the RSS. Prior to murdering the Staines family his hatred had focused against Muslim truck drivers who transported cattle to the slaughterhouses.[13]

'Most Indians and Hindus *abhor* this politics of hate', writes one Indian journalist, Peter De Souza,[14] and this abuse of Hinduism is rejected strongly by the vast majority of Hindus who make up about 80 per cent of India's population. In May 1984, when communal violence flared in Bihwandi, Muslims ran for shelter to the property of a local businessman, Mohammed Ibrahim Ansari. In the mayhem, Ansari's factory was destroyed. Nearly thirty people – his workers and those who had come seeking his protection – were killed. Still, Ansari was able to say of his attackers, 'They are misguided.' Ansari subsequently became active in working for greater harmony in Bihwandi. Communal violence has prompted others across India to form peace committees in areas where there has previously been conflict. Our friend Siddartha uses his network as a journalist to establish an international alliance of journalists to promote more objective and compassionate writing on conflict resolution and peace building.

As I read the papers and the journals coming into the Centre's library, my understanding of events in Mumbai my first year in India was that the conflict tended to involve groups of the very poor pitted violently against each other. There were indications that wealthy and powerful interests used the simplistic identifiers of religion or caste to manipulate those on the fringes for their own political and economic gain. It struck me that the poor were always being manipulated – I am not talking only about India – and are the ones who suffer most in any social or physical calamity.

This had been demonstrated vividly to me in December 1984.

---

[13] Christopher Kremmer, *Inhaling the Mahatma*, ch. 14.
[14] P. De Souza, in Ramin Jahanbegloo (2008), *India Revisited*, Oxford University Press, p. 162.

'*Caa-pee, caa-pee, caa-pee*', the vendors chant outside the train window as it stops at Vijawada Junction. '*Chai, chai, chai.*' We purchase milky coffee in small metal cups. With well-practised timing, the vendor collects the cups just as the train slides into movement again. The sweetness of the coffee stays in my mouth. We are in a train heading north from Chennai to Delhi. It is a long journey of around thirty-six hours and once in Delhi, we will visit a number of government departments in the ongoing pursuit of funding for the Centre's adult education or environment programs.

The train rocks steadily north from one state to another, and on into Maharashtra. It stops a while at the city of Nagpur, and we are about as close to the geographical centre of India as anyone can be. The season is right and we buy small sweet oranges from vendors through the carriage window. On a whim, Benjamin bargains for a colourful tin bird and a wooden flute. Nearly twenty-four hours after leaving Chennai, we arrive in Bhopal, about 800 kilometres south-west of Delhi. We are now in the state of Madhya Pradesh and this is its capital. I am sombre as the train screeches to a halt in this major rail junction. It is impossible not to feel the pall of one of history's worst industrial accidents which blighted the city just one year previously. I close my eyes in a moment of respect for half a million people whose lives were changed with that catastrophe.

Bhopal is normally a bustling noisy place. In the pre-dawn hours of Monday 3 December 1984, the morning shift workers had poured into the station as usual only to find signalmen and stationmasters collapsed, still holding signal levers in their hands; dead engine drivers in their cabs dutifully waiting for signals which were never going to turn green; clerks at the booking windows keeled over with ticket boxes and cash safes wide open.[15]

What had happened soon became all too horribly apparent.

---

[15] V. Anand (2002), 'The Bhopal Gas Tragedy', http://www.irfca.org/articles/bhopal-gas-tragedy.html, accessed June 2009. A version of this appeared in the *Indian Express* newspaper in December 2002.

Taking sides with the poor

During the night of 2 December, water had leaked into a storage tank in the Union Carbide pesticide factory. It set off a chemical reaction which released huge quantities of a gas known as methyl isocyanate (MIC) from a shaft thirty metres above the city. Shortly after midnight, plant officials became aware that MIC was possibly leaking into the atmosphere. It was nearly two hours before the warning sirens were sounded. The winter weather conditions were such that there was little dissipation of the gas and it swirled heavily away and down from the factory. Clustered around were the homes of the city's poorest families. Long before the sirens sounded and before the local authorities had been notified, the gas had seeped in under doorways and through windows as people slept. Screams of pain sounded as they ran outside, confused and breathless. Their throats burned and soon they were coughing and vomiting. When the first victims ran in terror from their dwellings, they increased the amount of poison they inhaled.

Between 7000 and 10,000 died during the first few days, and a further 15,000 died in the following years. In addition, there were tens of thousands of people left with permanent total or partial disabilities. Children and the elderly were the most vulnerable, with a large number of young children dying painful and horrible deaths. Twenty-four years later, around 100,000 people still suffer chronic and debilitating illnesses for which treatment is largely ineffective.

As I slept peacefully in our flat in Chennai, effects of the accident were being experienced up to ten kilometres from the factory far away in Bhopal. Almost thirty tonnes of MIC had been released into the night sky. MIC gas is poisonous at low levels, but it is only discernible by smell at much higher levels. Nearly twelve more tonnes of unidentified chemicals were in the cloud that spilled over Bhopal. A government report described, how within hours of the leak, all the hospitals of Bhopal were full of gassed victims. Doctors, medical students and volunteers worked round the clock but they lacked information about the gases released and could only offer symptomatic treatment. Following the incident, there was a 50 per cent abortion rate amongst pregnant women who lived in the most severely exposed areas.

At the time, Union Carbide blamed sabotage by workers for the presence of water in the storage tank. In reply, workers in the factory maintained that the water had seeped into the tank during a routine washing of pipes on the evening of 2 December. The water had pushed through a faulty valve, which, they claimed, had been known to be leaking since November. Even Union Carbide managers disputed the sabotage claim and one independent chemical engineer commented that the sabotage theory should not be used 'to divert attention from the underlying failings of design and management that created the conditions for a disaster.'

The state government department responsible for overseeing safety compliance had documented at least six accidents at the plant in Bhopal prior to December 1984. The company itself had noted possible risks both in processes and in the plant. Standards applied in Union Carbide plants on United States soil were not adhered to in the case of Bhopal. In 2010, a court case identified thirty major hazards in the Bhopal factory. There had also been problems caused by high staff turnover, staff reductions and low salaries. There had been cost-cutting so that parts were not properly replaced. One journalist had warned about potential disasters; at least one lawyer had argued against excessive environmental contamination. The state government had not enforced enquiries after earlier accidents, nor followed them up with better regulation and safety requirements. In particular, the company had not established a comprehensive emergency plan for warning local communities and authorities should a leak occur. Subsequently, in December 1984, there was a delay in warning police and residents, and hospitals were not informed about the nature of the chemicals.

The fact is, according to the Indian Council for Medical Research, nearly all the people in the area most severely affected by the gas leak (up to 86 per cent) were from the poorest class in Bhopal.

Taking sides with the poor

After the accident, Union Carbide withdrew from the disaster area, leaving a contaminated site. Twenty years after the accident, chemicals still lay around the ruins of the plant, and continued to poison the groundwater on which the people of Bhopal depended. The Supreme Court of India ruled that there had been indiscriminate dumping of hazardous waste and non-existent or negligent practices by the company and lack of enforcement of controls by the authorities. Consequently, the groundwater, and, therefore, drinking water supplies had been damaged. The Court ordered the state government to supply fresh drinking water through tankers to people whose potable water supplies had been contaminated by pollutants from the plant. In 2004, the state government had yet to implement the Supreme Court order to provide fresh water to these communities.

For the poor, the community pump or well is critical to their survival. For the families living close to the old plant the contaminated groundwater is their only source of water. In 1997, thirteen years after the MIC leak, the state government covered 250 hand-pumps around the plant with red paint; they posted signs warning that the water from the pumps was unfit for drinking. In the absence of any other convenient source of water, most people in the surrounding communities continued to use water from the red pumps.

What must it be like to go each day to a poisoned well and draw the water you need for your family – for washing, cooking, drinking? The poor know what the chemicals have done to hundreds of thousands of their familes and community. They have no other option. That is poverty.

For me, the Bhopal tragedy illustrates how it is always the poorest who are most gravely affected when environment degrades, justice is delayed and when good structures and processes are lacking.

The poor work. And work. The day creeps on slowly and they edge forward, pacing their movements with slow measure as if to match their supply of energy to the day's demands. The marvel is: they go on and on and on. Food collection, firewood gathering, food preparation, food consumption, sleep, food collection. If you're old, you sit on the edge for some time, fondling the baby, watching the younger women or men. On the edge: that's for old grey gummy grannies – on the edge of the road catching the thin shadow of the neighbour's house; on the edge at the entrance to the family's thatched mud hut; on the edge away from the cooking circle around the fire.

The poor are tough. Sinewy men in rolled up checked *lungis* or baggy shorts ride out early in the morning sitting on a load of gravel or bricks on the back of garish green and yellow trucks. The trucks boast slogans in red and blue paint, 'We two, our two'. They return in the evening, their bodies white with dust, their singlets grimy. The women are resilient. Pushy women jostle onto buses and get a seat while others hold back. Swaggering women, baskets of flowers or fish or fruit stuck on one hip, hair a little unkempt, walk back from the market to set up their roadside stall for the evening. And there are cunning women, like the one who crushed up against me in an overladen lurching bus. I thought she was pregnant, and marvelled at how hard her stomach felt as she pushed up against me. Only when I reached home and discovered my wallet missing did I realise her pregnancy was perhaps a clay pot beneath her sari. I didn't begrudge her the rupees she garnered through her initiative, but I was sentimentally pleased to recover the purse from the bus company and find my token twenty dollar Australian note intact.

I do not know how these men and women see the future. Perhaps they do not have time to wonder about a future beyond the next day. Perhaps the future is a dangerous place because it is too crushing to hope for something which is unlikely to happen. Maybe it is best to keep on with the present demands and to keep away from waters which might drag you down. Life is in the present, in this slum, in the next load of washing for the employer, in the free meal for the child at school, in managing a drunken husband.

Taking sides with the poor

The visibility of the poor in India raised questions for me about the invisibility of the poor in Australia, especially in cities. What is it like to be desperately poor in an environment which places so much emphasis on buying and having? I recalled a very brief period a few years before my marriage when I was unemployed and receiving unemployment benefits. For those few months, price tags on the simplest items became a symbol of exclusion for me, something that I could not consider; I dreaded my visits to commonwealth unemployment offices; my self-assurance slipped.

For the urban poor that I saw in India, their assurance of survival came in small ways: rags and papers from garbage bins to be collected and sold for re-cycling, tiny dried fish lined up on hessian sacks by the side of the road for sale to others from our colony, a plastic bag of fresh jasmine buds to thread and sell to women for their hair, packets of milk for delivery, dirty cooking vessels to scour, bricks on a building site to be heaved, broken *chappals* to be fixed, twisted umbrellas to be mended, buffalo dung collected and the pavement swept. It was salvation without illusion. Salvation with nothing to spare.

As I sat at my desk in the Centre or moved around the city, and on my visits to rural areas, I had many opportunities to observe the daily life of the poor. To be poor is to live with reduced options, like the residents of Bhopal who collect contaminated water from a pump painted red, knowing it is contaminated; or the children sent to work in factories which endanger their health and who have diminished long-term prospects because they are deprived of education. To be poor is to live with short-term horizons, like food for today and money to pay back the lender before his goons toss you out of where you live. To be poor is to be dependent on the manipulations of those in power, who might provide shirts at election time for the right vote, or free drink if there is a score to settle against someone, or who might provide a loan for sexual rights over a daughter or wife. To be poor is to be trapped in a culture which has a far longer history than your personal history, like the bonded labourers of Tamil Nadu. To be poor is to be those who in time of crisis and catastrophe, such as in floods, monsoons, development and accidents, feel the greatest pain and have the least defence.

The following extract gives a sense of what it means to be poor as expressed by a *Dalit* ('Untouchable') poet in 1973. The poem, 'Mother', starts with children waiting alone at home in the dark in the early morning while around them they smell the food which other families are enjoying. One day, their mother is bitten by a snake and dies.

> ... In our nostrils, the smell of food. In our stomachs, darkness.
> From our eyes, welling up, streams of tears.
> Slicing darkness, a shadow heavily draws near.
> On her head, a burden. Her legs a-totter.
> Thin, dark of body.....my mother.
> All day she combs the forest for firewood.
> We wait her return.
> When she brings no firewood to sell we go to bed hungry.
> One day something happens. How we don't know...
> The day ends. So does her life...
> Mother is gone. We, her brood, thrown to the winds.
> Even now my eyes search for mother. My sadness grows.
> When I see a thin woman with firewood on her head,
> I go and buy all her firewood.
>
> Warman Nimbalkar[16]

---

[16] Waman Nimbalkar (translated by Priya Adarkar) taken from *Poisoned Bread: Translations from Modern Marathi Dalit Literature*, edited Arjun Dangle, http://castory.wordpress.com/2008/09/21/mother-by-waman-nimbalkar/

In the mango field[17]

THE DAY AFTER the horrific accident in Bhopal was a Tuesday. I'd been home alone for a week while Benjamin had been at the rural centre. I left home in the freshness of the early morning, catching an already-crowded bus across the city and then another heading north towards our training centre at Cheyalnagar.

About thirty young people from nearby villages had gathered for a week-long environmental training program, funded by the government of India. Our goal was to educate participants to take leadership in environmental action in their own places. The experienced Ekambaram and new recruit Dorai were assisting Benjamin and Durairaj in leading the program. As well as taking part in lectures, films and discussions, participants had planted seedlings of large trees (tamarind and eucalyptus) in a badly-eroded area; they visited villages, sang environmental songs and distributed seedlings and educational materials; they did additional planting on the Centre's own model reforestation site with fruit-bearing trees like drumstick, guava and neem.

I had been caught up with other work back in the office but I

---

[17] A version of these events was previously published as 'Dorai – Education for Development: Some Consequences and Risks', in *Community Development Journal*, OUP, vol. 23:3, July 1988.

was joining Benjamin and the rural development team at Cheyalnagar for the day to evaluate and plan their programs.

The bus was late leaving the city. It was further delayed by political processions in a large village along the way. The normal journey of two and a half hours extended to four, so it was about 11.30 by the time I was walking the last kilometres along the dusty road from Palavakkam village bazaar to the one-acre base we called Cheyalnagar. About half way along on the verge of the road, I passed a cluster of four or five thatched huts. They were small, no more than a metre and a half high and wide. This was the home of the Irulas, Indigenous people, who made their living primarily as snake-catchers. The men were small and wiry, scantily clad, their skin burnished dark. The few women in the group were bone-thin, their faces carved with endurance. No one was around the huts as I walked past that December morning, but I recalled the day when Benjamin and I had been caught in a sudden storm as we walked from the bus stop in Palavakkam village towards Cheyalnagar. The downpour had caught us unawares just when we were approaching the Irula settlement. A woman in a ragged sari had beckoned us. We crawled in through the small opening and crouched in the woven shelter. Within the darkness of the dwellings, under a roof of leaves, we waited for the storm to pass. I'd been touched by the hospitality.

I continued on. Being December, it was not unusually hot, but it had been a drawn-out trip and so I was pleased to see the familiar roofs of the two permanent mud-and-thatch huts on the Centre's land. I noted the newly-erected shed which replaced the one blown down in a storm. The walls of the shed were woven from palms, the roof was thatched and it looked well-made. There was the usual jumble of bicycles at the gate. Muthu, the watchman, was standing, as he often did, by the side of the shed.

As I neared the gate, I realised something was different. It was too quiet. I knew many trainees would have left for home, but there were always some who waited around after a program, filling in time before they returned to their villages. Today, there was no activity. Usually, from far off, I would hear voices long before I reached the prickly thorn-bush fence designed to deter village goats from the carefully-tended trees and bushes. I would hear the hard sounds of guttural Tamil spoken energetically, because the speakers were young and idealistic and the only way to speak Tamil is with an explosion of consonants. All I could hear was the lonely bleat of goats somewhere nearby and the crunch of gravel beneath my leather sandals. I entered through the gate, walking along the side of the shed to the entrance which faced away from the road.

Benjamin stood there. He looked ghastly.

'What's happened?' At first he couldn't speak. Then, he told me, 'One of our staff members has drowned.' His face contorted. 'Dorai, a fair chap.'

I knew Dorai of course, although he had only recently begun working in the rural program. He was around 25 years old, strong and good-looking. With his physique and light-toned skin, he stood out amongst the small wiry frames of other young village men. He came from a village not far from Cheyalnagar. His role included coordinating and leading adult literacy classes and working with the villages on the environmental program. Sometimes, he assisted Durairaj or Ekambaram when they held awareness-raising and animation meetings.

'We haven't been able to find his body', said Benjamin. He was distraught.

The day had begun as usual. Dorai had ridden a cycle to the community well in Palavakkam to fill large stainless steel vessels with drinking water for the day. When he'd returned, he'd gone with Durairaj, Ekambaram and another staff member for a bath in one of the two lakes near the centre. The lake at the front of Cheyalnagar is shallow, but the second lake, about three hundred yards behind our huts, is deep. It is also thick with reeds and Benjamin had warned them not to bathe there. Dorai had told his colleagues that he could swim. He dived in and swam some twenty metres out into the lake. His companions could not swim well and simply bathed at the edge of the lake. Dorai joined them in the shallows while he soaped himself up, and then once more swam to the centre of the lake. When Dorai cried for help, Durairaj and his friends watched helplessly. Women working in the adjacent paddy fields came running. What could they do? The women held Durairaj back from the water, telling him not to risk his own life.

Their shouting brought the local village watchman and staff still remaining at the camp. Then the cooks who had been hired for the training session came. Workers passing by on the road heard the commotion and joined in. Benjamin cannot swim, but others dived in. The water was reedy and cold. They were frightened of being caught themselves. Since Dorai could not be found, Benjamin sent someone to get local divers, who make their living cleaning wells; they couldn't find him.

Finally accepting that Dorai had drowned, Benjamin asked one of the staff members to go and break the terrible news to Dorai's family.

'Bring them back with you', he said. 'They should be here.'

I had arrived about an hour later. We stood there, too distressed to talk. Around 11.45, Benjamin asked Durairaj to draft an official statement and lodge it with the nearest police station, in a village about ten kilometres away. Durairaj left on this errand taking two companions. Gradually, Dorai's family members began to arrive. They were keen to recover the body as soon as possible and take it back home. Again, some Centre staff and others made an attempt to find him. Again, failure: we were powerless to give Dorai's family even the comfort of seeing and receiving his body.

The day was creeping forward without direction. The police still had not come. At around 3.00 p.m., Benjamin and I went briefly to the spot from where Dorai had gone swimming. We stood and looked. Helpless. When we returned to our compound, the small area

In the mango field

around the huts had filled with hundreds of people. Inside the property, there were different groups, talking, gesticulating and watching. Villagers and labourers from Palavakkam gathered. Some of them had seen Dorai alive in the village early in the morning when he'd gone to collect the drinking water. Members of another small organisation and some of the course trainees had heard about the death and returned. There was a growing group of family members and their friends. As time passed, more and more onlookers came to see what was going on. Everyone had an opinion. Superstition held sway. It was congested and confusing.

Adjacent to our land, and divided by a stranded wire fence, was a field with a grove of large old mango trees. Here, in the shade of the mangoes, some of the local landlords had gathered. They had twenty or thirty men with them, probably employees of some kind. In the centre of the landlords' group was a Mr Reddy, a man well-known to Benjamin. Reddy was bitterly opposed to the work that the Centre had been doing in the area. As the long hot day hung suspended around us, whispers of 'murder' began to blow in the dust raised by the feet of the villagers coming into the compound and to take shape around the two small mud huts. Rumours and fears passed back and forth as individuals moved from one group to the other.

The men with Mr Reddy were claiming to those around them that the Centre staff had assaulted and killed Dorai the previous evening and had burnt his body. They gave no reason why this might have occurred. Improbable as these allegations were, the landlords were surrounded by villagers who were largely ignorant and in bondage both to superstition and to the men spreading lies.

It is difficult to write about my experiences within India without mentioning caste, a complex institution, difficult to comprehend in a way that does it justice. Text books typically describe caste in terms of the four major varnas – *Brahmins*, priests; *Kshatriyas*, kings or rulers;

Vaisyas, business people and farmers; *Shudras*, labourers – and those who fell outside, or beneath, this occupation-based system ('outcastes' or 'untouchables'). The Colonial British distorted caste by emphasising hierarchy at the expense of diversity in what was a flexible and dynamic social and cultural structure. The system had myriad refinements within it, with thousands of castes with many regional variations, and smaller units, all linked in some way to observances of ritual status and purity.

Benjamin's interest in establishing CHDSC was with those who were the poorest and weakest in Indian society. Often, although not always, this meant the Centre worked with *Dalits* – outcastes and untouchables – for whom Gandhi had earlier coined the word *Harijan*, or 'children of God'. Because the caste system discriminates against certain kinds of occupation as unclean, poverty and low-caste status are linked.

Most Indian villages traditionally had (and many still have) *Dalit* or *Harijan* colonies, at some distance from the main village, ostensibly to protect the ritual purity of caste villagers. This adds another burden on the backs of the poor, who have to walk further for normal provisions and services, or to collect water from a village pump or well. In some instances, they have been barred from using the well because they would contaminate it. Discrimination based on caste no longer exists in a formal, legal, sense in India, but the law written in custom and prejudice takes longer to change than the passage of a bill through Parliament, especially in rural and more remote areas.

Much of Benjamin's educational work with the young rural villagers was to alert them to their rights as workers for fairer pay and to empower them to seek rights through peaceful joint action. When he first set up the training centre at Cheyalnagar, one particular group of land owners, or landlords, as they are called, including Reddy, invited him to their homes. Benjamin is, after all, from the area, the son of a doctor, and known to them. They would be happy, they said, for him to come and eat with them and take tea with

In the mango field

them. There was, however, one condition: that anything he said to the *Harijans* was said in their presence. Benjamin had declined. The landlords interpreted this as a clear statement about where Benjamin, and the Centre, stood on such matters: that if there were sides to be drawn, Benjamin was certainly not going to be on their side. They were correct. Not all landlords, of course, belonged to this group and there were those who applauded the work Benjamin was doing. The firmness that he had taken with Reddy and his allies, however, was to provoke consequences.

One of the strategies that Benjamin and his colleagues used to raise villagers' awareness of their rights was street theatre, or people's theatre. The performances drew their subject matter from the lives of the people in the villages and the target audience was always the poorest in the village, especially the unemployed youth. They were low-cost informal productions that developed fairly spontaneously as they progressed. For example, actors played out the roles of high-caste villagers insisting that a non-caste villager get off his bicycle and remove his sandals as he went past the high-caste villager's front gate. Then, another actor demonstrated peaceful resistance, refusing to remove his sandals and encouraging his fellow villagers to do the same. The actors would then stop the play and invite their audience to talk to them about what had happened.

Other topics for such theatre might include how the labourers deserved proper wages, or how the landowners were taking advantage of them when they paid them for only a few months of the year and then lent them money for weddings at 25 per cent interest, or even 4 per cent, simply for money to pay the doctor's bills. The discussions they stimulated were about the power of people who work together to get their rights. They tended to satirise old prejudices and so were often raucous and good humoured.

One night, in May, 1982, Benjamin had organised a Street Theatre workshop performance in the Harijan Colony of the village. Afterwards, as evening came down and Benjamin was waiting for a bus back to Madras, some organised thugs challenged him and attacked him. He was only saved when the bus came and his colleagues pushed him on board, and so he returned home. Subsequently, he heard that the police were looking for him. Benjamin returned to the village and asked the people who knew him to gather to meet with the local police chief and explain what had taken place.

Two days later, led by Benjamin, the Centre staff gathered with more than a hundred volunteers from local villages and went to the police station. Once there, they discovered that the landlords had filed charges against them, claiming that Benjamin and his staff had beaten the landlords and their servants. One of the landlords involved in this incident was Mr Reddy

The Centre staff and other volunteers asembled at the police station were fearful that trouble might erupt while they were visiting the police. However, for Benjamin, this was people's theatre in real life – precisely the kind of false charges and twisting of justice that they were fighting. His staff and volunteers were disciplined, orderly and subdued. Once again Benjamin and his companions challenged the false charges made against them. The impact was quite abrupt: the landlords changed their minds about their allegations and the false charges were dropped. Of course, a humiliation such as this would not be forgotten easily

Now, two years after that incident, it was the same Mr Reddy who had gathered men in the nearby field and was now spreading rumours implicating Benjamin in murder. Young Dorai had become a pawn in someone else's game. It was becoming dangerous. I had no idea how it might end.

Until the body could be found, nothing was happening. The day was passing. And, still, no sign of the police, even though Durairaj had lodged the statement with them and had returned some hours back. Ever-faithful and diligent, Durairaj suggested that perhaps we should

In the mango field

offer an incentive to search for Dorai. So Benjamin offered the men some money if they could find the body. There was not much response. Finally, with much prodding, two of our young men joined five others in the water. Evening was coming and the water was quickly becoming cold. After only half an hour, again the divers had to give up.

With some desperation, Benjamin called together all the Centre's members and supporters who happened to be present. About 100 of us gathered on the sand floor and within the casuarina walls and thatch of the training shed. What should we do? The strategy was unclear. It was decided to send for professional divers. Meanwhile, in view of the landlords' stirring, twenty or so men agreed to stay overnight. In addition, there was also the watchman and his mother and wife, Durairaj, Ekambaram, Benjamin's brother Alphonse, Benjamin and me. We moved across to one of the small mud huts and waited.

As night came down, the training shed filled with the wailing of female relatives of the drowned boy. The menfolk of Dorai's family walked around outside, mute. Around nine o'clock, fresh coffee was made for everyone. Someone had sent for a snack for Benjamin and myself – his first food for the day, my first since an early breakfast back home in the quiet good order of our flat in Indira Nagar. In the dim yellow light of a kerosene lamp, we sat on a platform raised from the clay floor of the hut, savouring our coffee and a simple country porridge called *uppuma*, grateful for the kindness which had thought to bring us this food.

It was dark and the police had still not come.

In the circumstances, anything was possible. We feared that the landlords could even organise experts to find, remove and mutilate the body and then foist their charge of murder and burning on us. Volunteers set up a watch post on the rough ground near the lake keeping vigil through the cold night armed with lanterns, torches and sticks. After sunset, we needed to rely on kerosene lanterns or fire for light. It was very dark. Late in the night, I fell asleep on the mud floor of one of the thatched huts, ready to be woken any time by fire or some attack, and with the dry wailing of the women rising and falling at irregular intervals throughout the night.

December 5th dawned early. Dorai's male relatives went to the lake, followed by the women. Our staff and some volunteers joined them. The landlords and their crowd had gathered again under the mango trees in the adjoining field. At around 8.30, the body was found. Initially, some people, cowed by their presence, wanted to take poor Dorai's remains to the landlords under the mango trees; others suggested leaving him just outside our fence on a table by the side of the road in the sun. It was craziness. Common sense prevailed and the body was brought into the training shed and laid out upon a table. Our hope was that now, finally, we could help Dorai's family carry him back home with them.

The landlords, with their men around them, still refused to allow the removal of the body by the relatives. We did not want to force the issue and risk the possibility of a physical confrontation over the dead body of our colleague. Yet the continued presence of the body meant that the frenzied wailing of the women was attracting more and more villagers and passers-by. There were over 500 people around the Centre's small compound. Besides, it was already now more than twenty-four hours since Dorai's death and the day temperatures were quite high.

Then someone noticed that Mr Reddy and some of his followers were wearing crude paper badges with 'RSS' scrawled on them. Given what we knew of the Rastriya Seva Sangh, the Hindu revival group which is both fundamentalist and in some instances fascist, this introduced a sinister twist. We suspected that the landlords were trying to provoke some kind of religious-based division and strife. It reminded me of the bitter violence at Bhiwandi on the edge of Mumbai only a few months before, and other disturbances between Muslims and Hindus too, nearer to hand, in Hyderabad, the capital of Andhra Pradesh.

In the mango field

The handmade badges introduced menace into what was already a tense situation. Some Dalits from the village, including some of our staff, questioned what this meant, since most of them were Hindus also. Are the RSS the only Hindus, they asked? What about us?

By this time, the landlords had told the relatives that they would not let the body be moved because Dorai had been murdered. They encouraged the family to join with them, telling them they could get a large compensation for them from the organisation. The organisation, they added, had created trouble in other villages and was a disturber of the peace.

When Dorai's body was found to be completely smooth and unmarked, the landlords changed their story. Now they claimed that the Centre staff had not assaulted and burnt Dorai's body after all, but injected him with poison. They urged the relatives to seek money from the Centre on the spot. Initially, Benjamin refused to enter into any such negotiations, sending the local staff members, Durairaj and Ekambaram, to handle it, but, intimidated by the threats, they pleaded with Benjamin to speak with the landlords. For his part, he did not want to give any credence to the power they were highjacking, assuming the role of police, jury and judge all within themselves. Finally, he relented.

I was a foreigner and a woman – a double handicap in this situation. I had nothing to contribute, but there was no way I was going to let Benjamin go alone into this kangaroo court. So I walked with him across the field to the crowd under the mango trees. Ekambaram and Durairaj came with us. Parallel – at about fifteen metres – walked a group of young landlords saying clearly 'This time we shall finish you.' We walked towards what was now a crowd of about seventy-five men. They immediately closed around us in a wide semi-circle. We stood alone in the centre. The landlord who was leading the agitation was younger than I had expected. He was a trim man, dressed in a black *vaishti*, wearing beads around his neck and with the markings on his forehead of someone who is going through the forty days of cleansing and prayers which preface a pilgrimage to Sabarimala. On his shirt was a rough RSS badge. We did not know how many of those surrounding us really believed the landlord. To a fundamentalist RSS person such as Reddy, Benjamin's marriage to a foreigner probably was just another point of disdain. Apart from that, I was of no interest to the landlord: I was a non-presence.

Reddy then proceeded with his court of inquiry, first bullying an older relative of Dorai into questioning Benjamin. The old fellow initially thought that Benjamin was the inspector of police. Benjamin refused to answer him, saying that he was interested only in solving the problems caused by the landlords' fabricated murder rumour.

So Reddy took over himself. He seemed to enjoy his role as a bully. He spoke mostly in English, which meant that most of those standing around him were unaware of what was actually being said. He demanded that Benjamin explain what had happened. Benjamin refused to do so, for this would give recognition to Reddy's legitimacy to preside over the situation.

'Why was the matter not reported to the police, Benjamin? And if so, do you have a receipt from the police? Let me tell you, there was no complaint registered with the police, because I have been there myself to see. There is no report.'

His approach was clever, calculated to undermine Benjamin's confidence in Durairaj who had been sent to report the accident the previous day: to goad Benjamin and his staffer into an argument. Durairaj became agitated, but he remained quiet. Reddy seemed determined to control the situation. From time to time, Benjamin reminded him that he was going to follow only the appropriate legal and administrative procedures, and that this conversation was not part of them. He appealed to Reddy to consider the plight of the family and release the body.

Then Ekambaram, a *Dalit* himself, and a cocky, sturdy man, stepped further forward into the circle and spoke up to the landlord.

Reddy turned on him.

In the mango field

'How *dare* you speak to me', he sneered. 'Don't you dare speak to me!' His voice was oily with derision. The response of the two men amazed me. In an instant, Ekambaram shrivelled. Physically deflated. He became smaller. Both he and Durairaj, as one, folded their arms and lowered their heads. Just as the downtrodden had done for centuries before authority.

'This is going nowhere', Benjamin said in exasperation. 'There can be no resolution this way.' So we turned to walk the long distance back to safer ground. As we left the mango field, I heard Reddy's voice again. His warning was clear, 'I will do nothing while the body is here, Benjamin, but once it is removed, I will destroy you.'

Back within our compound, Benjamin addressed the many people still milling around. He explained to them the facts of what had happened. He described the work that the Centre had been doing in the area and he passed on to them the threats that the landlord had made. He appealed to them to be sensible and to let Dorai's family take the body home. They listened in silence as he spoke, in Tamil, with authority and passion.

Then we withdrew with the staff to one of the two huts. Outside the wailing rose and fell, emotional bursts followed by weary silence. As the tension and sad howling mounted, we began to take some precautions. The huts were used during the year by Durairaj and his team for adult education classes and so, along with gardening tools, there were bundles of slates on which the villagers practised their writing. We hid all the gardening tools, anything that could become a weapon, under the slates and covered them with bags and baskets. We disengaged the two gas cylinders we had brought for cooking for the training camp; a couple of staff members drained the precious kerosene from the lamps and the storage drum out upon the ground. Once more, we sent a team to bring the police and the village administrative officer.

Then there followed long negotiations over the compensation that the Centre would pay for Dorai's accidental death. There is a ritual with negotiations in India that cannot be hurried. Benjamin and I remained inside while Durairaj and Ekambaram went to negotiate. The Centre staff denied culpability for the death. Five hundred thousand rupees, two hundred thousand, fifty thousand, twenty thousand, ten thousand. During the back-and-forth, another more conciliatory landlord and the village administrative officer had arrived and they agreed that the family should be given some money. So 7500 rupees was offered and an agreement signed, couched in language that emphasised that Dorai's death had been an unfortunate accident and that it was offered in sympathy towards the family. The Centre staff would also give personally what they could. It was a settlement coerced over the body of Dorai so that the body could be taken for burial.

In the meantime, in the afternoon of the second day, the police finally came. They interviewed various people, but did not speak to us. Benjamin recounted to the village administrative officer the story of the physical attack by the same landlord some two years earlier. Since the drowning had been reported to the police, which is not always the case in remote villages, a post-mortem was to be performed. So, at around 4.00 pm on 5 December, the body of Dorai was carried on a cycle rickshaw and allowed to leave. With a small band of supporters, we walked the few kilometres back towards Palavakkam village. As we waited at the corner tea shop for the bus back to Chennai, Benjamin bought us tea. It was hot, sweet and comforting.

During the hours I had spent in the stuffy heat of the hut, I had thought only of the immediate: what might happen and how we were going to get out of the situation. I have a healthy fear of crowds and how easily they can be turned into a mob. I worried about Dorai's family. A tragedy had occurred: a young man had died. His family had lost a healthy young son. Yet they could not even take his body home to observe the normal rituals and grief; they had to endure the indignity of his body being left in the heat away from his own place.

In the mango field

And all because the landlords tried to shift the focus from the human to the political and use the situation to settle old scores and damage the Centre's reputation.

Only back in the Centre did I recall how little the Centre had done to provoke such hatred. In the course of three years at Cheyalnagar, what had been achieved? Activities amongst young women and men in the area had been low-key and modest: training camps with youth drawn from the various local villages; a short-lived tailoring and weaving project; inter-village games; adult education for about 900 men and women under the national government's program; local community organising with three or four simple processions involving about 400 people; a hunger strike or two with about 100 people protesting their right to basic public services, such as water, and against corrupt officials; an environmental program of education and planting – a few trees and shrubs on less than an acre of dry stony land. All in all, it was a program which was unpretentious and even sporadic.

What the Centre had tried consistently to do was to educate the local youth in their development: to help them become aware of the significance of their situation and to place it in a perspective of politics, society and history; to lead them to believe that if they worked together they could make some changes; to build confidence and some leadership from among the poor. In all their work, Benjamin and his colleagues had tried to establish a direct relationship with the poor.

When Benjamin ignored the landlords' invitation to take tea with them, he was signalling that he was working directly with *Dalits*, talking to them and befriending them, and, in so doing, refusing to grant the landlords the power which was no longer rightfully theirs. Traditionally, local councils of significant people had made decisions of common concern to a village. Many of these had worked well, governed by the integrity of the people involved. In the changeover to a new *panchayat* – local government – system involving representative elections, legal procedures and administration, some local people of influence and wealth had hung onto the traditional powers, overriding the new order. The landlords were further irked because the Centre – Benjamin – had refused to yield to them matters which, by the Constitution of India, were now vested in the police and judicial systems. The Centre refused to fold its arms and hang its head before the landlords. I sensed it was these attitudes, rather than the actual work achieved, that had provoked the landlords to reprisal. Such an episode shows the extent to which a few people would have liked to control the lives of the many poor. I believe it ratified our efforts in the area.

Violence hung over our heads during the siege at Cheyalnagar. Dorai was a quiet young fellow, who despite his confidence as a swimmer became trapped in reeds while taking a bath. Through him, I learned about the danger embedded within work that sought to bring social change. We humans rarely relinquish power voluntarily. When those who are poorest begin to exercise greater control over their lives, those who have previously held power over them tend to respond in anger and hostility. Dorai became a pawn in one small struggle between the powerless and the powerful. Working with the poor, I was learning, is not for the naive and faint-hearted.

Whorls of belief

AFTER GRUELLING HUMIDITY in the middle months of the year when temperatures often moved above 40 degrees Celsius, my first year in India slid mercifully into the less intense heat of the late monsoon season. Between June and September there had been some rain as the south-west monsoon cast its shadow over Tamil Nadu and the showers brought temporary relief that sent many locals into their cardigans. The real rains came towards the end of the year when the north-east monsoon dumped Chennai with some 400 millimetres of rain in about four days. Rain swept in over the coast. The city came to a halt. I remember one time when Benjamin was absent on some business during the height of the monsoon and I spent three days alone, and, like everyone else in the city, relying on candlelight. Winds battered the wooden shutters on our windows. Water blew in under doorways and the room we used as a study was inches deep in water. Books on the lowest shelf were destroyed. The entrance to the office became impassible, knee-high in muddy water.

During the monsoon, the map of Chennai was transformed. Deep muddy brown lakes appeared where previously there had been open fields and vacant blocks; roads were submerged. Across the city, even the deepest gutters flooded over the roads carrying with them all their accumulated rubbish. On the low-lying grounds where thousands lived under black plastic, the rains reminded those who had least need of reminding that life is fleeting and transient. They picked up their children and their few cooking pots and moved to higher ground to wait it out. After the worst of the rain had gone, I returned to work, making my way as usual on foot. For a number of weeks like everyone else on the stretch of road which led up to our office, I waded in water at least knee high, squelching who-knows-what between my toes.

After its concentrated assault, rain continued to fall many days during December. The air was cleaner and cooler. For the locals, this time of year meant winter. Some of the office staff started shivering, the cooler conditions and the rain and moist living arrangements bringing on fever. For me, it meant evenings and early mornings when the temperature fell to around 21 degrees Celsius.

I remember one such evening. The early evening sky was translucent. I stood on the balcony mesmerised by the lazy stirring of fronds of the coconut tree by the front gate. The crows were settling for the night. Evening light in India is luminescent, softer than in Australia, and at this time of year it was magical. The rains had washed the dust from roofs and leaves. A holiday had reduced the reek of diesel and other fumes. In my light cotton *churidar* dress and trousers, I was in that blissful zone of being neither cold nor hot. It was Christmas night, my first since our wedding.

As I stood there, revelling in the uncharacteristic freshness, I felt just a little adrift. It was not simply a matter of homesickness. It was more a nagging realisation of something larger. Christmas had come quite unannounced. There had been little commercial fanfare around Christmas in Chennai. The only sign prior to the feast had been large paper stars, decorated with patterned holes, which a few Christian households had hung over the bare light globe at the entrance of their homes. I didn't miss the commercial humbug one bit, but as a holiday, if not quite a holy day, for many in Australia, Christmas was certainly a high point in the year. As well as a religious feast, I think of it also as a time when the normal clock stops and there is a change of pace

Whorls of belief

until the festivities on 26 January signal that it is time to rewind the workaday diary-driven cycle once more.

Christmas Day is a holiday in India, but I was beginning to realise that first December that it was just one feast, even a lesser one, in a panoply of religious holidays in the Subcontinent. I was very conscious of being a minority as a white woman in suburban Chennai, but Christmas had shown me in a fresh way, that as a Christian, I was in a minority as well, one of maybe less than three per cent of the Indian population. I was no longer part of the dominant culture. This was a new experience. It threw me back on my own resources in terms of making sense of what was for me an important religious festival. I realised that I needed to adapt to the role and to start from scratch in developing what might become our own family rituals, and, in time, traditions.

While enjoying my quiet moment on the balcony that evening, I tried to make sense of my mood of suspension. It was the experience of transition from one way of celebrating this religious feast to another that I had not quite worked out or accepted yet. It challenged me to think of its meaning for us as a family and therefore how we might mark it.

My husband is a generous man and over the years has lavished more beautiful jewellery on me 'than a giraffe could wear', as my mum used to say. However, the rituals favoured by Benjamin and his family around events such as Christmas and birthdays tended to be low-key with no emphasis on gift-giving. So on this first Christmas in my new family, I had fashioned a small stylised tree and featured a Japanese nativity print which had been a wedding gift, creating a small festive corner in our living room. We sent cards to our family and friends back home in Australia. On Christmas Eve, we attended midnight Mass at our regular church. We visited friends and had lunch with Benjamin's father, Doctor Mathew, and Kochamma. We carried fruit and sweets and exchanged them when we visited. Lunch was fried fish, curry and rice. It had been a pleasant and relaxed day.

Yet as I stood on the balcony that Christmas night, part of me grieved, just a little, for potatoes, pudding and custard.

I found this experience of 'outsider' salutary, especially as an Australian. Migration has peopled our land with communities of difference. When I returned to Sydney a few years later, to a place where I was known and amongst my other family and friends, my time away gave my return an element of doing so as a migrant, and I felt identification in a very small way with those who have made harder and longer transitions.

India is a kaleidoscope of cultures, languages, festivals and faiths and all of them are celebrated. There are also many different calendars, so the year whirls around different spirals of festivity, and somehow manages to reach the starting point again each year. In the 1950s, India reduced thirty calendars into one when the Gregorian model became the official one. Outside public life, other systems persist. One used by Hindus for religious purposes dates from the first century of the Common Era (CE). It is based on solar, star and lunar phases and so the dates of many holidays vary from year to year and from state to state. Muslims use a schedule dating from 622 CE; Buddhists calculate their dates based on the death of Buddha in 483 BCE; and Zoroastrians from 632 BCE. The calendars of different groups are very important in governing auspicious and inauspicious times. In the great accommodating way which is India, there were holidays for Republic Day and Independence Day; there were birthday holidays for Gandhi, Buddha, the Prophet Muhammad, Jesus, Lord Krishna and the Sikh founder Guru Nanak; there were New Year holidays for the Gregorian calendar, the Islamic calendar, the Hindu calendar, the Tamil calendar; there were seasonal, regional and local celebrations as well. In the months between my arrival in Chennai in early May and this first Christmas night, religion had been a large part of our lives. Festival and feasts whorled around. Religion occupied my attention in other ways as well.

An early learning for me was that there are many ways of

being Hindu just as there are many ways of being Sikh or Buddhist or Muslim or Jewish or Christian. Benjamin had an old friend who was a very senior police officer in the Indian Police Service (IPS). Outside his home there was always at least one police jeep, waiting for his next move. He was also a devout Hindu and something of a philosopher. As he discoursed with Benjamin, he habitually ended a thought with *Inshallah*, the Islamic version of what is familiar to me as the traditional Irish 'God willing'. Over the years, he developed serious illnesses in which one complication led to another. Suffering from severe diabetes, he developed a critical heart condition; his eyesight became affected; he became virtually unable to walk. Still, in the midst of his discomfort and incapacity, he maintained his demeanour of acceptance and faith, retaining the spirit of *Inshallah* until his death.

In 1984, the Islamic month of Ramadan, which honours the revelation of the Qur'an to the Prophet, more or less coincided with June. During the holy month, observant Muslims had fasted from sunrise to sunset and no food or water had been taken. Fasting, as in all religions, was undertaken as a spiritual exercise in the pursuit of goodness, patience, sacrifice and humility. Ramadan is a time for Muslims to make a special effort with prayer and good works, ask forgiveness for sins, pray for guidance and help in refraining from everyday evils and try to purify themselves through self-restraint and good deeds. Charity, especially towards the poor, or *Zakat*, always important, is given even higher priority during this time.

By the end of June, Ramadan had moved to the joyful celebration of Id al-Fitr, Festival of Breaking the Fast, the most important Muslim festival. We had observed the coming of the feast in the preparations that went on in cleaning and freshening houses around us. Id is a time for new clothes. There were special morning prayers and people wished each other 'Blessed Id.' We visited Tahzeen and Tanveer in our old neighbourhood. In later years, when I was a little more attuned to what was happening, I would see through our kitchen window in Indira Nagar the party of lepers and beggars who would each year gather on the opposite corner at this time, and I knew that our neighbours were observing their Id duty of giving alms and good food. An invitation to visit Muslim friends at Id was always welcome, as one could look forward without disappointment to a wonderful *biriyani*.

Years later, in January 1998, Benjamin and I were in Chennai with our three children. It was Ramadan. There were very heavy rains. We were to stay with our friends, Professor Syed Zafrullah and his wife Praveen, for two nights. Professor Zafrullah met us in his car that was far from new. We piled in. Sheets of rain made visibility difficult. The windscreen wipers didn't work. Every hundred metres or so, Syed, seemingly unfazed by this, would reach out through the driver's window to wipe some small tunnel of fog off the window. Meanwhile, in the back seat, rain had begun to drop down on us through some rusted joints. We edged along as our host navigated in virtual darkness a street which torrential rain had stripped of its thin crust of bitumen, opening up deep craters. The children loved the experience.

The highlight of this visit, however, was the hospitality which was opened to us during Ramadan. While the family fasted between sunrise and sunset Praveen prepared our meals within the fast period and made us feel warmly welcomed. I was profoundly touched by this kindness. Their son, Nazrullah, then a tall slim boy of about twelve, played with our son, while our girls hung around his sister, Fauzia, a shy and dignified fifteen-year-old.

About ten years later, I witnessed another example of courteous respect. Nazrullah, now a tall young man, was spending a few days with us in Sydney, taking a break from his post-graduate studies in Adelaide. He had brought with him a student friend from Pakistan who was a few years older than himself. After lunch, which we enjoyed in the garden, I served cake, made by one of our daughters. Nazrullah, very courteously, declined, on the grounds of religion. His friend very quietly counselled him, saying that the Prophet had taught that it is better to eat the cake and risk offending a religious rule than to break the greater rule of courtesy. It was a gentle exchange between one young man and a slightly wiser one.

Most Hinduism is practised at home and in daily life. When I visited with my friends and colleagues, such as Lakshmi or Janaki, I noticed the *puja* area they had set aside. A special nook, or even a room, would display images according to the family's particular devotion within Hinduism. Often, it was set up in the corner of the kitchen or living room, much as I had set up my corner at home to mark Christmas, or the prayer spaces set aside in Catholic school classrooms. There would often be a coconut or banana and marigold-like flowers left in the *puja* area. Sometimes there might be a small silver bowl of sandalwood paste ground by the priests in the temple. In Australia, I enjoy being able to share the savoury holy basil (*tulsi*) from my garden with Hindu friends to use in their *puja*. Early in the morning and late in the evening, my friends lit the small brass oil lamps, burned incense in blessing, and sanctified the day's chores or the evening's sleep with their prayers. In some homes, women started the day by drawing a prayer in intricate geometric designs in powdered chalk on the doorstep.

In many ways, each day was a cycle drawn within the larger annual one – call to prayer at dawn from local mosques; Hindu priests riding their scooters in the early morning to do *puja* in the nearest temple; prayers at home from those of all religions. On television, regular time was given over to long in-depth interviews between spiritual gurus and a group of disciples. And in one of the two major daily newspapers, *The Hindu*, I read with interest the daily column devoted to Hindu philosophy, even when I couldn't quite comprehend its meaning.

Some time late in the year, I saw another face of Hindu piety. Benjamin and I had gone to the station to catch an overnight train. As we waited on the platform, a sudden commotion disturbed us. There was the sound of drums, cymbals, and loud chanting. A large group of rough and ragged-looking men moved towards us. Their hair was wild. They were bearded. Most of them wore black *vaishtis*, although one or two wore saffron-coloured ones. Ash was smeared on their faces. Around their necks were beads made from berries and sandalwood. They carried sticks and bundles. I was glad Benjamin was with me.

'Pilgrims. Going to Sarabimala', he said, undisturbed. 'There's a temple in Kerala. The Ayyappa temple. Millions go there each year to honour Lord Ayyappa. They have to walk through forests and rivers. Something like fifty kilometres.'

I remained uncomfortable with the group's noisy presence. Every now and again as we waited with other passengers, their drumming and chanting started up afresh.

'Only men can make the pilgrimage, although I think small children and very old women can go', Benjamin added. 'Ayyappa was celibate, so he shouldn't be tempted.' I was pleased when the time came to board the train that the group was not in our carriage.

Later on, I learned more from Shirley, who was a Christian married into a Hindu household. Her husband, she told me very quietly one day, was preparing to go to Sabarimala. That meant that for forty-one days beforehand, he couldn't shave, he bathed twice daily, he couldn't smoke and he couldn't have sex.

'It also means that during menstruation, I cannot be in the room with him. So that I won't contaminate him.' I got the sense that Shirley had mixed feelings about Sabarimala.

In the cleaner cooler post-monsoonal air that I was enjoying on the balcony under the stars on that evening of my first Christmas after our marriage, I wondered what the year ahead would hold. It seemed to me that it could hardly be more eventful than the previous eight months.

New Year started with a bang – on my head.

On 2 January, Benjamin and I had possibly the best *biriyani* we

Whorls of belief

have ever enjoyed, and there have been many. This one was neither in the home at one of our Muslim friends, nor at a wedding, but in the Connemara, one of the five-star hotels in the city. We were visiting our friends, Rosalie and Sampath, who had recently returned to Sam's home city of Chennai from Mumbai. Sam is a chef, a top chef, and has worked in prestigious hotels in a number of countries. His new position was as Executive Chef in the Connemara and he and Rosalie were living in the hotel until they found more suitable accommodation. I was meeting Rosalie for the first time. She was tall, younger than me and with an easy friendliness that I found relaxing. When she turned around, I stared at the thickness of her plait swinging heavily down to her waist. We laughed and talked our way through a fun evening. The *biriyani* in question, prepared under Sam's supervision, came to our table sealed in clay pots, the fulsome flavour of the mutton locked in and the spicy meat fragrant and tender.

We said goodbye fairly early, and reluctantly, but Benjamin was going as a consultant to a slum improvement project in Nagpur and was leaving on an overnight train. We mounted the Bullet to ride home. We didn't get far. It was a small accident really: a moment when Benjamin and an oncoming scooter rider were locked in indecision as to who would turn right across each other's path first. Stop. Start. Stop. Start. Revving. Moving. Stop. And I was tipped, heels-over-head, from my side-saddle pillion seat onto the middle of the road. I would rather not think of the sight I presented in the movement from the bike and prefer the image of lying prone there on the bitumen. It created a minor stir. The witnesses seemed embarrassed that a foreign woman had fallen in their midst, almost as if they were responsible. I was only mildly shaken with a superficial cut to the back of my head. After a brief check-up at one of the more highly regarded (that is, more expensive) hospitals, I was sent home. My husband had enough confidence in my sturdy Hunter Valley constitution to continue on with his planned journey.

This minor incident is worth mentioning only because it was

sandwiched between the evening with Sam and Rosalie and a historic gathering in which I was to take part the next day. The event was an International Conference that brought together representatives of the main religious groups in Asia. I rose early and caught a bus across the city to Gurukul Lutheran Theological College which was hosting the six day meeting, initiated by German theologian, Michael von Brück.

It was an amazing and privileged assembly. There were fewer than eighty people there, but they included the XVI Dalai Lama and Hindu, Muslim and other Buddhist holy men. As well as Benedictine Fr Bede Griffiths, there were Christians from both Western and Orthodox traditions. I recall that the speakers were all male, but the other participants I joined included women as well as men of all religions, from Asia and the West. It was colourful, with Catholic nuns in full white habits or simple cotton saris; women in western and eastern dress; men in business suits or Gandhian homespun cotton (*khadi*), *jibba* and *vaishti*.

Hindu monks quoted Muslim stories and Christian scriptures; the State Governor of Tamil Nadu, in opening the conference, gave a theological and philosophical address which drew on sources from major religions and western philosophers; the Dalai Lama spoke simply about happiness; a Muslim academic urged us to speak out boldly against injustice, oppression, prejudice and hatred 'practised by people of our own community' to 'pave the way for a just and peaceful world in which our children and their children could live in an atmosphere of peace and good will.'

We began each day with a Buddhist Zen meditation and during the day met three more times for prayers that were recited from the different religious scriptures. And if the words of worship were sometimes a little unfamiliar to us, the spirit of the meeting held us together. Our purpose was clear: to live for a few days according to our aspirations of being one family under God, which meant, in the words of Bede Griffiths, for religions to 'give an answer to the pressing economic and social and political problems of today'. If religions cannot do that, he continued in harmony with all the speakers, '... they are not fulfilling their proper function.'

Bede Griffiths, a convert from Anglicanism and a graduate from Oxford in journalism, had been ordained as a Benedictine monk in 1940. He had lived in India since 1955. In 1968, aged 62, he had moved to an ashram near Tiruchirappalli (Trichy) in a southern part of Tamil Nadu. He was a mystic, seeking the one-ness in all the great religious traditions. There, at 'Shantivanam', he pursued his life search. The ashram became a centre where pilgrims and scholars from all around the world came to study or simply to speak with him. At Gurukul, that January in 1985, he was among people who held him with both respect and great affection. An elegant figure in saffron robes, his longish hair was silver like his beard, and thick bushy eyebrows hung over his etched face. His hands were long, a scholar's hands. Two years later, he published a complete commentary on the *Bhagavad Gita*, which is part of the great Indian epic poem, the *Mahabharata*, and one of the most important Hindu scriptures. No doubt he was working on it at this time. I met him there at Gurukul but I am disappointed that, during the years I spent in India, I failed to organise myself to visit Shantivanam Ashram which was just an overnight train ride from Chennai.

The Dalai Lama contrasted with Fr Bede in his red robes, bare arms and with his round bald dome. He came across as a cheerful man, his eyes smiling behind shiny spectacles as he addressed us and when he spoke it was with homeliness. I sat there, pinching myself, that I was actually watching these two revered holy men in conversation before us.

When I look back on this experience, I want to revisit it. I sense that I might have wasted the richness of the opportunity, not because I did not appreciate it, but because I had not lived long enough or learnt enough at that time to grasp its significance. I am heartened to realise that Bede Griffiths, to whom Hindus had given the honorific title of

Dayananda, meaning 'Bliss of Compassion', came to his ashram only at the age of sixty-two.

Two weeks after New Year 1985, we celebrated the feast of Pongal, which is very much a local celebration, being New Year in the Tamil calendar. As I understand it, Pongal is a harvest festival, celebrating the sun, rice and the humble ox. The festival lasted for several days. It created an opportunity to make a fresh start, by cleaning up around the house, getting new clothes and meeting other families in a spirit of good will and peace. The specialty of Pongal was a dish of the same name. Rice is cooked in milk, coconut, raisins, cashew nuts, and lentils, spiced with cardamom and sweetened with jaggery, an unrefined sugar associated in India with spiritual and healing properties and made from sugar cane or date palms. The result is a rich and tasty delicacy. Benjamin and I visited a number of friends and ended up eating far more than was good for anyone. Sharing the hospitality of Pongal is partly what the feast is all about.

An interesting part of the festivities was a day dedicated to the humble beasts that pulled the ploughs and wagons in the cultivation of food. It was called 'cattle Pongal' (*Maattu Pongal*). Buffalo and cattle wandered the city streets with their horns painted red, blue, green and yellow. Some wore garlands around their thick lowering necks. This is their day, a tribute to their contribution to the production of food throughout the year. In some villages, I was told, communities celebrate a bull-running on the fourth day of Pongal. More aggressive young bulls are chosen, their horns sharpened and prizes attached to the animals' heads. They are released to run through the village while youths try to grab the prizes as they pass.

On 26 January, when the rest of India celebrated Republic Day, Benjamin and I included Australia in our celebrations. This happy concidence of Australia Day and Indian Republic Day on the same date continues to be a personal pleasure for us. I cannot recall exactly how we celebrated 26 January in 1985, but we probably marked it by watching tennis on TV.

Linking my worlds

SOME TIME IN MID-APRIL, I went alone to the Customs House on Beach Road. My business was for custom officials to cancel the bond against my goods which I had shipped to Chennai on what was known as 'Transfer of Residence' in May 1984 after the wedding. India was going through one of those periods when the country's trading borders were fairly rigid and duty on imports prohibitively high. Hence, the requirements for people taking up residence in India were tough to prevent imports which might circumvent the high duty. The value of my books and personal effects which I had shipped had been 28,000 rupees; the bond we had to guarantee had been 63,000 rupees (worth about four years of our combined Indian salaries.)

My business was with Mr Narayanaswamy, the same official who had appointed himself my Indian 'father' when I had first arrived in Chennai after our marriage. I was going to meet him, not at the airport, but at the Customs Office in the city proper, across the road from the Port. On this occasion also, as on every visit I made to a government office, I wore a sari. It was done as a courtesy and with respect for local customs and it seemed to please people far more than it bothered me to wind, pleat and pin myself into it. Once dressed, I found saris comfortable and elegant to wear. As I rode in the autorickshaw towards the Port and discerned the faint brininess of the air, I chuckled to myself recalling the three days it had taken us to clear my same personal effects through customs.

I made my way up a staircase which needed a scrub and a coat of paint like every other government institution I visited in India, and located Mr Narayanaswamy in a large open room with about a dozen other staff. Like him, they were dressed in pressed white cotton shirts and white trousers, and sat at uniform wooden desks. The Customs Office was bright, with windows facing towards the Bay of Bengal. There were piles of files all over the place. They tilted off the tops of cupboards; there were tidal marks of dust where a broom had skirted around stacks of them on the floor; on every flat surface they sat, mounds of dusty folders tied into bundles with red cotton tape, and looking like they dated back to Colonial days. They were similar to the ones I had seen in the Tamil Nadu Department of Welfare and in the Department of Adult Education and even the same as the mountains I had seen in the Department of the Environment in Delhi. I wondered, as I waited, if they were really all the same files just relocated from place to place.

I sat on the plain wooden chair in front of Mr Narayanaswamy's desk. He beamed at me.

We had just begun our business when the customs officer was visited by an elderly gentleman in white *vaishti* and shirt. There was a shuffle of chairs and greetings. The visitor sat down on the second chair facing the official behind the desk. It was clear the two men were long-time friends. The newcomer presented Mr Narayanaswarmy with two rupees. It was a donation, he said, towards the renovation of a temple in his friend's village because the temple fund, he explained, was being plundered by a wealthy landowner. They talked on, largely in English, which might have been for my benefit, although they appeared to ignore me. This was not at all displeasing to me, as I was enjoying the conversation and I had learned that, in dealing with Indian bureaucracy, it is wise to be in no particular hurry.

Linking my worlds

The older man shared his views on the dangers of affluence which exposes people to pride and egoism. (Was this deliberately directed towards the woman from the affluent West?)

'The things one acquires lead a person to think they are superior. But God will always win out.'

'God is more than human, all powerful.'

'Take Hitler – he led people to the arrogance of a superior Aryan race. (Was this another message for the very white woman beside them?) He created Poland just so that war could be generated and power won.'

'What about the nuclear bombs?'

'Ah, that's God's way when it gets too bad. When it gets too bad, God will wipe out the world!' I was becoming confused by this God who both created and destroyed. But then, I had not been brought up on the Hindu deity, Shiva. I wondered how it affected my adoptive guardian's approach to his customs duties.

'But God is present in everything, isn't it? God is in the ballpoint pen, in aeroplanes, in tanks, even in a bomb, because God created the image which became the thing. The thing can't be without God's image of it.' This was getting heavy in the humid office air.

'And for what we have, what we have been given, we must give too. We have been given money, so we must give. We have been given aeroplanes, so we must give.' And so, back to the two rupee donation.

Mr Narayanaswamy turned to me as his visitor left. 'Faith can move mountains', he smiled with a flourishing lapse into Christianity.

Mr Narayanaswamy talked to me then about himself and his family. He earned, he said, 2500 rupees a month; his wife was paid 1000 as a teacher in one of the city's public schools. His son brought home 700 and there was an additional 2000 coming in from rents, bringing their monthly income to over 6000 rupees. (In 1985, on a combined family income of 1400 rupees, that sounded like a fortune to me.) The family approached this as a family, with his son giving all his income into the common household pool, which I knew was a frequent (and laudable) practice. I was fascinated, but at the same time, I didn't want to forget why I had come to the Customs House in the first place.

Like many others in Chennai – of any religion – the family used some of their income to run a not-for-profit primary school up to Year 5 for about 200 poor children in the northern areas of the city.

'We must try to do good and share what we have', Mr Narayanaswamy said. I was warming in a guarded way to him and suspected that he was really very soft-hearted and sentimental.

'My son is going to marry soon. In June. He is a good boy. We have found a good girl for him. She is one of ours. This is important for us to see him settled. Then we have done our work.' I wondered if he was thinking of retirement after the expense and obligation of his son's marriage had been completed.

'My wife and I go every week to my village. We need to prepare for the wedding', he added. It occurred to me that this was a serious commitment on the part of the man and his wife, as his village was nearly seventy kilometres south west of Chennai, especially when both of them worked full-time.

'We must do *darshan* for blessings, you understand?' I nodded, vaguely aware that he was referring to the act of seeking divine presence and blessing. He had another more practical purpose as well: he also went to keep an eye on the upkeep of the local temple and its plundering landlord.

As usual in our meetings (for there had been others), I refused his repeated offers of gifts from the customs warehouse. As usual, I politely and very insistently refused his gushing offers of financial assistance. Just once, I had accepted a gift from him, and that, because in the open office area, it had become very difficult to keep on refusing: it was only a small hand towel, pretty enough and brand new. *Made in China*, the label read. I suspected it had been confiscated, one way or another.

Linking my worlds

I was not surprised that the simple task of cancelling my bond took an hour and a half to complete. During that short time, I had been given glimpses of the altruism and compassion common to all the great religions as well as different ways of doing business. On this occasion, I didn't mind the time spent one bit.

In time, I strengthened my links within Benjamin's family, as he took me beyond his immediate family to meet aunts, uncles, cousins, cousins's cousins and in-laws' in-laws. As is the case in most families, we met with some of these extended family members only occasionally, but were closer with others. In particular, from time to time, we made the three hour journey south to Puducherry (the former French territory previously known as Pondicherry) to visit two aunts, younger sisters of Benjamin's father, Doctor Mathew, and members of a French congregation of religious women, known as Cluny Sisters. One aunt, Sister Ignatius, was a solid woman. She became ill around this time, never recovered and spent her last years in a coma. Her sister, Sister Isabella, a tiny spry woman, became a special favourite of mine.

The Cluny Hospice, where the two Sister-aunts lived, is a large complex of freshly painted buildings behind a long cream compound wall in the French quarter of 'Pondy'. Inside the wall, neat gardens bloom beside freshly-swept gravel paths. The concrete floor of the covered veranda stretching past the chapel is smooth and polished to a low sheen. The cloister runs beside a courtyard that is neat, trim, watered and green with vegetables and flowers. Elderly residents move slowly as the aged move, hobbling along in simple *chappals* or thongs. In this sanctuary, the elderly poor live in dignity and calm watched over by a god of cleanliness. If, as we learnt as children, cleanliness is next to godliness, then God is very present in the Cluny convent and hospice.

On one of our visits there, we found Sister Isabella with another Sister who was incapacitated and being fussed over by two Sisters.

They called her 'Mother', and there were lots of laughs, touching, closeness as they worked with the semi-comatose Mère Octavia, a French woman who had worked for decades in India and wanted to die there. The younger religious and carers were warm and unaffected, mixing respect with cheerfulness. The love shown by the Sisters to the other women in their care was likewise joyful and somehow lighthearted. In this ambience, Sister Isabella, already about 70 years, was busy spreading her own special warmth.

I found out from Sister Isabella that, during the summers of 1938 through to 1940, an uncle of hers, one C. J. Varkey, would visit her family's home. She was then in her early teens, nearly twenty-five years younger than her brother, Mathew. Sister Isabella remembered her Uncle Varkey's visits clearly. He was a generous uncle to her, supporting her in her religious vocation in practical and financial ways.

This Varkey Uncle of Sister Isabella was the relative from whom Benjamin's father, Doctor Mathew, had sought accommodation when he had first gone to Chennai to study medicine in the 1930s. I had become a little curious about this relative, Mr C. J. Varkey, but Benjamin could tell me little. A fairly painstaking Google search identified him as one of the 'prominent Syro-Malabar Catholics in history' , a 'Catholic notable', one of the 'notable South Indian Catholic elite', a 'public figure' and 'a strident advocate of Catholic educational rights'. This was more than enough to intrigue me and sustain my burrowing for the crumbs I could find.

I did my own sleuthing and discovered that C. J. Varkey, a professor of history, had won a seat in Congress for the Indian Christian Constituency of Mangalore in the Madras Presidency in 1937. He was appointed Secretary to the Minister for Education, and then Minister for Education within the Madras Provincial Government, led by Sri C. Rajagopalachari. In this capacity, he participated in a number of national education committees. At least one of the meetings he attended was presided over by Mohandas K. Gandhi, who,

Linking my worlds

at this time, was promoting his Wardha Scheme of education. C. J. Varkey became an enthusiastic promoter of the ideas for national education laid out in the Mahatma's plan, although they created controversy in some quarters. He wrote a number of books on education, history and church life.

So it turned out that Benjamin's great uncle, C. J. Varkey, was a politician and nation-builder. In addition, he was an academic, a churchman and an educator, and it was these that linked him in a special way with some of my own interests. I would love to have had the chance to meet him.

Around this time, my husband built on the ties we had established to create an organisation known as the Indo-Australian Association. With his usual clear vision and sense of what needed to be done, we developed the necessary formalities. He found support amongst Chennai's professional and business community and, with encouragement from the Australian High Commission in Delhi, we embarked on a number of activities. They included hosting visiting Australian politicians, business people, sports people and public figures such as Helen and Bill Caldicott. It would be only natural a year later, when the Australian cricket team came to Chennai, for the Association to arrange an event to honour them. Few tests end in a tie, but in September 1986 it happened. Dean Jones was there, David Boon and Allan Border. More importantly from my perspective was the legendary Bobby Simpson, who was there as the team's coach. Here was a name that I had heard my dad speak of so often with admiration. I was delighted to meet Simpson, simply for my dad's sake, although by then, Dad had lost his characteristic enthusiasm for all things sporting. Later, after we returned to Australia, the Association would continue to flourish.

The management committee sponsored promising students on short visits to Australia and awarded individual Indians or Australians who had contributed to promoting Indo-Australian relations. The Indo-Australian Association, just one of Benjamin's initiatives, lives on still, over twenty-five years later. But in telling this part of my story, I have gone ahead of myself. We are still in 1985 and important things were going on in our household.

Not like this

ALL THIS TIME, I held on to Australia with the gentle thread of my mother's weekly aerogrammes. There were letters to and fro between others, of course, family and friends, but Mum's arrived each week, as faithful as the dawn. Hers took just four days to reach me from home, whereas my replies back took about eight days.

The encounter with the landlords in the mango field had given me a sense of vulnerability. It reminded me that taking the side of the poor rarely goes down very well with those who have something to lose, either in the first century or the twenty-first. I worried (a little, and, then, less and less,) about what might have happened had things gone differently at Cheyalnagar. More importantly, the event had sharpened my identification with the poor. Perhaps 'identification', or, more accurately, 'allegiance' to the poor, but I still did so from the security of the many back-ups I held onto: my education, family, and the comparative wealth that Benjamin and I enjoyed. I certainly hadn't written to Mum and Dad about the incident in the mango field – not that they needed to know – and, in fact, have still not discussed it much with others in my Aussie family.

Mum's letters were invariably cheerful, with all the domestic detail that forms the mortar in the bricks of family life. Dad scrawled a somewhat briefer, more generic, greeting on the back flap of the thin blue sheets.

My brother, Bernard, had been diagnosed with inoperable lung cancer in November 1984. So when Easter came round in early April, Benjamin and I were on a brief visit back home in Australia. We spent a little time with Bernard and his wife. He was gaunt and yellow with the radiation therapy he was undergoing. We all knew his illness was terminal and there was grace in the way he and his wife spoke and helped us all to speak matter-of-factly of his impending death. Before that, however, he arranged a trip together with his wife on a houseboat on the Murray River. Benjamin and I returned to Chennai in mid-April 1985.

In June 1984, when we had been attending the conference in Puntamba, amongst those I had met was Father Anthony Murmu. In a short time, the conference in Maharastra had slipped from my mind. Then, shortly after our return from Australia to see – that is, to say goodbye to – my brother, we had learned that there had been a fatal accident involving one of the conference participants. He and his family had been in their jeep when it had rolled over. Then, bad news gathering up like storm clouds, not long after, we began to hear startling rumours that Anthony Murmu too had died.

One morning in July, I was working in the Centre's library, perusing, with no particular purpose, one of the incoming journals. There, I learned more about Murmu's death: he had not died after an illness, or as the result of an accident. The rumours were confirmed. Murmu had returned to his home state of Bihar after the conference and continued his work with his people, an Indigenous group known as Santhals. He had died there in April while in police custody in the village of Banjhi in Bihar. I was shaken.

The sense of danger I had felt during our own encounter at Cheyalnagar brushed past me again. An incidental meeting a few months before linked me with this man, even superficially, in a chain of events leading to his death. It is something that has touched my life, one of those events after which I see everything a little differently. I am still trying to understand the cruelty and injustice of that day in 1985 in that distant village. The little I knew of his death was in contrast to the person I had seen in Puntamba. Because he was someone I had once met, and because of our own experiences of being threatened, I felt some kind of connection and I wanted to understand why Anthony Murmu had died.

So, over the years since then, I have sought out and spoken to Jesuits who had known him and been his friend. I have communicated with tribal groups who might have known him and in this way, ultimately, I reconnected with Xavier Dias, Anthony Murmu's friend, whom I'd met also at Puntamba and who still carries on his work seeking justice for tribals in the remote northern regions of India.

The more I searched out Anthony Murmu's story, the more I realised my understanding would always be incomplete: glimpsed from outside. I will not detail here the large story that I discovered; like other such stories, it is long, complex, and caught up in layers of history, politics and culture. It is enough, as part of my story, to say that his started with the fact that Anthony Murmu was a Santhal from the State of Bihar. While it is very much the story of one local region, Sahibganj, and its villages – the history, the people, the faith and the politics in which Murmu lived –it is also a universal story of the struggle between the powerful and weak, between evil and good, between despair and hope.

Anthony Murmu was born a decade or two before India's Independence in 1947. He entered the Jesuits and was ordained, and for some years served in Jesuit ministries. He stayed close to his origins as a Santhal and a tribal. A Jesuit who knew him during this time described him to me as an idealist and devoted to his people: he came from a tradition associated with struggle; he carried the same clan-name as some of the greatest heroes of that struggle and overlaid his Santhal identity with Jesuit spirituality and commitment to action and service. He also happened to have been born into one of India's poorest and most violent states.

In the course of his work as a Jesuit priest, Anthony Murmu became more and more involved with the struggles for autonomy of *Adivasis* (the Indigenous peoples) in his own region. In a time when civil liberties were being violated under Mrs Gandhi's Emergency period of government, he became involved in efforts directed at the restoration of democracy and civil rights. Somewhere along the way, he made the decision to run as a candidate in national elections for the Parliament of India lower house, the Lok Sabha, that were finally called early in 1977. The cost was high as he was required to stand aside as a Jesuit and as a priest. On 23 March 1977, Father Anthony Murmu began a term as a member of the sixth Lok Sabha, concluding on 22 August 1979. Following his term in the Lok Sabha, Anthony Murmu, still known as Father Murmu, returned to work with his people in Banjhi village.

The official report was that Fr Anthony Murmu was killed in police firing, which was held to control a protesting crowd. This official report fails to address the fact that he had been arrested *before* the shooting began and was already in custody. His palms and skull had bullet wounds. One hand was almost severed. An independent report released in Delhi in September 1985 found that 'Fr Anthony Murmu was killed in police custody in Banjhi, not in the police firing on April 19 in which 14 tribals were killed.'

I have learned also through his friends that Father Murmu continued to cling tenaciously to his religious ministry. 'I am a priest forever', he would say, 'anointed by the Holy Spirit.' When he was buried in the presence of his brother and of police officials, he was given a final indignity: this priest leader among the Santhals, who had also been a Jesuit and a Member of Parliament, was buried in a strange town; he was not permitted to return to his village, nor given the last rites that as a Catholic and priest would have been so important to him.

Anthony Murmu was a voice for the poor. He was one with them. Men and women only continue to fight, when they have something to hope for. For many of the poorest, there is no fight for freedom and justice, because they see no hope of attaining it. Anthony Murmu could hope, and he shared that with his community. It appears he was killed in a place used to store grain. The hands with which he had reached out to connect with his people in communion and to offer healing and guidance had been mangled The open palms with which he had offered service had been nailed with bullets, his blood mixed in with the grain.

A poignant death for one who had raised wine and bread aloft in sacramental memorial of another bloody death.

A former Member of the Indian Parliament, A. K. Roy, wrote just a few weeks after the Banjhi killings that the deaths of Fr Murmu and his companions 'in police firing near Sahibganj, Bihar, have perhaps already been forgotten as many of us are inclined to believe that tribals are born to die like this.'[18] My attempt to remember so many years later is a refusal to accept that anyone, anywhere, is born to die like this. Perhaps this one story can serve to remind whoever reads it about the capacity of women and men for evil and hate, so that we can resolve for a greater, deeper humanity.

Johar. It is a word, I learned, that has come to be used by different tribal groups of Jharkhand state as a greeting which transcends their different languages. But *Johar* is more than a word; it is a spirit, an attitude, a feeling and an expression of welcome, of gratitude, of praise, of togetherness, a salutation, an act of obeisance, a blessing. The tribal people of north India regard Anthony Murmu and his companions as martyrs. In Banjhi, their deaths are commemorated in an annual festival.

---

[18] A. K. Roy, former Member of Indian Parliament, letter to *The Statesman*, 2 May 1985.

Johar, Anthony Murmu. You and your companions should not have died in April 1985. Not like this.

Mum's aerogrammes continued to arrive, just as they had in previous times when I had lived away from home. In her careful elegant handwriting, she gave homely advice and on rare occasions there would be a line or two from Dad, often much the same each letter. As my brother's illness progressed, so did Dad's dementia. Always the manager, the man of action and initiative, he found himself confronted with something beyond his control: the coming death of his son. Bernard was just 45; Dad was about 83. Whatever else had caused his declining well-being, Bernard's illness, surely, pushed him to extremes. Mum wrote little to me about how the dementia that was distorting Dad's life was leaving her lonely and in the company of a stranger. Over the months, Dad's few words scrawled more and more into vagueness. And eventually ceased.

This was one of those times when I felt acutely the pain of being away from my Australian home. I was at a loss in terms of being able to do anything. I relied on my siblings to keep me informed, but they, too, protected me somewhat with limited information about just how horror-filled these months were for Mum. It is a family episode, in which, to this day, I have had only partial involvement. I still feel that loss.

The year went on, busy and distracting. In November, Benjamin and I travelled to the USA for a conference where we were both giving papers. Our flights were being paid for and this gave us the opportunity to make contact with funding organisations in Europe with which we were involved through the Centre. That was, more or less, how we relaxed in those days, rarely as tourists, but enjoying each other's company as we travelled.

On the way out of India, we made a brief stopover in Delhi, enjoying the gracious hospitality of Nicola and Graeme Feakes at the

Not like this

Australian High Commission for two nights. Then we flew to Frankfurt. To save time and a night's accommodation costs, we took an overnight train to Paris and met with contacts at the United Nations Education, Scientific and Cultural agency, UNESCO, and then on to London, where, once again, we met with academics, donors and potential supporters of our environment programs. Our end point was New Jersey, but before that we took a flight to Montreal to visit our old friend Raymond Cournoyer, whom duty had taken back to Canada. We had last seen Raymond on the night of the accident in which Benjamin broke his foot. Now Raymond was campaigning for the fiercely partisan Parti Québécois movement in national elections. In the depths of a Montreal area winter, I remember clear night skies and fumes of frozen breath as we left public meetings to walk through deep walls of snow back to the car. Afterwards, we sat with Raymond and his brother and family over a meal where the main course was the politics of French Canadians. Raymond was fired up and intense. He was to lose in the election but it was not for lack of effort on his part.

We attended the conference in New Jersey and gave our papers. The conference was being convened at a large resort-type hotel in a remote place outside Jersey City, NJ. Towards the end of the conference, the hotel staff left a message to say my father had died. No personal communication. A scribbled note. Desperately, we rang Australia. There was no reply. Even though Dad had been suffering from dementia, I hadn't anticipated his death. Having received this message and unable to reach my mother, I was convinced that she and my family were at his funeral. I sat on the bed in our room and sobbed. How could I be so far away at such a time?

What we didn't know was the message given to us by the hotel staff was already days old. When we finally succeeded in making contact with my family, it was to discover that Dad was alive, even if far from well. It was my brother, Bernard, who had died. By this time, the funeral was over. We returned home to Chennai, carrying the sad knowledge of my brother's death some ten days earlier. Once again,

I felt removed from my family in a time of sadness. Worse, I hadn't even known Bernard had died and so came late into my family's grief.

It is hard to grieve when you do not have the consolation of passing through funeral rituals in the company of family. I needed to remind myself of Bernard's absence – even though we had lived our separate lives for many years. For this reason I was especially grateful to my sister, Margaret, who thought to record the funeral Mass and send it to me. Once home in Chennai, I set aside one evening for my own memorial for him. I quietly played the tape and mourned Bernard for the older brother he had been.

Meetings

ON 4 OCTOBER 1985, BENJAMIN was admitted to the Chennai Bar as a lawyer. I couldn't go and take pride in his achievement in person because I had been laid low with an infection which left me in some discomfort. My disappointment in missing the ceremony was mitigated by the visitor we were hosting at the time, publisher David Lovell. During my time in India, I had continued my engagement with a curriculum project I had directed for Collins Dove in previous years. So, in between my work at the Centre, I was also editing a set of forty-two short stories for use in values education in Australian primary schools. This was the excuse which had brought David to stay with us in Chennai. He was a welcome and cheerful guest and I was delighted that he was able to go with Benjamin to the office of the Tamil Nadu Bar Association for the ceremonial swearing-in, while I was forced to wallow alone at home in my misery.

Other visitors were likewise welcomed over the years. We loved having visitors. An academic associate from the USA brought with her a sculptor friend. Jody had created large bronzes for a number of public institutions in the USA. She was charming, modest and adventuresome. Later on, we were to enjoy her company once again when she stayed with us in Sydney. This time, she was en route to a holiday trailing down the rivers of Papua New Guinea. Other visitors included Bill and Helen Caldicott, well-known peace activists. Later, their daughter brought a friend to stay for a while as they journeyed around India. They were bright and carefree young women, full of fun. It was to prove eventful for one of them in particular, who was to meet her future French husband while they were both volunteering in Mother Teresa's place in Calcutta.

Another group of young Australian visitors brought with them an added sense of responsibility for me. One of my nieces, Margaret Thomas, a nineteen-year-old student, arrived in a group of about fifteen students and teachers. It was one of those exposure tours which staff associated with the institutions that were to become Australian Catholic University had organised over a number of years as a way of building understanding in young teachers about other countries, cultures and the needs of the poor. The leaders of this tour included our friends, Peter Hancock and Tony Doherty, and also a young teacher who was to become a good friend, Paul Roberts. The group spent a few days in Chennai and we assisted them with breakfasts and by planning three days of seminars on topics such as poverty, development and women. We arranged visits for them to different organisations working with the poor and also to visit Benjamin's village and our rural program. They then left us to continue on for some more weeks in the west and north of India.

I had the clear sense that my eldest sister, Patricia, and her husband, Geoff, were more relaxed about their daughter's trip because Benjamin and I were there in India. But India is a big place and young women have their own minds. Despite our warnings against eating food from wayside stalls and not drinking unboiled water, my niece ended up in hospital in Mumbai, on a drip, with severe gastro problems and dehydration. Having recovered from this, she proceeded to explore for herself what we have all witnessed in the movie *Gandhi*, by riding on the top of a train in the far north. Fortunately, neither my sister nor I were aware of these antics till after they were over. It is

Meetings

not surprising that this young woman joined Australia's development assistance agency, AusAID. She has served in the Philippines, in Dili immediately after Independence and in Papua New Guinea, and is presently based in New York with the United Nations Development Program (UNDP).

One particular meeting during this time continues to stir my imagination.

A few scrawny trees twisted against the skyline. Here and there, sticks of thorn bush struggled through the taupe flinty crust which stretched away towards the horizon. Heat shimmered off rock. We had finally arrived. The desolation numbed me.

Heartilly welcome Mr Benjamin & Mrs Anne. The banner had been hung between two spindly sticks and we drove underneath it to enter the colony of Prakasam Nagar in Andhra Pradesh. Our jeep moved on a little further towards the heart of the settlement, a huddle of about thirty thatched dwellings squatting close to the ground. Small children played close by the houses while women were threshing grain known as ragi, or red millet, into the flour used as a staple food in the area. The villagers had grown the grain themselves, our guide said. As I stepped from the vehicle, I wondered how anything could grow in such an exposed, barren place.

Benjamin and I had been asked by the Australian Council of Churches to visit Prakasam Nagar and monitor the digging of a well they had funded. I have no technical expertise pertaining to wells, but I was confident I would know if one had been dug or not, and if it were functioning. So we had come to this outpost which was in Andhra Pradesh, the state adjoining the northern border of Tamil Nadu.

The journey had given us a good sense of the colony's isolation. We had travelled north by train from the city of Chennai the previous day and spent the night in a guest house near the large township of Cuddapah, which is the administrative centre for one of the districts in Andhra Pradesh. While we were there, a procession had approached noisily and caught us up in their midst. They were mostly men, peasants from the surrounding rural areas. I did not know what it was about. Some men carried large country-made shotguns which they fired in the air. It was noisy and threatening. The group halted in front of a building, apparently a government office, and fierce rhetoric was thrown to the crowd. Our host knew some of those involved and he and Benjamin seemed reasonably relaxed. Knowing the conditions of many agricultural labourers in our own adjoining state, I assumed that the protestors had a good case to argue. At the same time, I was also mindful that Andhra Pradesh is one of those states linked with the cycle of oppression, terrorism and counter-attacks associated with 'Naxalites' – a wide range of groups engaged in extremely violent struggles on behalf of landless labourers and Indigenous people against landlords and others with vested interests. The newspapers I read daily often reported horrific stories about Naxalite atrocities, especially in Andhra Pradesh.

On 25 May 1967, in a village called Naxalbari in the state of West Bengal, nearly 2000 kilometres to the north of Cuddapah, local thugs had attacked a man who had been given use of land by the courts under tenancy laws protecting the rights of tribal people. The victim's associates had retaliated violently against the landowners who had sponsored the original aggression and claimed the land back. The Naxalbari uprising gave its name to a movement that has continued to express itself in various guises across parts of India, and is synonymous with mayhem, anarchy and fear. While Naxalites originally claimed to represent the most oppressed people in India, they have often terrorised the lives of the Indigenous peoples whom they claim to represent.

So with this basic knowledge I found myself surrounded by the demonstration. With some unease, I wondered how I had ended up in the middle of this noisy group. There was no way I wanted to jeopardise my Indian visa because of some accidental association with

Meetings

people painted as terrorists. As it happened, the demonstration passed uneventfully.

The next morning we went to the office of Youth Voluntary Services, one of thousands of non-government organisations throughout India working with the poor. The organisation provided us with a jeep, a driver and a guide who was working with the villagers we were about to visit.

Three hours after we had left Cuddapah, the driver turned the vehicle off the sealed road on to a narrow country road. We bumped along for about fifteen kilometres until we came to the village of Thumunkunta. Here, the thatched dwellings pushed forward, reducing the road to a narrow track. The driver edged the jeep through the dusty sand, giving children and chickens plenty of time to scamper aside.

'About ten more kilometres', our guide said as we passed the huts on the outer rim of the village.

The torrents of centuries had cut deep gouges in many places. The road became two faint tracks which climbed steadily upwards over rocky ground. At one point we crossed a stream and the water washed strongly against the floor of the vehicle. Then up again from the river bed over shale which allowed little grip for the tyres. We moved very slowly. A bullock cart could make the journey in the dry, travelling even more slowly than the jeep. In the wet, any travel would need to be by foot.

The vehicle lent to us in Cuddapah had a faulty mechanism which leaked fuel into the cabin and around my feet. My curiosity to visit the remote community was tempered as the journey progressed with the sobering realisation that my sandals and sari hem were soaking in diesel. The longer we travelled, the further up my body the diesel crept.

I was uncomfortable. More than the physical irritation, my imagination played nervously with the possibilities of fire. The risk was probably quite unlikely, but my anxiety was not listening to reason. I was wearing a dark green Indian sari, its six metres tied firmly around me. The fact that the sari was synthetic added to my unease. By association, I recalled some of my recent reading about brides burnt to death in so-called kitchen accidents by in-laws disgruntled with the dowry they had been given by the bride's family. The fact that the practice of dowry had been prohibited in Indian legislation since 1961 did not seem to have curbed an old problem.

As I sat soaking up the jeep's diesel, I recalled the horrific deaths of these young women. Caught between such sombre musings and fascination with our present assignment, I had been relieved when our vehicle had driven in under the welcoming banner and our journey was over. I reminded myself to stay clear of any cooking fires.

As villagers gradually became aware that we had arrived, they interrupted their work to join the meeting. Watching them as they began to gather under a thatched shelter, I was in awe of the tenacity of spirit it would take to plant seed here year after year, and then the resilience needed to wait for a crop to survive and to ripen. I searched the lean faces for some understanding of their dogged determination. They gave nothing away.

Eventually, about thirty-five women and men settled in a circle on woven bamboo mats – men on one side with the men of our party, and me with the women and children on the other. The villagers were thin and dark. Most of the men wore the usual wrap-around checked cotton *lungi*, tucked around their waists and hanging to the ground; some had their *lungis* folded up in half, the way they were worn when the men were working. They wore shirts or singlets and a towel flung over their shoulder or wound around their head; the women's saris were shabby and their hair was dry and ill-groomed. The young girls wearing the half-sari normally worn by their age-group sat together on the outer edge of the circle, no doubt enjoying the interruption to their work and the distraction we provided. Younger children climbed around the women and girls.

We listened to their story. They had not been a natural

community, but marginal and disparate families who had come from different parts of the state to settle on land granted them by the government. Each family had been given five acres of seemingly inhospitable stony ground; they were twenty-five kilometres from transport and other services; their water supply was the river that we had crossed earlier which was a considerable distance from both the fields and dwellings and a single pump. They had also been strangers to each other when they first were brought together, being largely from different Adivasi groups.

With Independence, India had developed its own Constitution. This was the creative gift of Bhimrao Ramji Ambedkar, one of the first *Dalits* to complete higher education in India. Highly regarded as a scholar passionately determined to fight social oppression, Dr Ambedkar became the first Minister for Justice in Independent India in 1947 and was appointed chair of the committee responsible for drafting the new nation's Constitution. Mindful that the tribal peoples were among the poorest and most disadvantaged in the country, Dr Ambedkar and his colleagues singled them out for special protection in the Constitution draft. When the Indian Constitution was promulgated on 26 January 1950, it identified for special mention a listing of 'Scheduled Tribes' and attempted to make provisions for their well-being. A few years after Independence, in his address to an All-India Conference of Tribes in March 1955, Jawaharlal Nehru assured Indigenous people:

> Wherever you live, you should live in your own way. This is what I want you to decide yourselves. How would you like to live? Your old customs and habits are good. We want that they should survive but at the same time we want that you should be educated and should do your part in the welfare of the country.

Forests and waterways and lands which had traditionally provided the home and livelihood of tribal people were protected in legislation for their continuing use. They had close ties to their environment in what has been described as 'an intricate convivial-custodial mode of living'. Despite the good intentions of the nation's leaders and the commitment enshrined in the Indian Constitution and in legislation, Indigenous peoples continued to be exploited. Their access to traditional subsistence resources was whittled away.

The *Adivasi* peoples of India are among the poorest in the country. In 1991, some six years after our visit, there were around 4.2 million *Adivasi* people within Andhra Pradesh alone. They belonged to about thirty-three different groups, each with its own system of subgroups. Each community has its own culture, traditions, crafts, livelihood and dialect. Compared to the general state population (and this applies in other states as well), they have lower rates of literacy, school retention and land ownership, and higher rates of infant mortality, poor health and morbidity. In government documentation, the literacy rate of just over 17 per cent for Scheduled Tribes in Andhra Pradesh is lamented as 'abysmally low'. This 17 per cent disguises a literacy rate for Scheduled Tribe women in the state of only 8.6 per cent, symptomatic of the particular culture of disadvantage experienced by women and Indigenous women in particular.

It appeared that the community of Prakasam Nagar Colony was an effort by the government to re-settle families to compensate for their land being otherwise used for roads, dams or other developments. Given the harshness of the environment in which the families lived, and their impoverishment, it would be easy to be critical of this re-settlement at Prakasam Nagar: to lampoon possible government reports, or politicians' speeches, which might have cited this venture for acclaim for having looked after the poorest of the poor. Development, in a context as complex and large as in India, seems to happen only in miniscule increments. Even then, the gains and the efforts of genuine legislators and administrators can be compromised by inconsistent application, bureaucratic obfuscation or simple corruption.

We had not been told exactly who we were meeting on this visit to Prakasam Nagar Colony. The families, gathered so arbitrarily, had obviously developed some kind of kinship of survival. The men showed us the beginnings of the first well: piles of broken rock around a pit and at the bottom a small brown puddle indicating they had reached the water level. Much of the work so far had been done by hand, slow breaking of rock with rudimentary tools. I imagined the months it had taken for the villagers to make this much progress. Much more work lay ahead. But the impact would be enormous for the community, especially the women, who would be saved the arduous and time-consuming task of walking long distances for their daily water supply.

Now that they were assured of better access to water, the women's conversations turned to their next requirement. Their children needed nourishment.

'What we really need is buffaloes', they said. 'Then we can have milk for the children.' It was a joy for us later to report to the Australian donors that the villagers' resilience had endured and that the money was being well spent and to argue in support of their request for more wells and for buffaloes.

Their requests were reasonable and modest. However, I had the discomfort of realising that, simply by being a foreigner, my presence was raising expectations that I could not meet. *Foreigner*, especially for the less educated and sophisticated, can equate to miraculous solutions and abundance of wealth. As we sat there under the broken shade of thatch, conversing through interpreters, I knew that we would probably disappoint these people. Two people who simply came to inspect a well were incapable of extricating this community from their impoverished place in a system whose roots went centuries deep into the society's structure and culture. It was not the last time that I was to experience this kind of inadequacy.

As we continued to talk, a man and woman joined the meeting. He remained standing at the edge of the circle. She stepped straight to the front and sat down, not where we women sat, but amongst the men. Instead of a sari, she wore once-vivid skirts of a gypsy, layer upon layer of faded pinks and greens and blue. Her jewellery also was distinctive. Most of the women and girls present wore a simple plastic bangle or two. The gypsy woman arrived with a jangle of traditional jewellery: heavy dangling silver ear rings, hair pieces, a nose stud, beaded necklaces. Both forearms were all but covered with white and blue bangles that clattered when she gesticulated. She wore a faded pink cotton shawl over her head. She was as thin as could be imagined, wiry, with something in her of that tough high country itself. She mirrored the trees in the colony, sparse and weathered, with a persistent hold on life and dignity. Her clothing was worn and torn, but she was, indisputably, a lady of style.

She sat confidently, offering her opinions readily. I wondered about her relationship to the other women in that isolated colony: her colour, their drabness; her spryness, their languor; her confidence, their air of acquiescence. Her energy startled the landscape and in some ways challenged its harshness.

I wanted to know her better and I later discovered that she was most probably a Lambada woman, a member of a nomadic tribe originally from Rajasthan, who over the centuries have wandered to the southern states of India. The Lambadi women are famous for their dancing and for their colourful dresses decorated with beads and mirrors, silver ornaments and other bangles and jewellery. In the capital city of Andhra Pradesh, the Lambada (sometimes called Sugali) women can be seen sitting on pavements, stitching for the tourist and export market clothing, as they decorate textiles with mirrors and embroidery. In the 1991 census, the literacy rate among Lambada women was even lower than that for other *Adivasi* women, at 5.68 per cent. While the government has established a program whereby these pavement women can get loans to set up more durable businesses, it appears that many are unaware of them or are unwilling to take the risk.

I also learned that, even now, it is not uncommon for Lambada women to sell their girl children, because of the costs of raising and marrying a daughter. Authorities in India are working to eliminate the abuses that involve Lambada women, as well as other *Adivasi*

Meetings

groups, in Andhra Pradesh and neighbouring Tamil Nadu around the sale of babies and the way in which the ignorance and poverty of these women in remote settlements are exploited. The women worry about the dowry that a girl child will require for marriage; they worry about their perception that girls are unable to generate any family income; they worry about the drunken anger of their husbands when they produce yet another daughter.

When the meeting had finished, the women, keen to offer hospitality, gathered around us. The gypsy woman engaged with me in a friendly manner, more relaxed than many of the women I had met in city households. It was my first encounter with the greater personal freedom and social equality enjoyed by *Adivasi* women, as compared to other women in India. We struggled to connect using gestures, many smiles, a few words we could find to share and guesswork. What did she make of this? For me, she had a spirit which defied her austere existence.

Our work done and tea taken in little clay cups, we made our farewells. We drove back under the banner of *heartilly welcome* and began the descent towards more hospitable land. I looked back. The gypsy woman was watching us. She and her husband were etched against the skyline as she stood beside him on the rise, claiming her world under a large black umbrella.

Motherhood

AT LAST, MY SUSPICION was confirmed and I had the perfect answer for all my Indian relatives who had been offering wishful, and not-so-subtle, hints for fifteen months. I was pregnant.

I delighted in my pregnancy and prepared for the birth with relish, methodically and wholeheartedly. I stockpiled little garments and edged towels with picot crochet. I found satin ribbon in the market on Main Road and used it to add the luxury of satin-edged towels for the coming majesty, only to find that with the first wash the ribbon bled, its dull gum green blurring on the edges of the brown towel recalling a baked brown Australian summer landscape. Nappies were not available locally, so I bought light handloomed cotton from Co-optex and cut it into squares which I then hemmed. No other princess has ever had handcrafted nappies so lovingly made. For the small merino blankets, similar to those seen on certain airlines, wide red satin ribbon. A risky indulgence given previous experience with local ribbon and threads.

I had plenty of time to make these things for our child as I spent many evenings alone. After work, I would walk back home, while Benjamin would use this time to make work-related visits around the city. If he were going to the northside, for example, he would save up a few visits in that area to save time later on. Consequently, he often

Motherhood

arrived home to eat his dinner between nine and ten at night. It was not exactly how I had imagined our life together, and, in truth, some nights were pretty lonely, but I knew I would not have been the only woman in that kind of situation. As well as preparing for our baby, I had letters to write, books to read and a diary to keep. Spontaneous phone calls to friends or family for a chat were not on the agenda because in those days the quality of the phone system was more frustrating than the loneliness.

During this time, I thought a lot of Mum, naturally enough, because of the important thing happening to my body, and also because, when she wrote, she would offer little tips for me in her letters. More so, I was beginning to wonder about her life and feelings. Funny – I had lived all my life and not thought of how she might have experienced marriage and family, how she felt about her relationships. Dad had often been away from home for work and, yes, for golf, as well. Mum spent most of her time in the house. She was always so dignified, gracious and reserved. Now, in the quiet evenings of our flat in India, I began to imagine Mum less as my mother and more as another woman, one who had gone ahead of me and had experiences that paralleled some of those I was trying to negotiate.

During the months of anticipation, some treasured parcels from home added to my preparations: my sister Carmel sent beautifully embroidered bibs and linen. A large fluffy koala arrived in the mail one day. Another mail brought a furry kangaroo. Books. Cards. Letters. Our friend and neighbour, Prabha, who with her family had recently returned to Chennai after some time in Australia, lent us a low rocker cradle which had soothed many generations of her family. The wood of the cradle was smooth and I loved the idea that over decades, so many children had slept in it.

During this time, our household affairs took a big step forward. After struggling with our own cooking for over a year, we engaged some assistance in the house. Our stomachs and lives were cheered by the culinary skills of Chinnasamy, a big man with a kind heart, whose name translates literally as 'little god'. Chinnasamy would plod along slowly, arms swinging, head down. On his cycle, he rolled along with knees out. He arrived each morning around 6.30; he cleaned a little, but more importantly, prepared our breakfast and lunch. He took his own breakfast sitting cross-legged on the kitchen floor. Promptly at quarter to nine, he would leave to take his children to school, carrying our lunch and water flask. By 9.00, he was at the office to spend the day steadily gardening, cleaning and doing odd jobs. Around 6.00 in the evening, he and I would walk home. Once we reached Main Road, he would fall back and walk a few steps behind me. He would cook our evening meal and leave.

'Good morning, Madam', he greeted me, unsolicited, each day.

'Good night, Madam', he said as he left, again unsolicited. And in between, especially if Benjamin had already left for work, he would speak of his hopes and dreams. Mostly, they focused on his two sons.

'I am not a servant', he told me, repeating Benjamin's words when he had hired him. 'Madam works and gets paid. Sir works and gets paid. Chinnasamy works and gets paid.' He was fast and efficient, preparing a tasty meal quickly. He went out of his way to prepare meals to please me – 'Chinese noodles, Madam?' – ideas he had picked up at places where he or his wife, Saraswati, had previously cooked.

During my pregnancy, he coddled me with gentle breakfasts of *idiyappam*, 'string-hoppers', the steamed noodle-like cakes made from ground rice, served with warm, sweet coconut milk. The disaster that Benjamin and I had created when we had tried to make this delicacy enhanced the flavour of those made by Chinnasamy. He was a superb cook and patiently showed me how he made some of the more basic dishes.

'If I had gone to school, I would not be a cook', he confided once, as I savoured my breakfast. He could sign his name but could not read or write beyond that. Whenever he purchased vegetables or eggs, he faithfully brought me little slips written out by the stall-keeper who had a shop on the edge of our compound. Determined that his sons would have the chances he had missed, Chinnasamy paid to send his two little boys to a school with the magic allure of being run 'by an Englishman'.

Chinnasamy revealed his very determined views about 'nice' people and the 'not nice' based on some clear-cut principles. The core one was respect and dignity. He told me about Edel, the German woman for whom his wife, Saraswati, worked. I sensed that Saras, as he called her, might have been an extravert foil to Chinnasamy's shyness. Edel insisted that Saraswati sit at table with the family for their meal. One day there was a visitor, a local from Tamil Nadu. The visitor demurred when she saw the 'servant', Saraswati, take her place at table as usual. She spoke to Saraswati angrily in Tamil, upbraiding her. Edel picked up the tone immediately, and promptly introduced Saraswati to the annoyed visitor as 'my sister'.

While Edel rated highly in Chinnasamy's scale of niceness, her husband came in rather lower. 'Loud people who shout and get angry are not nice', he ruled, and it was apparent that Edel's husband fell into the loud, angry and 'not nice' category. Other elements in his taxonomy included people who worked hard (nice), and 'English' people (clean), Tamils (unclean). He was full of these prejudices and it was easier not to challenge him.

Chinnasamy carried lots of gossip on people around Chennai and the state – 1000 rupees spent by three foreigners on one lunch, especially for drink; some English man (I interpreted this as perhaps a westerner, not necessarily English) with a Malayalee wife, or one with a Tamil wife, depending on the story: 'nice madam', 'not-nice madam', all were categorised. He chattered away confidently and intimately, 75 per cent in Tamil, 20 per cent English with a gap for guesswork, so I felt some guilt in betraying his trust in me in being able to follow only about half of his stories.

Chinnasamy and his wife and two small sons lived in a single-room dwelling not far from ours. The house was brick but it leaked with every rain. He wanted to fix it himself, but the owner of the house would not permit it. When the monsoon came and water levels rose, his house was always flooded. He seemed quite philosophical about this regular calamity. His focus was on a bigger agenda: dreaming a future for his boys in America. He had recently bought a second-hand bicycle for taking the children to school, but it had problems and the tyre had been abominably patched. All of this, cheerily told, was also possibly a wistful endeavour to soften my heart to offer a higher salary from my obvious foreign-backed wealth.

Chinnasamy noticed the letters coming for me and would ask after my *Amma* and *Appa*, and then *Anna*, referring to my older brother, Bernard, before he had died from cancer. This served as an excuse to talk to me about his own family. His father, he said, was dead. His older brother, Periyasamy, used to beat Chinnasamy when he was a child. Now *Anna*, his older brother, enjoyed the family land and its produce while Chinnasamy and another brother and sister lived in Chennai. When their sister married, each gave 1000 rupees, but not the older brother.

Adding to Chinnasamy's resentment was the fact that his wife Saraswati 'had an operation' after her two children, as did the other brother's wife. Not so the older brother's wife, who already had three children. In the same spirit, Chinnasamy ended the family name tradition (*Chinnasamy* means 'little god', *Periyasamy*, 'big god') and named his sons Ramesh and Suresh. Now his ambition was to take driving lessons, eventually driving a lorry so that he could earn more money and Saraswati could stay at home and take care of the house and children.

Chinnasamy left us, of course. He was too good to be true and he received an offer too good to turn down. Edel and her husband, who already paid Saraswati over six hundred rupees a month, offered Chinnasamy a position as gardener for 200 rupees a month.

Motherhood

To cap it off (and he was well worth securing) from their United Nations salaries, they threw in a new flat worth another two hundred rupees a month and the children's school fees. This left Chinnasamy's family with an income very close to our own. We were definitely outclassed and outpriced.

Even this lasted for only a short time, as happens. The couple was transferred and the last we heard Chinnasamy was back cooking, this time in a small restaurant nearby.

My pregnancy was not without some anxiety, but then, I suspect, every pregnancy brings with it an uncertainty that is all the greater because the anticipation is so treasured. In my case, I was well into my thirties. Also, in the first few months of the pregnancy, I had contracted a measles-like infection after visiting a local school. We didn't think it was rubella – but how could we be sure? So we moved forward, loving this child absolutely, but nervous about possible complications.

Coming from a family of eight children probably gave me some preparation for becoming a mother but it didn't prepare me for childbirth. I'd always learned from books. I treasure them. So, finding myself pregnant in a foreign country with my mother eight days away by aerogramme, I naturally turned to books. But books can only go so far and our unborn daughter was not yet a reader and didn't quite keep up with me. I sang nice songs to her, spoke earnestly to her, and, as a doctor in Bangalore whom I had met in the course of my pregnancy advised, I thought lots of good thoughts.

I cannot think of our baby's birth without sentiments of gratitude to Pope John Paul II – an unlikely-enough association. In February 1986, the Pontiff had visited Chennai and other Indian cities. In preparation for his visit, the roads on which his convoy would travel had been resurfaced and the deep gutters freshly whitewashed. Much of my journey from our home to the hospital for my regular visits with my gynaecologist overlapped the Papal route. So for the last three months of the pregnancy, when I appreciated it most, the autorickshaw journey was as smooth as one could expect from such lightweight three-wheeler transport.

Our infant's birth re-established the fact that there is little point in planning details too far in advance. Friends' cars had been lined up for an emergency take-off. Delicate discussions about whether or not Benjamin would attend the birth had been executed. Our friend Priscilla had made arrangements to spend some time with me after the birth. My gynaecologist, Doctor Gita Arjun, had explained that I would spend the first part of labour in my own room and only go to the labour ward at the end. In the event, all these details become more or less irrelevant.

On the evening of the tenth day after the baby's estimated date of arrival, Benjamin and I set off quietly and leisurely, a procession of two: the bags and I in an autorickshaw proceeding with uncharacteristic care as though carrying a bomb along the papally-smoothed roadways; and Benjamin, the outrider, putt-putting behind on the Bullet motorbike. I was admitted to the ward unceremoniously. Our friend, Priscilla, a fellow educator and academic, arrived and we three walked to a nearby hotel for a *dosai*. Then I was left to settle in, unpack my bags and set up the makeshift kitchen/storeroom I had packed to help cover my food arrangements for the stay in hospital. In addition to some food, I had also brought the package of materials as requested in advance by the hospital: in fact, everything that might be needed for the birth of our child, including even the practicality of catgut to tie the cord.

The enema around 10.00 on the morning of Friday 2 May was a bit of a shock and my first experience of this kind. I was amazed by the rapid reaction. Then I walked along to the labour ward – hardly at all as I had envisaged it would happen throughout all those months of waiting, reading and planning. While my body continued to resist all persuasion for the birth to be induced, Benjamin appeared in the labour ward. Worn red shoulder bag swinging, motorcycle helmet in hand, his khadi cotton shirt damp with perspiration in the mid-

Motherhood

summer heat, he presented a comforting everyday touch in contrast to the sterility of most labour wards.

Some three and a half hours later I was being transferred to the operating theatre upstairs by means of a wicker chair with long carrier poles on each side, a plantation chair, I think it is called, in some throwback to the glories of colonial days. At the front, a small-built gardener grasped the poles, whiles two of the burlier *ayahs* – women helpers – carried the rear handles. By then, I was far from comfortable, but my greatest distress was that none of my friends or family was there to witness this carriage-in-style.

The daughter whom we both had anticipated with such delight was born at 1.50 pm. We called her Mariam, the name of Benjamin's mother, but also a name which has resonance in the great religious traditions of Judaism, Islam and Hinduism as well as Christianity. I woke to meet her after a general anaesthetic only around 5.00 pm. She was already three hours ahead of me. The eight days spent in the hospital were quite special. Temperatures soared into the forties. Benjamin continued his work in the office, with the additional task of providing me with all my water, buttermilk and food. He would appear early with toast and coffee, or later in the day with buttermilk and some dahl.

Priscilla also helped with meals, as did other friends, especialy Rosalie (she of the long plait) and Indira, a Hindu lady who worked with us in the Centre. Most importantly, the room had a second adult bed as well as the baby's crib. So, for a number of nights, we three – Benjamin, baby and I – were together. On the alternate nights, Priscilla proved herself indeed a godly godmother spending the time with us and caring for both the baby and me wonderfully. On our return home, my sister-in-law, Elsey, stayed for some days while we settled in. After she had returned to the village, another of Benjamin's sisters, Gracey, also made frequent visits.

About eight weeks before Mariam's birth, Sister Wenceslaus (Wency), Benjamin's eldest sister (baptised Jubilee), had brought us a young girl to help in the house. Selvi was a stocky young woman of about sixteen, or seventeen. She helped me by running the household errands for milk and vegetables as well as some cleaning. By the last few days of my pregnancy, Benjamin and I were confident that we had just about trained Selvi so that she could assist with some simple cooking, washing and cleaning after the baby was born. Then, two days before the birth, we were instructed to settle the young woman's account and send her to her guardians, an aunt and uncle, so that she could be married. So Selvi came and Selvi went. On 11 May, she was married to begin her own new role as wife.

There were a few challenges after Mariam's birth. Chinnasamy had gone. Selvi had gone. I had never had a baby before. We had no house help. The powerlessness that I had felt in my first year – years – in India had a new reason to flourish. It was true at work, where I was restricted by my lack of language. In domestic matters, it showed up in shopping, in dealing with all sorts of door-to-door vendors. How should I negotiate over the cost of sharpening our knives? Even the basic everyday matters of cooking different food with just a gas ring? The complication of being a first-time mother, and, what's more, as the medical records indicated, an *elderly prima gravida* in a foreign country had left me delighted with our baby, but nonetheless fragile, dispirited and exhausted.

> There was a cockroach in my coffee this morning. Not a big one really – not much more than a centimetre, just a baby. It was not a good omen for the day ahead. Had it fallen in? Had Rosie simply overlooked it? Had it been pushed? (Diary, 1986)

When I saw Rosie for the first time, I had cried. Not for Rosie. For myself.

One Sunday, the doorbell disturbed our afternoon nap. Mariam was twenty-three days old. Benjamin answered the door to say Wency had come and she had brought someone to help. I craved sleep as only a new mother can, but I was also desperate for some help with cooking, shopping, grinding, collecting milk, cleaning, washing of nappies, as well as storing and boiling water. 'Good ol' Wency', I thought, 'always generous-hearted.' As principal of one of her congregation's schools in the poorer part of the city, Wency was keen to help her older students find good safe employment. She also had a heart of gold in reaching out to Benjamin and me in our new role as parents. This time she was bringing salvation with pigtails.

There were two small girls in the living room. 'This is it – the help?' I said incredulously to Benjamin. I was a little less than gracious.

'Just one of them', he replied, 'the smaller one.'

The smaller one, a lovely looking girl, appeared to be around fourteen or fifteen years old but could have been younger or older. Two pigtails with odd ribbons and big round eyes: this was to be my pillar of strength now that there was a new baby in the house. I sat in the cane chair in which there were always tiny insects that pinched and itched and tried miserably to hold myself together while Benjamin conducted the interview. Rosie was hired: sixty rupees a month, board, lodging and toiletries included.

Rosie settled into our family routine. She had completed about Year 3 level of schooling and could read very little. I was trying to get into the language for myself. As I struggled with my own attempts to read and write Tamil (with its 247 characters, including twelve vowels and eighteen consonants), the teacher in me insisted that I try to continue Rosie's education as well. There was no point. Rosie was as interested to learn how to read and write as the crows outside the window. Teaching her to iron a shirt was likewise meaningless. Why do that when the *dhobi wallah* (laundry man) came by every afternoon and ironed shirts on the footpath outside our window with his iron filled with hot coals?

Not only did I fail to teach Rosie, I also failed in my own efforts to become Tamil-literate, barely mastering a survival Tamil which at least gave me a sense of what was going on around me. Sometimes as I moved around the city, I would try and practise my elementary Tamil reading skills. B-A-T-A, I would spell out laboriously to myself as the bus ground its gears through the traffic. Bata, a famous brand of shoes. Not much gained from that reading. S-T-A-A-R, I stuttered out to myself, discovering I was reading an English word in the Tamil script. My mastery of Tamil progressed as slowly as the bus. There was little hope that I would ever be able to discover the greatly loved literature of the Tamils for myself in the original.

However, I did learn from Rosie a whole new approach to language.

'Butterflower, Auntie', she aptly named the butterflies flitting around the flowers in the compound. 'Sleep coming, Aunty', she would announce as the baby began to grow listless and rub her eyes. Rosie herself rather enjoyed her own sleep, and perhaps she had worked out that with the baby asleep, she could probably slip away for a bit of a nap herself. At times, she slept more than the baby.

When vendors came to the door, Rosie was my international interpreter and economic adviser all in one. One day it was a seller of oranges; another, a cashew nut wallah. Invariably, Rosie's advice was stern and prudential, 'Too much, Auntie. Too much.' Her eyes large and stern. Often I took her advice, and other times, because I longed for an orange or a cashew, I'd take my own counsel. My highest-risk venture was to purchase some rugs from a vendor pushing a cart laden with his wares from door to door. They were vibrant and richly patterned, awakening my pre-conceived nostalgia for the exotic east. 'Too much, Aunty', Rosie warned me, but I wasn't really asking her on this occasion.

Rosie found some company at the little shop built into the wall of the compound about ten steps outside our front door. When she went to buy some eggs or garlic or tomatoes, the errand usually took at least twenty minutes. There she would be, chatting to this one or that one or listening in on the conversations of those who had come to buy. She relished her capacity for collecting news and gossip.

Motherhood

Each day, if there were letters, the postman would knock on the downstairs outer door. Like a bird freed from a cage, Rosie would hurtle down the stairs for the 'posht'. Then she would return more slowly, shaking her head seriously, to announce, '*Illai* posht, Aunty, no posht today', all the time hiding the letters behind her back. It was a simple game to play and one where my limited language met her command of English.

There were many frustrations and bad days. Days when Rosie simply didn't want to get up from her afternoon sleep, and wouldn't get up, until she reappeared scowling and sulky an hour later. Her English was limited, but skilled and fluent compared to my bumbling self-conscious Tamil. There was the time when Benjamin and I were sitting with a friend.

'Three cups of tea please, Rosie.' Originally my instinct had been to embroider such a request within the usual niceties. 'Would you mind getting us some tea, etc.' But in the communication which essentially takes place in the gap between two languages, such nuancing leads to more confusion than graciousness. On this occasion, Rosie held up four fingers.

'No, Rosie, three' (fingers of mine up in the air) cups'.

'Four cups, Auntie?'

On other days, international relations were strained over her personal hygiene, resulting in a ritualistic litany which flowed between the two of us.

'Rosie', I would say, 'that blouse is very dirty. Put on a clean one.'

'Bath time coming, Auntie', meaning, why waste the effort of dressing twice? So, I would wait, and if I remembered and was not distracted and if I had the energy for the argument, I would remind her,

'Bath time, Rosie.'

'*Nalaiki*, Auntie', she would bargain. *Tomorrow*.

'*Inoiki*, Rosie', I would insist. *Today*.

'*Aperum*, Auntie.' *Later*, she bartered, risking more wrath than she deserved.

'*Ippo*, Rosie.' *Now*, I rejoined slowly, emphasising the syllables with as much authority as I could.

Rosie usually won.

When Mariam was still very small, I would sometimes take her in her carry basket to the office and try to do my work there. It proved demanding. It was more practical, and better for her, for me to stay at home and work on documents and reports on the computer which was in our study. Driven by the amount of pending editing and writing for the Centre, Benjamin and I finally hired an ayah, or a nursemaid. We started off looking among the ayahs working for the foreign community. This included diplomats and United Nations personnel on anything up to 40,000 rupees a month, perhaps more. By then, our combined income was a little less than 2000 rupees a month. We hardly compared. What a laugh! We figured that if hiring an ayah enabled me to earn even her salary, then we wouldn't be behind, and some of the other household jobs would get done.

So, avoiding the 500-plus rupees girls, we hired a woman who had the impeccable distinction of coming to us after working for Mahatma Gandhi's grandson, and, before that, even his daughter-in-law. Mind you, the Mahatma's grandson did give us a mild warning about the value of locks and keys, but that was amidst general good feeling towards the woman. Benjamin engaged Kamala for 300 rupees a month, plus lunch and afternoon tea. On her first day, perhaps because she realised there was a foreign (read, *wealthy*) wife in the house, or maybe because she had quickly assessed how little I knew about running a household in India, Kamala asked us to pay her 400 rupees. This was not a bad pay rise before the job had even begun. We negotiated a figure somewhere in between. She was very experienced, both as cook and baby ayah. Because she was responsible and worked quickly, I had the confidence to leave Mariam with her when I needed to leave the house or was simply down the stairs in the study. I also was glad that she could give Rosie the training that I couldn't.

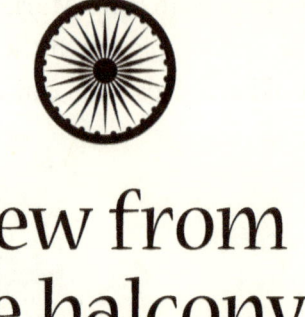

View from the balcony

I CELEBRATED MY FORTIETH birthday the day Mariam completed her first twelve weeks. My life had taken a somersault, surprised by the overwhelming totality of being a mum. Now, I began to understand what love meant. I hadn't grown up imagining myself as 'happily married with children' as the big goal of my life. I had come to it all a bit later and having enjoyed the satisfaction of completing and relishing study, a professional life and some creative output through the books I'd been involved with. I was totally absorbed in this new little person and her demands for food, attention, sleep (not enough at times) and her insistence on them (too much at times).

When she didn't feed well, I held her at my breast with my left arm and a book in my right hand as I searched for a quick answer to the mysteries of life. I soon learnt to abandon the books and simply follow my instinct. On afternoons when both of us were tired and she'd cry from colic, I'd hold her close and march vigorously up and down singing made-up lullabies, or, if feeling homesick, would play my Slim Dusty tape, not because I was a big fan of country and western, but because a friend had slipped it in my bag as an Aussie touch when I'd left home. By the time she was a few months old, I could bathe her

View from the balcony

in a large bucket – I would like to think of it as silver, but it was in fact stainless steel – and she clung to the rim and splashed playfully. I began to wonder how anyone could love someone so much, and still have heart-space for others. And so I thought of my mum and dad, and how, born in the middle ranks of their eight children, I had felt myself totally loved. Again, I began to feel I was beginning to understand something of my own mother in a new way.

One of the joys for me during our daughter's infancy was sitting with her on my knee on our closed-in front verandah. A parade of humanity passed before us, paying homage to our baby and inviting her into life. Cars, buses, cycles, scooters, motor bikes, lorries raced past at a frightening speed for such a suburban street. The trucks were invariably painted garishly with the owner's name proudly emblazoned on them – Southern Roadways, Murugan Roadways, Jesudas, and so on. They looked like old jalopies (but could be quite new) and rattled past with their load of bricks or 'jelly' (blue metal) and a nest of workers on top – sitting, often sleeping. In the evenings as they returned, jangling and empty, the men stood up at the back of the cabin, the wind whipping some of the day's salt and dust from their faces and stringy bodies. When I was out on the road anywhere, I was wary of these trucks.

'Lorries, Aunty', Rosie reported one morning. 'Crash!' Her arms waved and her eyes rolled with the excitement she had not-quite witnessed. 'Right here, *ingé*, First Avenue. The electricity office, Aunty.' Then she reached the juicy part of the story. 'One driver, Aunty, drinking', and she demonstrated with her arm up and hand to her mouth. 'Tch', she clicked her teeth in disgust like an old woman. 'Terrible Aunty.' The collision had occurred quite early, around 6.00, so Rosie's dismay about the drunken driver was not surprising. The vicarious adventure gave her extra excuses to visit Elumalai's vegetable stand and compare the horror with the other women.

The buses, too, roared along at a great speed, but always left a cooling flutter of fumes in their wake – a ripple pleasant for its cracking of the prevailing humidity but stifling in its diesel aura. In the evening, these homeward-bound buses were jammed beyond capacity, crammed inside until there was neither foot nor air space, and with young men hanging off the front and back doorways. Often these outriders had only one foot on with one hand grasping some bar connecting them to the bus. The buses tilted to the left with the weight of their constant over-burden.

The front balcony provided a natural play area for Mariam. As the months passed, she could crawl around there and then pull herself up to gaze through the floor-to-ceiling windows. Families constantly passed by on foot and wheels. Fathers pedalled their small children to school, a child perched either in front or back or both. I was always touched by the intimacy of these travellers: a dad's special time with these little ones (some as young as two or three years) close in front. Other children were ferried to school in creaky old cycle rickshaws with anything up to five or six children aboard. There were even some cycle rickshaws with little cabins on the back in which I've seen up to ten tiny tots packed. A cycle mini-bus, if you like. Children were sent off to school as early as three years old, uniforms, lunch boxes, books and all, even if for only a half-day.

For some families (us included), their vehicle was a scooter or motorbike. When I was on the motorbike with Benjamin, I was always conscious of what might have happened: potholes, sudden swerves, braking. In the early days, I carried Mariam, papoose-like, in a sling across my chest, as I sat behind Benjamin on the Bullet. Other mothers appeared far more relaxed. I was amazed to watch these families as they rode past our house, the women seemingly casual as pillion riders, one arm around an infant, one arm loosely on husband's shoulder, no safety helmet spoiling their jasmine-garlanded hair and sari floating and flapping in the breeze. I have never seen more than five family members on a two-wheeler, but I wouldn't be surprised if they carried more. Depending on their personality and vehicle, young men either putt-putted or roared along, as often as not with a helmet

View from the balcony

hanging from the steering handle or passenger's arm. This was one of the mysteries of the Indian psyche to me. Many years later, a young friend, George (whom I have known since his birth) told me, that finally there was a law that required drivers of two-wheelers to wear helmets, but it didn't apply to their passengers. This provoked me to reflect on what I like to call 'George's law':

> I have to wear my helmet,
> or they'll fine me. It's the law.
> But just for drivers, not their pillions.
> So whose head is valued more?

Mariam and I were entertained by a constant parade of bicycles and tricycles, imaginatively modified. Sometimes we might see a bike with large flat tray in the front or back, with four or five televisions or empty television cases, going somewhere, not to be discarded, but to be recycled and reincarnated. On others, we saw five or six gas cylinders, replacements being delivered to households; or timber; or wrought iron; or groceries from Rolex Stores down on Main Road. One day, the Rolex delivery boy was hit by a car just outside our window. I would chat to Mariam about the marvel of an ordinary cycle stacked with racks of eggs being happily pedalled by, not too fast, not too intently, the delivery boy seeming to enjoy the ride. Bullock wagons carried mosaic tiles for a new house nearby or for the one a little further along the road which was being renovated and extended. Before the tiles were needed, thin women had carried loads of bricks on their heads up skinny ladders until the building took shape.

We watched young boys and girls on their way to tuition, while their poorer contemporaries were fetching stores, and dark-skinned children of gypsies scavenged for paper through the rubbish that neighbours like the Vice Chancellor (that is, his staff) had thrown over their compound wall. The gypsy boys and men wore short shorts and their hair was often tied up in a knot of top of their heads; around their necks were bright beads which contrasted with their blackened clothes and nearly black skin; the girls and women swung grimy, full mid-length skirts. Some girls carried a baby in the cloth tied around their neck and hanging off their hip. They poked in the rubbish with long thin rods and collected their finds in bags slung off their shoulders.

In the evening, small family groups strolled leisurely by, the women bedecked with fresh jasmine sold by elderly women vendors. Sometimes a marriage procession passed noisily by on foot, drums banging and trumpet blaring, or a religious procession of Hindus or Christians with children, lamps, flowers and images, or a political caravan of trucks loaded with (paid) supporters, blasting out ear-piercing slogans or songs from old movies in which MGR had starred. MGR was then the Chief Minister of Tamil Nadu and a dearly-loved former movie star. Super-size cut-outs of him appeared at strategic times and places around the city. Religious beggars in black or orange dhotis came by in small ragged groups. At Id, beggars thronged the neighbouring Muslim household, clamouring noisily for food and coins. We even saw an elephant pass occasionally and a funeral procession, the dead on the bier amidst the cacophony of ritual Hindu farewells.

This was our baby's perch: her first insight into life. Here she sat in her father's lap as he sat cross-legged on the floor, the pair of them engrossed in the newspapers. Here she often took her midday nap. Here she crawled around as we sat with an evening cup of tea. Before her a daily pageant of India was played out just for her and she grew amidst its thrall and smell and sounds. And when it was quiet, there was still the bright sky and the gently waving trees.

The Bengali poet, Rabindranath Tagore, summed up my feelings during this time most aptly.

> This song of mine will wind its music around you,
>   my child, like the fond arms of love.
> The song of mine will touch your forehead
>   like a kiss of blessing ...
> It will be like the faithful star overhead

View from the balcony

> when dark night is over your road …
> And when my voice is silenced in death,
> my song will speak in your living heart.[19]

In February 1987, Mariam and I made a quick visit home to Australia. I was proud to show off our beautiful girl. My family oohed, aahed and goo-gooed most appropriately. It was in Mum and Dad's living room that Mariam finally got to her feet by herself, hanging onto the large carved wooden leg of their old oak dining table. After a delightful interlude, we returned to Chennai.

Late afternoon. Time for a walk, and perhaps some company if I'm lucky. I put Mariam in the stroller I had brought back from Australia and leave the compound and continue straight across the side street. The ironing wallah has finished for the day and only the coals from his iron are left on the pavement outside the Muslim house on the corner. I enter the next gate, number 13 1st Main Road, and make my way half-way down the side path to the house entrance.

Will Prabha, my friend not long returned from Australia, be at home? It's always a nice way to pass thirty minutes or so.

Today, I'm not in luck. Madam is out, I am told. So, back past our own gate and Elumalai's vegetable shop set in the compound wall watched over by the small elephant-god Ganesh in his rudimentary brick shrine across the street, and on this side by the few curious women clustered around the counter of vegetables and wire baskets of eggs.

At 1st Cross St, I turn left and wander in the shade, past Kim and Valerie's house on the left. No chance of a cuppa and a chat there today either, since they are visiting Val's family in the UK. I wander further along between two rows of large houses. Many feature tall

---

[19] Extract from 'My Song', *Gitanjali: Song Offerings* (1913), India Society of London.

candle-like ashoka trees, and within the frames created by the upright trees against the high cement-rendered walls I have a limited vision of upper balconies and flat roof tops, with their mixture of clotheslines, washing, pots and water tanks. On one roof, a woman stands, a still silhouette against the blue sky, stealing a moment's breeze and solitude.

Another good friend and supporter of Benjamin's and also a loyal Gandhian is Mr Oza. He lives about 150 metres along at the far end of the street, and is a former Secretary of the Government of Tamil Nadu. His house, a solid, flat-roofed two-storey dwelling typical of the area, is painted pink and cream. The crotons along the side wall have recently been watered. Crows squabble in a clump of coconut trees in one corner of the front garden. The cream Ambassador with its black and white official government plates tells me that the great man is at home.

The street ends one house later. I complete the circuit of the block and return home, once more past Ganesh, and through the narrow side gate which leads to our door.

After she had been with us a few months, Rosie surprised me one day by saying she had seen her *Chithappa* (uncle, younger brother of her father) riding by on a cycle.

'Did he see you?' I asked.

'No, Auntie.'

'Rosie called out, "Hello, Hello?"' I dramatised the possibilities of her trying to attract his attention.

'No, Auntie.'

'Brandy *Chithappa*?' I asked to determine which one of her uncles, knowing from Rosie's previous accounts, that one had a predilection for the bottle.

'*Illai*, no, Auntie', Rosie laughed. 'Yellow shirt *Chithappa*, Auntie.' This was a new Uncle in my repertoire of Rosie's *Chithappas*.

A day or two later, Rosie reported that she had again seen her uncle and this time he had seen her also – through the front windows. I asked for more information and she told me that he lived in Kasimode, a suburb at some considerable distance on the north side of Chennai. He rode his cycle each day to work right here in our own street at the electricity office.

I found this a little odd. Rosie had been to the Electricity Office a few days earlier to pay our monthly bill. She had not mentioned her uncle then or on any of her earlier visits. A return cycle ride from Kasimode to Indira Nagar each day was quite demanding. Why had this uncle not come to our house to see her? In truth, this was part of my unease, not knowing who this 'uncle' was and concerned on her behalf. Or if, in fact, he even existed.

From time to time, Rosie reported a sighting of *Chithappa*. The next notable occasion came soon enough. Rosie had broken her sandal. So I sent her off, barefoot, to Rolex to get them repaired. On her return, she reported that *Chithappa* had been standing at the corner smoking. Rosie's eyes danced as she babbled on excitedly,

'*Chithappa* said *Amma* is coming.' I had never seen Rosie's mother, or *Amma*. '*Amma* will bring new *chappals* and new blouses and new ribbons.' It sounded like Christmas.

The weeks passed and Rosie's *Amma* didn't come. As the feast of Deepavali approached, Rosie became very excited. It is customary in many Hindu households for everyone to receive new clothes at Deepavali (known as *Diwali* up north, but said as *Divali* in the south). For the women, especially, it is time for a new sari, and the wealthier one is, the finer and more exquisite the sari purchased. In the weeks leading up to the feast, there had been great discount sales with handloom cottons and silks being promoted at 40-50 per cent discount. Now, Rosie reported, *Chitthappa* had told her that her mother would come at Deepavali and bring her a new skirt and jewellery as well as the new *chappals*.

The festival is popularly known as the 'festival of lights' and it fell on 1 November that year. In the last days of October, the upstairs and downstairs wives busied themselves with cleaning, shaking rugs and washing steps in preparation for the feast. On the day itself, we woke at dawn to the sounds and smell of sulphur as a million fireworks were exploded around the city.

At breakfast, the downstairs children came in the spirit of good will and festivity bearing plates of sweets and *idlis* – the steamed white Tamil speciality made from ground and fermented rice and grain. Then the upstairs children arrived with still more snacks and savoury treats. Deepavali is a significant and joyful Hindu feast, celebrating the triumph of good over evil and the awareness of the pure, infinite and eternal essence called *Atman*, the individual's inner light. It is a time for forgiveness, compassion, love and inner joy or peace, as expressed in this prayer often used during the feast:

> God, lead us from untruth to truth. Lead us from darkness to light. Lead us from death to immortality. May all be happy. May all be free from misery. May all be filled with goodness.
> And to this, I say, Amen.

We watched people walking in the street outside the window, the mood relaxed and leisurely. Mostly, their clothes were new, the men's shirts crisp. 'Happy Divali', our friends greeted us when they rang. We visited other friends, stepping over a doorstep freshly decorated with flowers and chalked designs and enjoyed (in the spirit of inner joy) more sweets and snacks. Unfortunately, there had been no appropriate delicacies coming from our kitchen to mark the feast.

All day long the city sounded as if it were under siege with the boom and crackle of firecrackers warding off evil spirits. The air was smoky and acrid. In the evening, as the fireworks returned to the crescendo of the dawn, our neighbours burned numerous little clay lamps along their paths, on the windowsills and balconies to welcome the mythological Rama and Sita back home from their exile and sufferings under the tyranny of the kingdom of Ravana, symbolising the yearning all humans share for a world that is free from fear and filled with kindness.

View from the balcony

By the end of the day, I realised that there was to be no visit for Rosie from her *Amma*. No gifts or new clothes. No *Chithappa*. Late that night, inspiration – and the spirit of Deepavali – seized me. I took from my cupboard a very pretty, long swirling skirt. I had bought it on a whim some years previously in Chicago for the princely sum of $7.00, but I had worn it only once or twice. More importantly, I had never worn it in India, so in Rosie's eyes it would be new. It took me little effort to cut it down and remake it to fit the compact little Rosie, and I was energised with the determination to get it right for her. At 1.00 am, the skirt was complete and in the morning Rosie woke to get her Deepavali present a day late.

Our baby daughter's baptism was to take place the same day. We had invited many of our friends to join us at our place after the church liturgy for a meal of celebration. The smoke from Deepavali was still in the air. And it seemed only appropriate that when we gathered to celebrate the baptism of this little one, we did so with Christians, Hindus and Muslims alike.

A few days later, I took Rosie with me to a nearby shoe store and let her choose for herself the new sandals she wanted. Rosie never mentioned *Chithappa* again. Maybe, just maybe, he had served the purpose for which he had been introduced into our domestic discourse in the first place – to educate a foreign wife about her obligations to a little girl.

I take myself back to those days at home with the baby in Indira Nagar. Midday lassitude is settling its blanket on my eyes as I sit with the baby on the front closed-in balcony. On the street below, a carpet wallah pushes his cart into a patch of shade and squats in the dust chewing a handful of peanuts. A maid-servant dawdles past with a plastic basket of the leafy vegetable called 'greens'. Occasional cyclists pass, the backs of their bicycles piled high with large trays carrying tiffin boxes – fresh hot lunch for office workers. The baby's eyelids droop.

Pu-utt-putt-putt-putt. Twenty-five seconds to go. I wait for the distinctive roar as he guns the Bullet out of the corner from Main Road into the 300 metre stretch of 1st Main Road. Twenty-two seconds left. Stirring from the slump of the cane chair, I settle the baby with a quick kiss into the large playpen which occupies three square metres of the balcony. 'Appa's coming. I'll be back.' Eighteen seconds.

On cue, the engine is cut as the motorbike glides past the window and round the corner. I turn back into the main room through the open double polished teak doors and skim the terrazzo floor on thin leather *chappals*, knowing that he will be gliding the bike onto the grass verge by the narrow side gate. Eight smooth steps around the lounge to the doors at the top of stairs.

Twelve seconds. I ease sideways through the single open doorway, grab the handrail with my left hand and move down the top eight steps, passing the small study on the right off the landing. As I swing around to take the midway turn on the landing, I glance out the narrow window towards the street. His helmet is in one hand, his face dark with heat, his hair pressed flat and wet with sweat. He swings his rough-woven cloth bag from his shoulder, his long green homespun cotton *jibba* damp across his chest, as he stretches the tension out of his back and arms and shakes sticky jeans loose from his crotch.

Seven seconds. '*Ennappa, sawukiama*.' He greets the shopkeeper at his stand in the compound wall to the right of the gate. Down the second set of ten steps, as he pushes the gate open with his *chappal*. I grab the handrail firmly and balance for the last turn past the locked doors on the right leading to the landlord's quarters on the ground floor. He can make the outside door in three strides.

I take the last four small steps. Grab the padlock on the inside of the painted wooden door, slide it back and open the door, as he looms on the doorstep. My man is home for lunch.

A skein of silk

WOMEN MOVE IN AND ACROSS the pages of this book. Some are from India's rich past like the mythical Kannagi; some are her modern-day counterpart, the fierce Kasiamma; others like the nameless Lambada gypsy in the remote settlement in Andhra Pradesh; others like Rosie and her ilk, who serve the smooth running of household life; there are women from wealth and privilege, gracious and ungracious; there are the two wives between whose words we lived for most of my time in Chennai. Women have left their fingerprints all over this story as they have imprinted the story of India. Their lives are entwined, entangled with each other and with my life there.

Within the privacy of the compound walls, the yard where we lived was graced with the shade and fruit of coconut trees. Here Jyothi lived with her husband Elumalai, in the fully-enclosed space behind their shop, a rough wooden counter and lean-to from which they sold vegetables, eggs and bananas. The room was a narrow corridor of space about five feet wide and perhaps ten feet in length. During our time there, Jyothi gave birth to a child whom, with wonderful optimism, she and her husband named Lakshmi, after the goddess of wealth. It was on such occasions that I felt totally confined within my monolingual limitations, since my Tamil allowed no subtleties of conversation other than I could mime and mumble. When I visited them with a small gift to celebrate the new arrival, I glimpsed the narrow space behind Jyothi as I stood at the door. There were cooking vessels which she used to cook outdoors. Behind that, only a dark space without windows or ventilation of any kind. During the time that I enjoyed the spaciousness of our apartment sandwiched between the two wives, annoyed by Rosie, managing constant dust and water shortage, my neighbour raised her infant in this narrow room with all her water provided from an outside tap.

From our front veranda, sitting on the cane chairs into which my spine curled and out of which nasty little nipping insects emerged, I observed the daily procession on First Avenue. I struggled with the humidity and its constancy. It enervated me. I had learned early that fresh clothes would be clinging damp and dusty by mid-morning. So I admired the tenacious good order of those everyday housewives and young women who passed: their faces oiled and then powdered; hair massaged with coconut oil, washed and then pulled back with precision and determination; the fresh jasmine flowers pinned to the end of a long plait swinging across the back of a scooter driver, pillion passenger or pedestrian; the crispness of a cotton sari which had been starched and pressed to perfection. There were times when I thought such care was hardly worth the effort. Of course, few of these scooter riders would have laundered their own sari. The sari itself is a six-metre handful of cloth to pleat and pin. I am sure the locals could sleep late and tie their saris as quickly as I could slip into a skirt and blouse. While I was comfortable wearing saris, I never became so slickly competent in the donning.

Outside the city, the women who passed along the dusty road in front of the rural centre at Cheyalnagar had other priorities in their routine. Rising before full light, they would make their ablutions in the fields taking advantage of the darkness for some privacy. They would prepare breakfast, or reheat the evening meal remnants for their menfolk to take with them to the fields. Their saris were creased

A skein of silk

and limp as they set out, bare feet on the hard road, in their search for firewood for the family cooking. Each year the distance increased as the forest growth in the region diminished. The Centre's work with women emphasised training and education. The young women came and lived together for the programs, and for some this was their first experience of being away from home alone, of being involved in such discussions and in group living. The camps were small attempts to empower young impoverished women to take greater control of their lives.

It was because of women like those who joined us in these courses that towards the end of that first year, I became something of a serious dung-watcher – and not just because this was a practical necessity. One of the proposals which I had earlier developed had finally attracted funding from the Canadian International Development Research Centre (IDRC). I was commissioned to complete a study relating to the social dimensions of biogas technology and its potential for the poor. I developed a new interest in observing the number of good solid cattle turds, as well as to spot the dung which had been handcrafted and flattened out into thin *pattis* to dry by the roadside, on a house wall, or on a river bank. Dung *pattis* are the poor woman's cooking fuel. In mud and thatched huts, one can easily imagine the hazards to health and hygiene (let's not mention comfort) created by dung fires. Let me just say, that the carcinogenic effects on a woman of a dung-fuelled fire, compounded by poor ventilation, were estimated at this time to be equivalent to her smoking up to 400 cigarettes a day. Poor rural women generally take on cooking responsibilities from around the age of thirteen, and this means they are exposed to these hazards from an early age and for a longer period.

As part of the spiral of poverty, lack of adequate cooking fuels also undermines the nutrition level of a poor woman and her family: to save precious fuel, it is tempting to cook some foods for insufficient time and some pulses and edible oils are toxic if undercooked. The poor housewife will tend to choose cereal staples that require less cooking time, avoiding the more nutritious (such as maize or sorghum), leading to greater risk of contamination and undernourishment.

An alternative fuel is biogas, which has distinct advantages: with processing, dung of all kinds can be used to produce a safe, smokeless gas for cooking and lighting, as well as cleaner, more efficient manure from the residue. Because of these advantages, biogas has been much proclaimed as the fuel source for the masses. In reality, it is not quite so simple.

To complete this research, I interviewed experts in a number of institutions, both government and non-government, in both North and South India. My paper explored the social, human and bureaucratic reasons why biogas was not being adopted, and also the relationship of biogas to the needs and attitudes of the poor. Even a small biogas plant requires the equivalent of dung from at least two cattle for a day's operation. Having two cattle does not make you wealthy, but most villagers do not have even that.

As Coordinator of Women's Programs at the Centre, I had the chance to take a particular interest in other women in the large complex nation of India. It was through my avid reading of the journals that made their way into the Centre's library that I had discovered the women lawyers in Delhi who published the magazine *Manushi*. I read each edition eagerly as soon as it came into the Centre's library and I am delighted to see that it is still alive so many years later. These women pursued truth at personal cost, demonstrating principles which humanise society, even while revealing some of its ugliest sides.

Children and adults alike would often turn to stare at me in my long skirt or sari walking in dusty sandals along their suburban streets and I assumed that as an Australian in Chennai I was something of a rarity. Yet, there were other Australian women who were also part of this skein of lives and I will share glimpses of three, each of whom chose to link their lives intimately with women in India.

Nicola Feakes was wife of the then Australian High Commissioner in New Delhi. Nicola reached out to this (seemingly) lone

A skein of silk

Aussie woman far away down in Chennai, and on a number of occasions when I passed through Delhi, either alone or with Benjamin, she offered me the hospitality of her home. The Australian High Commission residence is elegant and welcoming. The smooth expanses of the residence lawn were a balm to my eyes and I had not seen such greenness since my arrival in India. I might have been momentarily distracted that I was sleeping in a bed where famous people of Australian public life had and would sleep, but this trivial thought was dissipated by the intelligence and graciousness of my hosts. When our baby was born, Nicola thoughtfully sent a gift, a kindness I will not forget. Nicola used her educational skills to work with the neediest in the immediate vicinity of the High Commission. She and Graeme added dignity and integrity to the Australian presence in India.

Benjamin had told me about an Australian religious sister whose life for many years had been entwined with the lives of children in the city. I was keen to meet her. We visited Sister Theodore one day at MITHRA, the school and home she had established for the disabled. MITHRA, another of those wonderful Indian acronyms, stands for the Madras Institute to Habilitate Retarded and Afflicted. *Mithra* also, happily, means 'friend' in Sanskrit. Sister Theodore had landed in Bombay (now Mumbai) on Anzac Day, 1951. She was 24. Home was a well-to-do family in Brisbane which she had left when she joined her religious congregation.

When the local archbishop had been looking for an appropriate memorial to mark the nineteenth centenary of the martyrdom of St Thomas in Chennai, Sister Theodore had suggested that he establish an institute for the 'physically handicapped and mentally retarded'. 'You do it', the archbishop responded. And she did.

She and her associates received the first eight students in 1977. Since then, she has battled with governments, with the relentless climate, with her own early doubts and with constant shortage of money. When I visited during the mid-1980s, the grounds were large and clay-baked, surrounded by a range of sparse classrooms and workshops. Children with all kinds of disabilities played on this hard bare surface. They were children who, without Sister Theodore's intervention, would have been kept at home, out of sight, and regarded as a punishment on their families for some wrong in their lives. Thousands of children have been educated and rehabilitated since then in programs for students-in-residence, day scholars, a mother and child interaction program, workshop (staffed by the students) and a Diploma course of Multipurpose Rehabilitation Workers.

'We take them', Sister Theodore once said, referring to children doctors have given up on, 'and we love them up.'

'And when the time comes to retire …?' she was asked when she was 80 years old.

'Who's gonna retire?' she replied in her broad Australian accent. A year later, she was planning a home for the elderly, because, as she told the Australian High Commissioner at the time, 'We get so many enquiries, I thought I'd better do something.'

After our daughter, Mariam, was born, I spent more time at home. As I mentioned earlier, I liked to take the baby out for a walk in the late afternoon. On these walks, I often stopped by our neighbours. Prabha who had lent us the cradle and was a very devout Hindu, was always cheery company and welcomed me into her afternoon schedule. On one visit, I casually glanced through a magazine on her glass-topped table with its centrepiece of ornate porcelain roses. As I flicked the pages, I found myself eyeball to eyeball with an academic from South Australia, whom I knew by repute for his creative and solid work close to my own discipline. Dr Norm Habel, the article reported, was the principal of an International School in Kodaikanal, one of the hill station towns in our own state, Tamil Nadu. I hurried home with the news, impatient to make contact.

A friendship with two wonderful people has resulted from this contact. Over the next year while both our families were still in South India, we met from time to time. Benjamin and I visited Norm, an ordained Lutheran, and his academic wife Jan in the beautiful hills

A skein of silk

of Kodaikanal, and I relished the cool nights, energetic conversation and long breakfasts. The early morning speciality of the house was thick fluffy pancakes prepared by a bright young woman called Selvi. More often, when business brought Jan to Chennai, Benjamin regaled her with his signature green-banana dish while our two Indian-born babies rolled together on the traditional sleeping mats made from woven leaves. Our friendship has continued as these two little girls have blossomed into beautiful young women.

In collaboration with local educators in Kodaikanal, and with generous support from the Jesuit community there, Jan and Norm had established a training program for the poorest girls in the area, young women from *Dalit* and *Adivasi* villages. They called it 'Grihini', which is a Sanskrit word meaning 'one who knows the house' (or domestic science) and they used as its image the *kurunji*, a local flower from the Palni Hills that blooms only once in twelve years. In their anniversary publication, Jan reflected on her involvement in this exciting venture in a way which I warm to.

> As a privileged educator, I felt uncomfortable and wanted to do something. I was arrogant enough to assume my Aussie orientation would provide some explanation, but it did not seem practical in these conditions. I often felt that I was part of the problem.

In a similar way, I often felt that my main contribution to the poor in India was that I had chosen to be there, when I could have been somewhere far more comfortable. I too felt I had little to give, and often bumbled along on the edges of conversations and culture. Many times I said to myself that my biggest contribution was to 'walk beside' the poor. There is nothing very grand about that.

At the Centre, within my job, I worked closely with other women. Janaki and Lakshmi, both trained social workers, were there for most of my time with the Centre. At other times, Indira and Meena were on the team. Together, we planned programs and attended to details and worked our way around the challenges of a multi-lingual office. More importantly, we enjoyed each other's company and the shared experience as women. Lakshmi's two sons were both under ten at this time; Indira was older and brought a wealth of wisdom; while Janaki and I each gave birth to our first child within weeks of each other and so travelled the journey of first pregnancy and having an infant together. All four were highly intelligent, refined women, of high caste background and comfortable in themselves. They were idealistic and brought that to their work. In later years, after she had finished working at the Centre, Lakshmi was to initiate a system of garbage collection in her suburb – an undertaking, in my view, of vision, practicality and determination.

Priscilla was another of those women of about my age whom I met in India and who was to become a good friend. It was Priscilla who spent time with me in the hospital immediately after our daughter Mariam's birth and became one of her godmothers. Like me, Priscilla was an academic involved in teacher education. She was a single mum with a lovely lively athletic daughter. On one occasion, Priscilla invited me to address the students in one of her classes on moral education, a subject which I had taught for many years in Sydney.

As I prepared for the session, I realised I would be teaching a class that involved women of multiple religious backgrounds: Hindu, Muslim and Christian. This was a good challenge for me. In Sydney, teaching at the institution that would later become Australian Catholic University, it had been easy enough (but not necessarily educationally sound) to speak within one religious framework. I enjoyed the session, although, typically for India at that time, the students were quiet and receptive, and therefore not giving me much insight into what they made of this strange-speaking foreigner. Perhaps, they couldn't get past my Aussie accent. I would have enjoyed doing more, knowing that I was the one learning through the exercise. However, my main duty lay with the Centre and I was very circumspect about the limitations I brought as a teacher because of my ignorance of the local culture.

Like many other professionals in India, Priscilla had established a voluntary organisation, known as Society for the Upliftment of the Economically Backward (SUEB). She managed this in her spare time. Unlike our Centre's focus on non-formal education, research and community organisation, SUEB's priority was the development of families and communities, with a special focus on women and children. The main activities of SUEB were to organise women into Self-Help Groups (SHG) and through these groups to help each other save and lend among themselves. Through providing micro-credit, they enabled women to undertake their own income-generating activities. This included micro insurance for social security. SUEB also offered leadership and vocational skills training to equip women to undertake community development activities in their villages and to start new income-generation activities. It was an idea that many other groups have also pursued all around India, including in Chennai itself through organisations such as the Working Women's Forum.

For a period of about ten years from the late 1980s, Priscilla worked at a senior level in a Christian development organisation based in Geneva, Switzerland. Her organisation's activities continued to grow. Priscilla estimates that since its foundation in 1986, SUEB has mobilised 16,000 women in about 150 villages into 1109 grass-roots Self-Help Groups. They have given loans to women for activities such as starting small shops, vegetable or flower vending, animal husbandry, food processing, and the like; trained thousands of women in leadership skills, typing, computing, spoken English and tailoring; provided trained teachers, teaching material, uniforms, books and tuition for about 10,000 children in twenty-four Panchayat schools and conducted a low-cost tuition centre for disadvantaged senior high school students.

All this, because of the 'spare-time' initiative of one woman.

Another educator of whom I became very fond was the mother of our friend, Professor Syed Zaffrullah, one of the Management Committee members of the Centre, a Professor of Commerce in the local Muslim-run New College. Zafrullah's mother was principal of a primary school, and was another of those warm, intelligent, professional women. On occasion, I 'presided' at ceremonies at her school, hoisting the flag for Indian Republic Day on 26 January, as I privately celebrated Australia Day. I cannot recall if it was from her school or from another that I learned a universal lesson about schools when I woke up ten days after a school visit with a case of some measles-like infection.

Another woman I recall warmly from my early days in India is Jamuna. At that time, she headed up the Department of Adult Education at the University of Madras. When we visited her at home, she delighted me by coming out of the kitchen to relax and chat with us. She was an earth-mother kind of lady, always cheerful, and one of those women who naturally include people in their embrace.

These are just a few of the women with whom my life in India became entwined. The dictionary defines *skein* variously as *a bundle of yarn*, *a tangle* and *a group of geese* in flight. Any one of these seems to fit this chapter. There are many other women I have not named: the friends as close and sure as family, some of whom have also migrated to Australia; expatriates who, like me, married into India, some of them making India their long-term home; outstanding administrators and women in public life who model all that is professional, intelligent and committed; the women within our Indian family. One of the richer experiences I have come to value in my life, especially as I have grown older, is the relationships with women friends, wherever they live. They form a brilliant thread holding my own story together.

Family matters

PART OF THE EXPECTATION upon every good Indian wife is to produce an abundance of hospitality measured by her expertise in the kitchen. The time has come for me to face up to the critical question: just what kind of an Indian wife was I?

I have mentioned that Benjamin and I had shared some cooking disasters, but there were two particular gastronomic flops which belonged entirely to me. The first occurred early on in my Indian life when one of Benjamin's long-term friends asked me to come to his home and make a 'typical Australian dish'. This invitation was troubling. Indians have particular cuisines: in the Punjab, you can enjoy all sorts of chick pea dishes, or meaty tandoori chicken legs; in Delhi, you eat thin roasted unleavened bread known as *fulka roti* or *chapati*; in Andhra Pradesh it is the hot spicy rice *biriyani*; in Kerala, it is fish curry or the Onam harvest festival vegetable dish, *avial*, rich with freshly grated coconut; in Tamil Nadu, they are rice eaters, with a plethora of scrumptious snacks, such as the steamed and fermented rice cakes called *idli*, paper-thin *dosai* pancakes and plate-sized *pooris* which puff up when the flat dough shapes are deep-fried. But what is a typical Australian dish? I could have served a lamb (rather, a mutton) stew. I might have fried some fish. If only I had settled for a fresh garden salad or a home-made soup. I didn't.

In the unfamiliar kitchen of our friends, with only a gas ring to cook on, there was little chance that my attempt at fried chicken, mashed potatoes and vegetables followed by stewed apples and custard would have a happy ending. It was, of course, disappointingly bland for my hosts, embarrassing for my husband and as mortifying for me as I had anticipated.

My reputation as an Australian and good housewife ruined by this effort, I was to produce yet another public failure, once again in the name of 'Australian cuisine'. The primary cause of this humiliation was the America's Cup of 1987; the secondary cause was my Indonesian friend and culinary fiend, Hennie, who lived nearby with her family. It was always a pleasant diversion to stroll the kilometre or two to their home and enjoy Hennie's lively company. The debacle would not have happened, however, had I not, once again, let myself be coerced into a commitment I did not want to make.

The 27th America's Cup was held off Fremantle in Western Australia between October 1986 and February 1987. For the first time in over 130 years, the event was not being hosted by the New York Yacht Club. This was because in the previous series Australia had done the unexpected and beaten the Americans at their own game. I have little sympathy with the whole profligate extravagance which was the America's Cup. Associated with it during this period of time was the profile given in Australian media and business to a whole gallery of high-fliers, who were, to put it kindly, cavalier in their corporate morality. In time they came undone. But, back in 1987, they were still in favour, and some of them were part of the America's Cup challenge.

I became implicated this way. Unbeknown to me, Hennie had entered into a wager with her friends, John and Nancy. John was the US Consul General based in Chennai at the time and Nancy was his wife. The bet was this: if Australia won the Cup, then John and Nancy would host a barbeque; if the United States won, then 'the Australians' would host it. There were very few Aussies in Chennai that I

Family matters

knew of. Hennie's husband was Australian and so she considered that she and I owed it to Australia to represent the home country in India during the challenge. Australia lost. The wager was called.

I knew John and Nancy a little. After Mariam's birth, I had attended some informal gatherings of expatriate women that Nancy hosted about once a month. The other women arrived in air-conditioned chauffeured cars; I arrived in a chugging three-wheeled autorickshaw. Some of the women talked about their planned holiday – a ten-day journey on a luxurious train through northern India. The cost for the ten days exceeded my annual income at the time. I lived my life immersed within the local community; as for many of these expatriates, they seemed to survive in India by protecting themselves against too much firsthand exposure. Each woman in the group had her own interesting story, but because of the surface differences I was never particularly at home among them, and never really gave myself the chance to discover who they were. So I was more curious than excited about the prospect of the barbecue of triumph.

With a confidence born out of ignorance, Hennie directed – it was nothing less – that I would make a pavlova for the occasion and I would decorate it with peeled mandarin quarters. As a cook, she had style and imagination. What she didn't know was that I had never made a pavlova in my life. However, I did have in my pantry an 'egg', one of those pre-mix pavlovas, which for some bizarre reason I had included in my trousseau. I was curious to try it out. Was it still in date? Who knew? And, as it offered me my only hope of delivering on the bet, I didn't care.

I purchased some mandarins for the occasion, quite a luxury in our household, and proceeded to discover that, if there is a technique to peeling quarters in a way which leaves them more or less intact, I didn't know about it. The only oven I had was a microwave and I also failed to take into account the difference between a conventional and microwave oven in cooking egg white. I knew that there was something special about pavlova, either that you cooked them very high or very low. So I put the plate with its beaten mixture in the microwave, which had been a wedding gift from my parents. I tried it on high for five minutes. The result was glorious. The creation rose like a white cloud at least twelve, no, fourteen, centimetres high. I was thrilled. My first pavlova. What a success.

The microwave timer clicked off. Through the tinted glass of the microwave, I watched the slow-motion collapse of my pride: the cloud had burst. I think I realised right then that the pavlova was already doomed, but there can sometimes be an urge for total destruction, once one has begun the downward tumble. So I gave the thing another five minute burst. Again, it rose, glorious, but this time I was not deluded. I knew what would happen when the appointed time was up. And so it did.

The next day, I carried my good glass plate burdened with its light burden of flat crust of sweet egg white topped with broken mandarin segments to the Consul General's house. I had decorated it as best I could so that the charred base was almost disguised. From above, it didn't look too bad, flat, perhaps, but how were the Americans to know anyway? I wore a good *churidar* tunic and pants and applied extra makeup to help me along.

The whole event was a parade of incongruities. Hennie's husband led the cooking of fish beside the smooth diplomatic lawns, while inside the spacious dining hall of the consulate we ladies sat down at a table which stretched for at least seven or eight metres. Rich brocaded Roman blinds adorned the windows at each end of the room. Our chairs were heavy and ornate. Magnificent cream silk with wide blood-red borders and a thinner purple stripe was laid along the length of the table. Each place setting was in heavy silver accompanied by fine crystal glasses. There was the hush that wealth provokes among the servers who came with water and dishes. My dessert was placed squarely in the middle. I thought of barbecues with my family around picnic tables by Lake Macquarie or barefoot in someone's backyard. This America's Cup barbecue of defeat became a celebration of cultural confusion and national humiliation – not just on the water.

In idle moments I wonder why I did it. Why let myself be dragged into something that was so much out of my element? The best I can do is to put it down to a vague sense of adventure, to try something different, and perhaps, also to the disorientation of my normal judgement when I was in such an entirely different place. Re-telling of the debacle has provided me great dinnertime fun for years. As for Hennie: she never asked me to cook again.

The grandest city I visited in my Indian sojourn was Delhi – New Delhi, with the polish of a diplomatic centre, and Old Delhi, with its tangled streets, magnificent Red Fort and Islamic minarets. The most peaceful spot I found in Delhi is Rajghat, Mahatma Gandhi's burial place, which is a simple marble platform set in sunken lawns and gardens, somehow sealed off from the noise of city traffic. Since our visits were built around work for the Centre, I regret that I did not take more time then to explore more of the city's historical places. We made a day's visit to Agra, the Taj Mahal and other historic sites in that dusty city. It was eighty kilometres travel each way, complete with Hindi movies in the coach, and the trip was worth every bit of agony inflicted by the eardrum-splitting music.

I was stunned by the Taj Mahal. In many ways, it was very familiar to me, but being there in front of it, the building's simplicity, intricacy and beauty were a wonderful surprise. (It was not even moonlight.) Back in Delhi, we enjoyed another historic light-and-sound portrayal one night in the Red Fort, with special effects from dramatised audio tapes and clever manipulation of coloured lighting around the different buildings and spaces of the Fort. Winter in Delhi can be as cold as in Sydney and I have memories of travelling by night in rickshaws with fog blurring the hard edges of buildings and our breath hanging solid before us.

Benjamin and I attended a national seminar on Human Ecology and Human Development in Delhi, and spent the next few days making the most of our rare sojourn in the centre of power in a whirlwind tour of government departments, institutes and other agencies with whom we had some working relationship. So, from 7.30 in the morning till late at night, we were away from our hostel in Hauz Khas for conversations with alternate technologists, department secretaries and directors, educationists, environmentalists, journalists, women's groups, research institutes: all having in common a commitment to development of people, although each one envisaged this development in a distinctive way. This was a fascinating exposure for me to the bureaucracy of India and of the development network. Benjamin's long-standing relationship with many of them made most of the visits pleasant, often involving a meal.

I travelled by myself twice to Delhi from Chennai in those years, each time making the journey by train, a trip of around thirty-five hours. As usual, I travelled second class, which meant non-air-conditioned and sleeping at night on simple wooden berths. I enjoy train travel. I even enjoy taking a Cityrail commuter into Sydney. So, for me, the trip from Chennai to Delhi was fascinating.

The physical landscape changed subtly as the train progressed north by north-west up through the middle of India, flat paddies giving way in parts to tall teak forests and the kind of hilly country I had never seen around Chennai. But it was the human dramas inside and outside the train which made these trips memorable. I sat in a compartment reserved for women and children, a nice touch especially for a solitary female traveller. On leaving Chennai, family groups settled in for the long ride, well-prepared with *chapatis* or *pooris* for their meals along the way. Not everyone purchased a berth, or some family groups were quite large, so sometimes during the night I would need to accommodate a child who might have joined me on my plank. I too had some of my own food supplies which I supplemented with a sustaining kind of omelette between two pieces of

Family matters

bread known as 'egg bread' which was hawked down the corridor early each day. I looked forward to the stations when I could expect to buy a sweet cup of early morning coffee and never tired of the gaggle of vendors as they passed along the platform, raising a chorus that had its own harmony. The train would shudder back along its journey and the sounds and aromas would trail away.

On one solo visit to Delhi, I travelled on to Rajasthan for a conference on women's development. I was asked to make some closing comments at its conclusion and regretted that my visit again had been so brief. In passing through Delhi, I had once again stayed at the Australian High Commission with Graham and Nicola Feakes and enjoyed their company.

My second visit alone to Delhi proved a disaster. It was in high summer 1985 and on this occasion I stayed in an institutional guest house. The accommodation was comfortable enough and typical of many local guest houses and hotels. The floors were uncovered concrete. Ceiling fans provided cooling. India had experienced drought in the past few summers and the Thar desert in the nearby state of Rajasthan was extending its reach. The hot August winds brought a fiery heat and relentless sand into Delhi, into the room where I was staying, into my nostrils and eyes. If I kept the hinged windows closed, I could scarcely breathe with the heat. If I opened them, the winds swept in with dust and sand. The floor under my feet was warm and gritty.

The thought of making my way alone around the intricate streets of Delhi, moving from dusty government office to dusty government office paralysed me. I fell into a panic. It is one of the rare occasions in my life that I pulled the plug. I called for help: I wanted out. Our good friend, Thomas Mathew, then CEO of World Wildlife Fund for Nature Conservation (WWF) bailed me out, put me on a plane and sent me flying back to the comfortable familiarity of Chennai, where it was in the mid-forties Celsius and humid, but without the desert sands of high-summer Delhi.

Despite these travels, my life was mostly quite domestic and centred around Mariam, our home and the Centre. Our small family was generally unaffected by the domestic complexity of the landlord and his two wives between whom we lived. But life in Chennai was always dominated by concern for water and I was reminded of this when I came across the following entry in my diary. Benjamin, I recall, was away.

> There were two inches of water in the black plastic bucket when I went to have my bath this morning. I used one inch to have my bath, leaving the rest for the baby's bath later on. Then one more tumbler full to clean my teeth. At least the nappies have been washed and hung and Rosie had a bath yesterday.

Like the water, our time in India, was, at least for the moment, coming to an end. A number of factors led us to the not-uncomplicated decision to move to Australia, at least for a period of time. Returning to Sydney was not necessarily our preferred option. Benjamin, who had been working extraordinarily hard in the Centre without a break since 1975, had hopes of completing a doctorate and had been accepted into two programs – one offered by the United Nations University (UNU) based in Japan and one in Warwick, UK. A crisis in the international money market led to the UNU funds not coming through. Still, Warwick was there with a welcome waiting for him. Normally, I would have welcomed the opportunity to live and experience another culture by living in the UK but there were practicalities, now we had a child, about earning enough money to live.

Coming as we did off the very low base of our meagre income from the Centre, we recognised that I still held a position back in Sydney at the Catholic College of Education. My employer had been generous in extending my request for unpaid leave three times; in fairness, I either had to resign or return. The overriding factor was concern for my parents who had obviously been through very difficult times with little prospect for improvement. Dad's condition was deteriorating and he was now eighty-three.

Family matters

And so, with compromise, especially on Benjamin's part, the decision was made in favour of Australia. Privately, I was relieved. On reflection, my inability to cope in Delhi's high summer was a signal that I was losing some of my usual resilience. I realised that I had become increasingly depressed by what confronted us in our work. I think this was exacerbated because I was – rightly, I maintain – sensitive about my limitations as an outsider in addressing poverty, injustice and development in India. But it was especially in domestic matters, in my own home, where I experienced the discomfort of lacking my own agency. As the daughter of traditional Australians of the 1950s and 60s, meaning for me as wife and mother was vested in relationships and in homemaking. Benjamin, growing within a culture where the minutiae of domestic life are outsourced to others, brought a different perspective. I was aware that sometimes Rosie, unfairly, bore the brunt of my frustration.

For Benjamin, the move to Australia was drastic. He was not someone who had dreamed of migrating to the West. It was not his choice. His dad, too, was elderly, although still going out to the village each day to his surgery. Independent as he was in most matters, Doctor Mathew tended to rely on Benjamin for certain things, and was reluctant to see him leave India. In addition to this, for Benjamin, our move also meant leaving the Centre which he had created and in which he had invested his energy and attention for twelve years, and entrusting it to others to maintain and promote. Besides, apart from the friends who had attended our wedding, he had no other connections living in Australia.

We began to pack.

We celebrated Mariam's first birthday with cake and tea at home with the office staff. The next day we woke to find that she had developed a bad case of chicken pox. It was mid-summer and the discomfort was obvious for her.

I was in the midst of packing up our goods and disposing of those things we were to leave behind. My preparations took me out into the city's summer heat as I visited shipping agents to arrange transport of our goods. Jan and Norm happened to be returning to Adelaide around the same time, so we were able to share a container for our goods, of which, in both cases, books formed a large part.

As I moved around the city, I found my eyes constantly irritated, thinking, at first, that it was simply dust. It turned out to be shingles in my eyes – the adult version, I believe, of chicken pox for those who have had the disease in childhood. My eyes were affected for a number of months, well after our return to Sydney, and I had begun to imagine ways in which I might continue my academic and teaching profession with limited sight.

We returned to Sydney on 14 June 1987, and were offered hospitality by the same friends, Maureen and Jim Cleary, who had done so much to help us celebrate our marriage before my Indian sojourn began. At first, Benjamin stayed at home minding Mariam while I resumed my teaching. Like many of those fears that loom up on sleepless nights, my fears about my eyesight proved groundless and after some months and medical attention, my eyesight improved. Benjamin had applied to Macquarie University to do his doctorate and we spent some weeks in faculty accommodation. By August, we had found a place of our own in the western Sydney suburb of Toongabbie, a wonderful lady nearby who cared for Mariam during the day and a chance for Benjamin to begin his studies and look for some work.

Then, on 20 August, in the middle of my teaching at the Teachers' College, he rang me. His father had died. Doctor Mathew had continued his routine of early rising, prayers and travel to the surgery in Kannigairpair. That morning, aged eighty-four, he had arrived as usual at the rustic clinic at 6.00 am. He treated two patients and asked the third to wait. Feeling unwell, he sat down to rest in his dispensary chair and quietly died.

Benjamin left that same evening, reaching Chennai in time for the funeral. He was to remain there, busy with what needed to be done and assisting Kochamma, for over two months. I know it weighed heavily on him that his father, of whom he was so proud, had died such a short time after our – Benjamin's – departure from India. It also delayed his entry into Australian life.

Returning

AS I DROVE THOUGH Castle Hill on my way to work in the first months following our return to Australia, I found the suburban streets unreasonably quiet. Where were the thin dark servant women on their way to the bazaar? No cyclist darted out across the street in front of my car – or not normally. The traffic insisted on driving in lanes and the large shopping malls were a tad overwhelming. I realised I missed Chennai and its chaotic roadways. Gradually, life in Sydney took over as I resumed contact with friends and family and as we busied ourselves as 'new arrivals'.

When you migrate, you lose immediate access to friends and family. This is less so, now of course, in our interconnected world. In 1987, when we returned to Sydney, we didn't yet have mobile phones for quick calls and text messages home, no domestic email, Skype or Facebook for staying in touch. When you migrate, you also lose your identity in many ways – the sense of self that is constantly reflected back to you from those who know you well. So, while you are busy about the practicalities of finding employment, housing and putting down roots into new soil, you also have to create a new identity for yourself to communicate to those who know nothing about you. This can be freeing, of course, as I had found when I had studied in the United States as a younger woman. You want people to know who you are.

Returning

There are also the other uncertainties of negotiating a way through the minefield of cultural norms and social idiosyncracies different from those in your home. Such as 'getting' Aussie humour. I had seen this in reverse when young travelling Australians had slipped into typical semi-sarcastic dry humour in the face of Indian bureacracy in the Chennai immigration office. 'You'll get nowhere with that, here', I wanted to tell them. 'Play it straight and courteous.' Or language – when something as trivial as a word like 'broom' (my word) and 'brush' (his) can lead to misunderstandings. Or getting an Indian tongue around what seems to me to be simple Irish-Australian names, as I still struggle with Indian places and names. Or social niceties around how late in the evening it is acceptable for someone to make a phone call.

The challenges for Benjamin were, as for all immigrants, enormous. In my early days in India, wanting not to offend, I recognised the need for me to take my lead in many settings from Benjamin, and over time even I felt limited by a kind of passivity this could provoke, and had wanted to act more from my own initiative. Now, with our roles reversed, how would he react? He was strong and individualistic. While I believed it was easier for people of diverse cultures to feel at home in Australia than it would be in India, I felt it had probably been easier for me to adapt to India than it would be for him to settle into Australia. Now, we were back on my turf. *And*, just as people had wondered before I went to India – *Would the marriage last?* – I sometimes wondered if our marriage would survive the strain of this new adjustment.

Not surprisingly, Benjamin entered into Australian life with the swiftness and vigour of a tiger. On his return from attending to family matters after his father's funeral, he set about finding employment. His first, short-term, job was one that, in his home country, was normally performed by the least skilled and lowliest workers: mowing lawns. Benjamin, who had never handled a lawn mower in his life, did this for three months during the exhausting summer days of 1987.

When I wasn't teaching, I would take lunch to him. When he wasn't cutting and edging, he found an outlet for his social work skills and experience, and his love of connecting with people, by listening to the loneliness of the elderly people whose lawns he was tending as part of the state government's Home Care program. By February, he was a NSW public servant in the State Authorities Superannuation Board.

This move had become necessary, despite his plans for higher studies, because, very late in 1987 we had discovered that I was pregnant once again. Twins. Mathew and Shanthi were born at Blacktown near our home in Western Sydney in September 1988. Benjamin was present at the birth. Mariam had turned two just a few months before and suddenly found herself outnumbered by these newcomers. It was a big adjustment for her and probably helped her develop both her strong sense of compassion and organisation.

I took a year's maternity leave and a further six months on half-time to give our family of three under-threes the care they needed. I was also able, during this time, to direct the publication of two more books for use in schools – one for each twin. In the midst of being absorbed by our feisty three-year-old and eighteen-month-old twins, we enjoyed a visit from our old friend, Canadian Raymond Cournoyer. In his usual gruff manner, he seemed to begrudge the attention the children demanded in the course of our conversations over dinner. It was a grumpiness that was easy to forgive in this idealistic celibate who had foregone the joys of parenthood, but who had given generously to others. When I visited Montreal in 2009, I was saddened to learn that Raymond had died two or three years previously after some years of illness.

Our home became a place where people of many cultures gathered and our children grew up with the sounds of Tamil and Malayalam in the air, even though it is of some disappointment to us both that they speak neither language. I blame this on their mother – me – because I had already learned with Mariam in Chennai that 'mother tongue' is critical in the early formation of language and my Tamil was certainly not what they needed to learn. At one stage, we took the children to Tamil classes but, since all the other children were from homes where Tamil was spoken consistently, ours struggled to keep up and failed to progress much beyond *Amma, ingé, va, va* ('Come here, Mummy'), and even I could have taught them that much. Later, the girls spent some years attending *Bharatanatyam* (classical Indian dance) lessons and have stored that experience somewhere in their psyches also.

We joined (or, rather, he joined and we followed) local associations of Tamils and Malayalees and served on their committees. In this way, as a family, we marked, not only the local calendar and the church's liturgical calendar, but also Tamil feasts, such as *Pongal*, and Malayalee feasts, such as *Onam*. On 26 January each year, we began to observe Indian Republic Day with the traditional flag-raising and breakfast at the Indian Consul General's residence before slipping into something more casual for Australia Day. Benjamin has always enjoyed throwing the house open and cooking huge quantities of different Indian dishes. Until they were in their teens and this became totally uncool, the children's birthdays were the occasion to convene their friends, our friends and relatives in a nearby park with massive platters of salad, sausages, rice, curries and, of course, the fancy cake I always made for each one's birthday.

Even before arriving in the country to live, Benjamin had been better informed on Australian politics than many educated Australians. Before our marriage, he had taken advantage of our visit to Melbourne friends to meet up with the late Don Chipp, founder of the (also-late) Australian Democrats Party; on the same visit, he met up with the first Indigenous Australian parliamentarian, Senator Neville Bonner, and joked about theirs being the only dark faces in a room of white ones. He had amazing political acumen and, not long after our re-settlement in Toongabbie late in 1990, became active in the Labor Party. His knowledge and awareness of Australian political life grew rapidly and his involvement increased around 1997.

Around the same time, Benjamin became increasingly available for people who needed advice or assistance in legal matters. Many of these people were new settlers also; many came from India, but also from Sri Lanka, Pakistan, Bangladesh, the Philippines and the local Anglo-Australian community. There was no restriction, and, of course, it was all *pro bono*. Almost every evening, after he had returned from his work with the NSW government (now in the Office of State Revenue), people would come to our home asking for help: he drafted letters; advised people in their job search; counselled groups or families who found themselves at loggerheads. On Saturdays and Sundays, he would set time aside from as early as 6.30 am and until late at evening. So many times, I have heard him answer the phone on a Sunday evening and after a while say, *Vaango, vaango, vaango* ('Come, come, come').

As happened, in 1997, I also took on additional responsibilities moving into the role of Executive Director of Catholic schools in the Diocese of Parramatta, a system of 75 primary and secondary schools in Western Sydney. With almost 4000 staff and a large budget, this was a demanding role which I held for nearly nine years. The consequence was that ours was a very busy household and, in attempting to balance my priorities of family and work – in that order – I restricted much of my involvement in external associations and functions.

In response to the growing community needs that presented themselves to him, Benjamin set about creating a community structure that would support the service he offered and in 2007, after due consultation, and with the support of similar-minded solicitors and other professionals, opened Toongabbie Legal Centre (TLC). TLC has taken off. It is, as I write, unfunded and run on the generosity of volunteers and now absorbs a lot of time and attention of us both. I was very pleased for him, when, after two terms on the federal government Australian Multicultural Advisory Council, he was appointed one of the first People of Australia Ambassadors in 2012.

To cope with our busy lives, and to attempt the balancing act

Returning

between our cultures, I developed a mission to find ways to cheat with Indian cooking – ways to prepare food that might reasonably pass as authentic but which I could prepare with no generational knowledge and without the patient, time-rich assistance of mother-in-law, *ayah* and aunt. It wasn't too much to ask for, I thought, and I had help at hand: there were all sorts of commercial preparations to help me in this mission, as well as Indian recipes written in an English style in books and on the internet, many Indian-Australian women friends and an abundance of Indian food shops.

So our three children grew up rolling different Indian breads; we do *idlis* (steamed rice cakes made from ground and fermented rice and black lentils) and the basic meat curries, vegetable curries and sweets. My confidence as an Indian cook peaked a few seasons back when an abundant harvest of limes on our backyard tree in Toongabbie tipped me into making a passable lime pickle that I felt I could share with Indian-Australian friends. Twenty-five years after our marriage, I was finally becoming a real Indian wife. A real Indian wife, perhaps, but one that is always negotiating her way between two worlds

Benjamin and I visited Sister Isabella in 2008, as we had on previous occasions, and as we do whenever possible. As our car drove into the large dusty town of Puducherry, I soon saw the familiar gendarmesque policeman directing a melange of traffic around his raised dais in the middle of the intersection. One of the distinctive relics of this former French territory, the traffic cop wore a white uniform, festooned with crimson braid and topped with a red kepi on his head. Most of Puducherry is like any other large south Indian town, but there is also a French quarter. A canal runs through this section and the buildings here hint at Parisian associations as they cluster in streets not far from the Bay of Bengal. A large old wooden guest house opposite the beach evokes images of comfortable, if unglamorous, holidays.

We waited for Isabella in a large room with plain cane chairs set in small groups. The room, like the rest of the building, looked out onto another courtyard, this one bright with roses and hibiscus, in the same impeccable order as I remembered. There was a soft shirring sound outside along the cloister. We waited. It took a while, but Sister Isabella finally shuffled in and joined us. She was wearing a traditional white habit with a full veil covering her head. Around her neck she had wound a thick brown-checked woollen scarf as protection against cold on a day that was nearing 28 degrees. There was nothing old in her smile. She held small brown hands out to greet us. Any small effort we might have made to come and see her was repaid to excess with her warmth. She quickly noted that the overhead fan was idle and trotted down to the far end of the room to switch it on for our comfort. Only then did she settle down to hear our stories and our answers to her many questions.

At our best calculations, Sister Isabella was then nearing ninety. She was sprightly and alert. There was no escaping the probing concern in her dark eyes. She asked after each of us and our family, by name, in turn, just as she has so often in her letters which she sends 'To my darling son Benji and my dear daughter Annie.' Each of our children is named in turn. She dictates these letters to one of the younger Sisters, and they brim with her love. So, too, on our visit.

'Are you going to church?' We pass that one easily.

'Does Benji say the rosary?' I tell her 'No, or sometimes', and try to persuade her that it is okay and that we are still on track. It is impossible to be offended by questions that from someone else might be seen as intrusive. For Sister Isabella, these are the important matters, matters of the soul and of happiness, and there is no mistaking the regard which prompts them.

A niece hasn't married yet, and it is beginning to concern Sister that she might be leaving it too late. She hasn't heard much from this one. She is worried about that one who has been sick. She prays a lot for another whose marriage appears to be troubled. And are our three children studying well? Are they saying their prayers?

'You look tired', she says to Benjamin, patting his hand with her wiry one. 'You must take care of your heart. Your health.' She turns to me, 'You must look after him.'

'Is there anything you need, Aunty?' I ask. 'Anything you would like?' She thinks a while about this. We have also asked Sister Mary, the superior of the convent, if there is anything our aunt needs. Sister Mary tells us that whenever anyone gives money to Sister Isabella, she immediately gives it away to the poor.

'A flask', she says after a while, meaning a thermos. 'A stainless steel flask, this big', hands measuring the air. She looked as coy as a child, as though no one had ever thought to ask her what she wanted. It was a simple request from a woman of large heart and few needs who spent most of her time thinking of other people.

'I cried when you did not answer my letter about my jubilee.' She had recently completed fifty years as a religious sister. I thought of the bundles of paper in various rooms in our house and was mortified. I was particularly glad we had come in person to see her.

'I am so happy to see you', she kept saying, holding my hand, and it was easy to see she was. I found her goodness washed off on me.

Benjamin and I ate our lunch while Sister Isabella buzzed around us, passing plates of cabbage and coconut *poriyal*, deep-fried fish crumbed with a chilli and spice mix, crisp fried *pappadums*, *sambar*, *rasam* and rice. 'Eat, eat', she urged us, which must be the first words Indian baby girls are taught so that they are the first words they remember when caring for guests and friends in adulthood. There was no point in being embarrassed that we as healthy people were being waited on and served by this venerable old lady: she would have done it anyway.

And then, the meal over, hands washed, the diligent attention to detail which had been her life came out, as she turned off the fan, put the food back in the fridge, turned off the light and locked the door behind us as we left. I was moved with admiration by the simple carefulness of it all. In Sister Isabella's worldview, being ninety was no excuse to give up on immersing herself in the lives of her extended family as well as the wellbeing of others in the hospice.

We have visited Sister Isabella on other occasions, three times with all three of our children. The other Sisters matched the children's ebullience with good humour and a sense of fun which moderated the chagrin Benjamin and I might have felt as parents to see our nine-year-olds haring around the ordered hospice pathways on a cycle rickshaw. On one occasion, we visited with a large party of Benjamin's family, and the sisters produced a banquet of chilli crabs, an indulgence which I had never experienced anywhere else.

That visit was memorable also for other reasons. We had hired a van and driver for the day. Dark fell as we made our way back to the city. The route included a section where roadwork was in progress for the creation of a dual carriage highway. Somehow, our driver got us and the van onto the wrong carriageway and for some kilometres we travelled against the oncoming traffic. My terror was compounded by the local custom of turning off headlights, until one encountered another vehicle. I imagined the news being delivered to my mother in Newcastle that Benjamin, the three children and I had perished on a road in India along with most of Benjamin's family. Sister Isabella and her sisters must have been praying for us that night because we made it back safely after all.

When I visited her again in 2011, with Benjamin's sister Angela and her family, Sister Isabella, then a perky 94 years, entertained a group of us in the hospice dining room. Without hesitation, she spoke to the other Sisters in Tamil, moved into Malayalam to speak to my sister-in-law and her family, and then into English when she turned to me. As I left to go, she fossicked in her papers, producing an old business card of mine, just to check that the email address was still correct.

The last time I saw Sister Isabella was in February 2013. She had been hospitalised and was weak, a tiny body in the metal bed. We had not said that we were coming but she immediately recognised me and sparked up with laughter when she saw our children, now adults, of course, with me and my husband. As we left, I was overcome with sadness, sensing I would not see this beautiful loving woman again. She passed away in October that same year, ninety-six and still full of grace.

In 2009, we discovered that land that the Centre had purchased in Chennai for future use had been fraudulently sold and a solid house built upon it by the new owners. I was in Canada visiting Shanthi who was studying in Montreal for a year; the Centre's Management Committee asked Benjamin to go to Chennai. He left immediately, with Mathew for moral support, for a week. On my return flight from Canada, after a delayed take-off from New York's JFK airport, and a diversion through Brisbane, we had time only for a quick phone call between Brisbane and Sydney airports. Some might see it as a fitting image of our lives together.

There have been the sadnesses: my father's death in 1991, Mum's death in 2000 a month after we celebrated her 90th birthday, three of our brothers-in-law, one year after each other, the last being Benjamin's brother, Alphonse, at the age of 68. Alphonse had suffered for three years before his death following a motorbike accident in which his leg was broken and badly injured. After numerous surgeries, his leg was removed late in 2008, but his life never recovered. The impact on him and Elsey was hard to watch, despite Benjamin and others offering whatever they could as support. Benjamin arrived in India on 26 December 2011. He visited with Alphonse and Elsey a number of times during the week. Alphonse died early in the morning of 30 December. Elsey remains independent but has the comfort of their foster son and his wife and children.

From time to time, I receive emails and poetry from Xavier whom I had met at Puntamba in 1984, and who had been the friend of Father Anthony Murmu who was killed in police custody. When Xavier and I had met at Puntamba, we had found common interest in *From Massacres to Mining* by Jan Roberts, a book on the colonisation of

Aboriginal Australia published a few years previously with which we were both familar. Some twenty-five years later, I received an email from Xavier. He recalled the book we had discussed at that time, but he needed to pass on some bad news.

> Dear Anne – a very good book indeed. But someone borrowed it from me and he kept it at the back of his bicycle. And, he added, a cow came and ate it up.

I was pleased to find a new edition of Roberts' book and was able to forward it to Xavier with the hope that this volume would not meet the same fate.

My colleagues, Janaki and Lakshmi, are there, just the same, in faces that have mellowed gracefully as their children have reached adulthood. When we meet, we easily resume conversations that are punctuated with years. In between, Janaki and I occasionally meet on Facebook. Dr Elsa Benjamin continued to share her motherly warmth and prayers, though the aches and pains of age until her death. Priscilla, who took such kind care of me when our daughter was born, still remembers her god-daughter, Mariam, and continues her work with women and families.

Doctor Mathew died on 20 August 1987. In 2012, Benjamin's father's will was nearly but still not settled. Given the time this has taken, given that some years have been spent removing the name of the lawyer managing the will for the family from the list of beneficiaries, I can easily understand Benjamin's desire to reform the Indian legal system. What I cannot understand is why he, or anyone, would want even to think about taking it on.

My Indian experience continues. Half of our family lives in India. My relationships with those in the community development field are alive. Our Sydney life is lived very much within parts of the diverse Indian-Australian community. The acceptance that I have experienced, both in India and Australia, by those who are Indian-born, is something which I don't take for granted. To the observer in the street, I was just another foreigner, an excuse for ten-year-old boys to practise their English. There were times when I believed that a white person such as I would remain a stranger in Chennai even were I to live there twenty-five years.

If I have regrets about the past thirty years they are that, in the busy-ness of our work with the Centre, I deferred some of my own interests in India: the visit to Bede Griffith's ashram, an inter-religious seminar around social justice I had considered, the language and literature, more leisurely times in relaxing places with my husband. But, I am a realist, as well as something of a romantic and I recognised, several times over, that my husband is always moving ahead to the next task, the next strategic achievement. In recent years, I have begun to explore India more on my own terms: it is no less exciting.

And so, I live in Australia, very much part of the Indian and broader sub-Continent communities. Having done this now for so long, and losing, I suspect, some of my earlier forebearance, I have become tired of well-meaning Indians half my age asking me, 'Is the food too spicy?' 'I cook the stuff', I like to tell them. I want to be known as knowing and belonging. After nearly thirty years of marriage to Benjamin, of having produced more Indian meals for our family than I want to count, the novelty of being a novelty sits edgily with me. What is really soul-nurturing is the place I have been given among the Indian-Australians who have known me for a longer period of time. They are my friends. From those with whom I worked or associated more closely, I have felt warmth and appreciation. It is simultaneously humbling and joyful to be accepted in this way, for in breaking out of a single cultural group I feel as though I became a larger person. I even made it on one occasion into the line-up of Malayalee women for an Onam festival in Sydney, doing a skit on family life. My ginger hair was, I admit, heavily disguised under a thick black wig.

India again

I VISITED KERALA, home state of Benjamin's family, for the first time on a visit to India some years after we had resettled in Australia. Even though our family is immersed in the Sydney Subcontinent communities, we wanted to take our children to India to meet with their family and to connect with their culture in India itself.

Each of our children has been to India a number of times. On one such occasion, we all travelled on the overnight train to Kerala, the children being about eight and six at the time. The few days in Kerala were long, full and fantastic. As we made our way up the west coast of India from the state capital Trivandrum (Thiruvananthapuram) by way of Thiruvalla, Kottayam, Ernakulam, Kochi and Trissur, we visited a large network of relatives I had never met before: every possible combination of Benjamin's mother's and father's and step-mother's family connections. One uncle-cousin had a penchant for family history; one cousin was a Carmelite priest who taught in a large secondary school. On the outside of the rendered walls of the school, someone had boldly painted: *The future of India is within these walls.*

Another cousin we visited was a religious sister who held a senior nursing position in a large hospital in Thiruvalla. While visiting Thiruvalla, we stayed overnight with the family of a friend,

Simon John, who was also involved in an organisation working with the poor. He drove us a little way out of the city. The road to the *Adivasi* colony where Simon John worked wound around through growth so thick it snuffed the light from the late afternoon. Under the surrounding forest, and in the unpowered settlement, the night was black. Simon led us to a single-roomed brick building. The people gathered there made way so that the children and I could sit on a low bench to one side. The only light in the room fell in three or four dim yellow pools from kerosene lanterns. I smelt the strong smell of bodies close together, and hoped the children would not comment.

As my eyes adjusted to the darkness, I could make out men, women and children sitting on the floor or standing around. Simon John addressed them from a low platform at one end of the space. He was trying to set up reading rooms and small collections of books in colonies such as this. There was discussion back and forth as he explored the people's issues, he and Benjamin responding in Malayalam. While this interaction was going on, the children in the room were creeping closer and closer to where I sat with our three children. We were far more interesting than the adults' business. The children scuttled up, leaning over our shoulders and peering up into our faces with nervous giggles. They were refreshingly uninhibited in their curiosity.

'Hello', I said, trying to put the whole of humanity into one smile. 'Mariam', I said pointing to our elder daughter. 'Shanthi', as I pointed to her sister. The children looked puzzled. Our two girls pressed in close to me, but our son was at some distance, happy to play with the boys around him. The children stroked my shoulders. One daring girl of about eleven poked at me tentatively with a finger, and then quickly grabbed her hand back.

'Hello', I smiled again, rather inanely, but not really having much of a repertoire for the occasion. Some women, too, crowded in, and brought with them the smell of smoky fires. One thin woman, who might have been thirty or sixty, held my hand.

Sometimes, the poor can appear threatening to those who are not poor. My husband was in his element on this occasion, drawing energy from an opportunity to challenge the poor to fight for their entitlements. My children and I were certainly outside our comfort zone. Yet, in the context of our friend's relationship with the community, it was a very friendly encounter. The children and women crowding in on us were simply curious – as well they might be – about this pale woman and her three children, thriving on an Australian-Indian diet of vegemite and curd rice. As our car drove back through the forest, I wondered about the challenges involved for the children we had left behind in simple things, like getting to school on a regular basis. I wondered again about the enormity of resolving the intense poverty of so many in India.

At Kottayam, we stayed with the mother of Ranjit Thomas and his family from Sydney, who like us, had come to Kerala for a wedding. It was an arranged marriage. The groom (Tony Mathai) was a dentist who spoke English with an accent perfected in thirteen years of schooling in Western Sydney. Sharon, his bride, completing a degree in dentistry, still lived in Kerala. The wedding day dawned hot. We dressed in our finery – the girls in traditional long silk skirts and top, one a brilliant royal blue, the other rich fuschia. I wore royal blue *churidar* pants and a top which was embroidered with pearls and gold thread. Benjamin, too, was in traditional celebration gear, white *jibba* and *vaishti*, above thin leather *chappals*. By the time we reached the church around midday, temperatures were reaching thirty degrees. Meanwhile, there was a delay. It was New Year's eve and another ceremony was taking place in the church. The bride, in heavy silk wedding sari and make-up, sat in her father's car and waited. And waited. An hour later, the wedding began.

The bridal couple belonged to the Syrian Catholic tradition of Kerala. There were no pews in the church. So people stood. The celebrants wore the elaborate headgear of the Eastern rites and much of the long ceremony was chanted in Malayalam. There appeared to

India again

be little opportunity for congregational participation and I found it difficult to follow the order. During the hour or so of the prayers and blessings, people wandered in and out of the chapel, chatting in groups in the shade of the white building. I felt for the bride who had already been through a morning of rituals in her home as she was prepared for the wedding with blessings from the many members of her extended family. Finally, the ceremony was complete and we made our way to enjoy the other part of the festivities with music, photographs, sweets, wine and *biriyani* served on banana leaf. Kerala is, after all, as the locals like to claim, 'God's country'.

After the wedding, we travelled on up to enjoy a few days in Kochi (or Cochin), a port city on the west coast of India. We took a cruise on the harbour (let's not mention the captain handing the wheel to six-year-old Mathew) , stopping off at Willington Island, where we took tea, appropriately enough, in this area named after a former British Viceroy in India in an old hotel dating from the days of the Raj. Across the harbour in the old part of Kochi, we wandered through Jew Town. As we made our way to the old Paradesi synagogue, now serving just a handful of faithful, we wandered past stores with spices spilling their aroma out into the streets. There have been Jews in India from the first century of the Common Era, and one of their contributions in the past was the development of the spice trade. 'Paradesi' refers to the 'foreigners' who founded this synagogue in 1568 – largely Sephardim Jews from Spain and Holland. While the whole building is beautiful, I was taken with the floor, which is composed of hundreds of hand-painted porcelain tiles originating in China in the eighteenth century. Each tile is unique, which, no doubt, has prompted rich hermeneutic over the centuries from presiding elders.

A highlight of our days in Kochi was an intimate evening in a small tiered theatre where the traditional Kathakali dancers performed. The performance began several hours in advance of the actual event, as the performers went through the demanding and intricate process of putting on makeup and costume. Kathakali is a form of dance-drama which draws its ideas from Indian mythology and folklore. Like many things cultural in India, it has a long history, in this case, almost 1300 years. The costumes, vibrant with reds, green, gold, blue and white, are exaggerated. So is the makeup, which is a large part of the drama as the performers make great use of facial expressions and eye movements. The faces of certain characters (the gods and heroes) are always painted green, with large black moustaches and eyebrows, their faces resting on a plate-like collar. The demons are painted with red beards. All have a mask-like quality. All the performers were male.

The theatre where we went with our children was small, so we sat just a metre or two from the stage as the dancers went through their elaborate mime and dance movements. The traditional performance began at eight in the evening and continued onto dawn the next day. The performance we enjoyed was a mere two hours and I was fascinated for every minute. In some ways, because of the makeup, the larger-than-life costumes, with large skirts extending out wide and high head gear, and the energetic movements, the performance can be a bit terrifying. However, our children were entranced and at the end, we could all relax and stand side by side with the performers for photographs.

We were in for one more surprise before our visit to Kerala was finished. We had not notified our family that we planned to visit Benjamin's father's village not far from the town of Trissur. We set off early in a hired car, our son, Mathew, squeezed in the front seat between the driver and Benjamin. The girls and I were in the back. Beyond the city, we passed by rice paddies and coconut groves and the usual agricultural traffic of carts, cyclists, pedestrians and other cars. The countryside looked much greener than I was used to in Chennai on the east coast, and there was a sense that perhaps people were better off. After about two hours, the driver slowed down as entered the village of Mattom. We drove on a bit uncertainly.

'Stop', Benjamin said as the car approached the bazaar. 'We'll ask these fellows.' A small group of young men in cotton shirts and checked *lungis* lounged against a wooden shop front. Benjamin leaned through the car window in his green homespun shirt. The villagers looked at the car.

'The Kakkaseri house? We are looking for Mr Kakkaseri Chakunny. Which way is it?' he asked the young men in Malayalam. One of the young men stepped forward.

'I am his son', he said. He was probably about twenty-four or -five, of average height and slim.

Benjamin laughed. 'Really?' It was a bit hard to believe. The young man looked quickly at all of us in the car.

'Yes. Why? Who are you, Uncle?'

'He is my father's brother', replied Benjamin. *'Ninde pér endo?'* Your name?

'Mathew', the young man replied. It seemed to be something of a family name.

'Can you take us there?' Benjamin asked and moved further across the front seat to make room for him. 'This is my wife, my son Mathew, my daughters Mariam and Shanthi.' Mathew squirmed his way into the big old Ambassador and slammed the door.

'He says he's Uncle's son', Benjamin turned to me, a mixture of amazement and mild incredulity. 'Well, let's see where he takes us.'

As the fortuitously-discovered Mathew directed the driver, the car moved slowly around a winding country road. It was only a short drive, but pleasantly shaded by tall trees crowding overhead. Benjamin and our guide chatted in Malayalam. The girls and I chuckled at the novelty of the meeting. Was this young man really our uncles's son? Kerala Mathew guided the driver to a small house set back about six metres from the gate. A path led to a veranda which ran along the width of the ochre-rendered building. We eased ourselves out of the car, shaking clothes from our sticky bodies.

I followed Benjamin towards the front door. As I did so, a framed photograph hanging on the wall of the veranda caught my eye.

'Unusual place for a photo', I mused to myself, thinking of the practicalities of rain, dust, monsoons and damage. It was only a small photograph so at first it was unclear. I moved nearer, mildly curious. Then, I went closer to make sure. I called out to Benjamin. I pulled Mariam over to see also. There was no mistake. Dad. On the wall of our uncle's house outside a small village in Kerala, was a photo of my father. As well as Dad, Benjamin was in the picture, holding Mariam, and I was beside them. Mariam was dressed for winter in an outfit she wore when she was about two: red pinafore, red stockings, and a red sweater and pixie hat knitted by Mum. 'Little Red Riding Hood', we called her. I looked again at the framed image. I couldn't speak.

The house of our relatives was simple but the welcome was total. The children were taken to explore the wonders of a small verdant plot. They watched as workers climbed bare-footed up thin araca nut trees, plucking the nuts, and then swaying their bodies so that the trees bent and they could swing from that tree to the next; they were given raw cashew nuts fresh from the trees to throw into the fire and roast; and they sat on their haunches around the kitchen cooking area – a mound of clay with a hollowed space for vessels in the top and a fire burning underneath. Meanwhile, we were enjoying family news over strong tea and snacks and gave the small gifts we had brought from Australia. Our family insisted that we stay for lunch. Neighbours were called. And a meal of welcome was prepared.

My memory of that visit to Kerala centres on the photograph of my father on the veranda wall. It linked two men from radically different worlds: Benjamin's father, Doctor Mathew, and my dad. Both had been self-made, determined characters who, at one stage or other, had seen the work they had built up destroyed, and who had then risen back above the adversity. Both had exercised strong discipline on themselves and their families. Both were profoundly devout men. If anyone would have understood why Doctor Mathew had called his house in Chennai 'Shojbom' – *Sacred Heart of Jesus bless our marriage* – it would have been Dad with his prayer books, grubby

India again

and worn at the edges, and his devotion to his chosen gallery of saints. While we had not sent word that we were coming, I wondered if the family bush telegraph or its local variant had been at work.

Whether or not, word had leaked about our possible visit, there could have been no more powerful way for our uncle (or perhaps his wife) to welcome the foreign wife and family of his brother's younger son. The family also celebrated the mesh of family in another way. We had not sent that photograph, or any photo, to Benjamin's uncle in Kerala. We frequently sent photos showing our children as they grew taller each year to Benjamin's immediate family in Chennai. Somehow, in seven years' traffic of news and chatter within the family, that photo had found its way, from the east coast of India to the west.

I returned to India a number of times over the years. My visit in 2008 was after a long break of nearly ten years and signalled the resumption of more frequent visits. Changes were obvious even before I arrived. On the flight from Singapore to Chennai, I was no longer one of a handful of non-Indians on the flight. Now nearly half the flight were passengers from Canada, Australia, Hong Kong and Japan, on their way to do business in Chennai. The commercial world had discovered India. As usual, we flew in late at night and made our way from the airport through quiet and darkened streets. I was curious to see what had happened since my last visit. How would it look? Would I recognise old haunts?

I was amazed by the transformation of the city. Information Technology had bloomed in India and, with it, fly-overs, high-rise buildings, billboards and salaries. It had become a city where conversations among some of the people I met circled largely around money. The chatter and the buzz were all about land prices and the salaries of the young in tens of thousands per month. I saw enormous disparities in disposable income between the young and the previous generation, the impact on lifestyle and culture significant. The Indian Tiger was roaring and the world was listening.

I asked about the poor in this new economy which had seen the costs of everyday items soar. There was a clear divide in the answers: from those who worked with the poor in development, the lot of the poor was harder; they had not gone away nor had they progressed up the income scale; the cost of living had simply risen faster than their incomes. For the others, the poor, who were less immediately visible, were assumed to be better off. On that first night back, jaded perhaps after a long flight, and caught up in emotion and excitement to be back in India after so long, I wept to see the bodies huddled asleep on pavements, and the same makeshift shelters of woven leaves pressed up against compound walls. Still.

The streetscape too had changed: cows and cycle rickshaws had been shifted out of the central area of the city; the city was much cleaner, although Buckingham Canal still gave off its usual stench. I looked out from the windows of the Tamil Nadu Bar Association one afternoon, trying to capture a photo of a red-capped bird that was calling from a large sprawling tree. Instead, I saw stunningly-beautiful old Mughal buildings at this historic end of the city falling into decay; a small tree had put its roots into some of the fretted red brickwork; another classic building was virtually eclipsed by the drab concrete cube of business offices. I was disappointed and angry. We sat in the dusk one evening, enjoying tea and conversation with a friend, as birds quarrelled in the large old fig trees of the Presidency Club. Nostalgically-clad waiters carried our drinks across the lawn, while foul fumes from the overgrown river running behind this stately old relic of colonialism wafted over us with the evening breeze. In the streets, housewives, servants and children still walked on the edge of pot-holed roads, covered in dust or splashed with mud, depending on the season. Once again, I experienced the same sense of frustration that a country filled with as much wealth and cleverness as India just doesn't fix some things up.

India again

My visit in 2008 was for just a few weeks and crowded with the catch-up conversations I had been saving for too many years. So it was only on the eve of our departure back to Sydney that I managed to go shopping for a few more colourful *churidars* to add to my wardrobe. As I was driven back home in the air-conditioned car through rows of dense peak hour traffic, I had lots of opportunities to observe life by the street-side close up.

At one point, the car paused. Between us and the pavement was another line of traffic. Here, motor bikes and cycles squeezed their way forward, fast enough to pass the rows of cars and buses, but slow enough to wobble their way through the constricted passageway, one foot dangling ready for balance. The pavement itself was less than three metres away. There was a hut there, its walls and roof constructed from woven coconut palms; the only opening, a gap between the fronds. On the dirt outside the hut sat two old women. Before them was a basket of jasmine flowers. I watched them as they sat threading jasmine buds into strings for later sale for women to tie in their hair. Seemingly oblivious to the visible pall of diesel and petrol, and to the blaring sounds of the traffic, they laughed and talked with each other. Were they worrying over their grandchildren? Lamenting a no-good son-in-law? Gossiping about a neighbour? Comparing their aches and pains? Or simply telling each other ribald jokes? One nodded and the other shook her grey head and licked gummy lips. And as our car moved on, I carried their image with me.

In 2007, the women of Grihini, the program in Kodaikanal in which our friends, Jan and Norm, have played (and play) such a creative part, celebrated its twentieth anniversary. This initiative, that had set out to enable young women to gain the literacy, practical skills and confidence to break free and develop a sense of their rights and dignity, had educated women from some of the remotest parts of Tamil Nadu. The venture has succeeded with intertwining of experience from

Australian education, Lutherans, Hindus, Islam, Paolo Freire's ideas, Indian education, local knowledge and Jesuit assistance.

In December 2009, I had the privilege of spending nearly three weeks meeting and talking to the women who had been part of the Grihini program and reporting on the impact it had in their lives. During this time I lived in the Jesuit monastery set amongst old botanical gardens and forest twenty minutes outside the hill-station town of Kodaikanal.

In the company of Grihini leaders, I visited the villages of some of the 1200 women who had completed the program over the years. My companions were a warm cheerful teacher and Director of the program, Dency Michael, the elegant Administrator, Ruth Alexander, and the senior Animator and nurse, Amali. From village to village, we travelled slowly, taking two hours to go just sixty kilometres on the steep winding mountain roads, often eroded by heavy rains. It was winter, the air was crisp, but, during the day, the sun was warm.

In the village of Poombari, where *Dalit* women and their families live in small, low, one-room dwellings without running water (but with government-supplied televisions blaring throughout the day) in a colony separated from the caste part of the township, the women showed me a large cement toilet block. It was due to their efforts, they said, that the authorities had relented and built it. Now the women can bathe with some privacy.

In the village of Gundupatti, twenty-four-year-old Saroja sat on the grass with her toddler daughter and confidently told me how she had been one of those who had helped force the government to build a road into their village, home to Tamils who had been repatriated from Sri Lanka during the troubled 1980s. Now there was a road that linked this remote high-mountain village, a bus that could take villagers to Poombari, some nine precipitous kilometres away, and there link them with transport to hospitals and services in Kodaikanal.

As we approached the village of Moolaiyar, young tribal women greeted us with smiles, flowers and fruit. We climbed by foot up through the stepped tiers of the village perched on the mountainside. The houses were more substantial here than in Poombari: solid brick and concrete, some with a divider between rooms. A white-haired man, the village President, wandered through our meeting. 'The Grihini women', he said, 'they helped us to get good houses. They talked to the politicians and we got them.'

And so, my weeks went on. In that time, I spoke with about seventy women, the poorest of the poor in many ways, but women who were confident, articulate and aware of their rights and power. One thing in particular stood out from their conversations: each of these women was determined that their children would receive a good education. Given that the oldest of these women had an average of only two years' schooling, given that even today many girls, especially in remote areas, are unschooled or drop out early, this was a proud ambition. And the Grihini women had lived up to their words, because I calculated that, on average, *their* children were receiving about seven years' education. In writing this, I can see Renuga, a young woman, seven months pregnant, two toddlers hanging off her worn sari. She had dropped out of school at Year 3; her husband had gone – 'not to return', nodded the older women in the village knowingly. Because of what she had learnt at Grihini, Renuga told me, she keeps her children and house clean and enjoys reading. 'Somehow', she said, 'I will educate my children.' Brave words.

I have no doubt that the Grihini program has continued and served over a thousand women in the Kodai area because Jan and Norm had the humility to respect the wisdom and experience of those with whom they worked. Since 2011, the program has been linked with a community college in the nearby city of Madurai and so graduates' work can be accredited, enabling some students to proceed onto university studies. Not bad for tribal women in this remote area.

While I was in Kodaikanal in 2009, I met up again with Selvi, the cheerful maker of fluffy pancakes in Jan and Norm's home during their stay in India. Since I first met her, she has faced hell. The short and horrible story of this vivacious woman is that, as a young wife, her husband had poured kerosene over her and set her alight. He then abandoned her. Selvi survived. She is traumatised and scarred. One finger melted away in the fire; the rest of her hand is deeply scarred. Nearly twenty years after the fire, her legs have still not healed. For many in her small town, she is regarded with suspicion because her husband abandoned her. She has limited access to her work as a servant because people associate her poor maimed hand as 'dirty'. Her husband has not been charged. Her fear of his vengeance, coupled with her belief that the police will only respond to bribes, have held her back from pressing for prosecution. Selvi's family made a deal with his family so that he would stay away from Selvi and her daughter. She still fears him.

Meanwhile, she has continued to work hard. When I met up with her again, I also met her daughter: a beautiful young woman now completing university studies: a tribute to Selvi's strength, love and determination. Selvi lives her life independently and cheerfully.

And what of the other people in my story?

Manimaran, the active assistant in the Centre, is now a police officer. He finally helped his family build a brick house. When I am in Chennai these days, I look closely at middle-aged policemen on point duty, wondering if I might see him. Rosie, my helper when Mariam was newborn, is married many years now and is probably a grandmother already.

Jamuna, the friend who had worked in adult education, has remained a friend and when we visit Chennai I try to see her. She has retired to her home village, not far from Ambur, on the far outskirts of Chennai. This is a big centre for tanneries and the nearby river has been devastated with pollution from the leather works around about. Jamuna has chosen to live here alone, except for one woman who ssists her. Her mission in her mature years is to bring the river back to

India again

life. In doing this, she is challenging powerful elements in a lucrative industry. I salute her courage.

Ekambaram, who dared to challenge the landlord in the field when Dorai died, worked in the villages on behalf of the poor until his recent death. Did Chinnasamy's sons ever reach America? I don't know.

And what of some of the organisations in my stories?

In Bhopal, the former Union Carbide factory is a rusting derelict. Containers of chemicals still lie around. The light sentences handed down in the court case in June 2010 have left many people dissatisfied. India, according to some, has not yet developed tighter regulation around the mining, production and use of asbestos by her own work force and, twenty years after Bhopal, pesticide poisoning is reported to be the cause of at least 22,000 deaths in India each year.

The Centre where we worked continues on in a reduced way for the present. Negotiations having failed, a court case is under way to rectify the fraud over the land. Benjamin is liaising with various groups in South India about cooperating on joint community development programs. He has a vision to provide accredited training for some of the building trades, such as bricklaying and plumbing, for those unable to study because of finance or access.

Pipal Tree, established by our friend Siddartha, continues to flourish near Bangalore as one of many life-giving centres within India. It is a place of dialogue in a beautiful natural environment which has created space for dialogue on religion, spirituality and personal development.

Now that Benjamin and I are able to return more often to Chennai, we do so with increasing regularity. India is a place where I write, where I find stimulation, in abundance, for poetry and stories – and that, too, is something that I now am able to do more often than when I was busy with a younger family and heavy work responsibilities. But the greatest joy for me in India now is the people. In particular, it is the deep joy of being able, even at this stage, to forge deeper, closer and warmer ties with my immediate family members there, as well as a host of other friends. And while I am relishing these almost-like-new relationships, I grieve a little for the lost years when that was not possible, because of distance or because of busy-ness. Or in my uncertainty, when I came there as a raw, if not so young, bride. Every time I visit India, I feel closer to the family and people of whom I am now part. And, for me, that is wonderful.

And, Benjamin and me? So far, we have survived together, although we continue to be as different as we were when we met in Canada in 1983.

The map

MY DAUGHTER HAS GOOGLED the Earth to me. Mesmerised, I sit before my laptop in western Sydney as a satellite catapults me to India. With my cursor, I locate Chennai where Benjamin and I made our first home. My life spins. Once again it is May, mid-summer Chennai, 1984.

My return to Chennai via Google reminded me of a particular experience during that first visit of mine in 1983. I had wanted to do some shopping, so Benjamin had taken me to a shop which was a marketing outlet for goods produced in village industries. Khadi Gramodyog Bhavan in Chennai was an exotic treasure cavern. It promoted the vision of a home-grown rural Indian industry independent of foreign (British) imports which Mahatma Gandhi had developed in the decades leading up to Independence. It is symbolised by the *charka*, the spinning wheel which occupies the centre of India's flag, the wheel of virtue and of progress. This goal of self-reliance relied heavily on khadi, or homespun cottons, silks and woollens. The store was filled with fabrics and handicrafts. As I stepped into its coolness from the brightness of the pavement outside, my first impression was the woody perfume of sandalwood. It drifted from the brilliantly-hued silks and the other hand-woven cloth and jolted my senses to take in the jewellery, brassware, carved trinkets and goods inlaid with ivory that crammed every corner of the place. The only purchase I remember from that visit was a small elephant attached to a keyring. The elephant was carved from sandalwood and was as fragrant as the incense in the air. When Benjamin saw it, he was excited.

'Rub it', he instructed, placing it under my nostrils. 'The fragrance is refreshed when you rub it.' The carving was quite intricate even though the animal was a mere three centimetres long. It fitted neatly in my hand.

Later, as we made our way through the city streets, passing tea stalls and schools, rickshaw stands and the Mylapore temple, the presence of the sandalwood wafted with us and became something like the spirit of my journey. I was rummaging through a drawer at home in Sydney one day when I come across a little sandalwood elephant keychain. The chain had broken which is probably why it was in the drawer. The wooden body had become a little grubby amongst old textas, paper clips and scrap paper. It was one of many such inexpensive sandalwood souvenirs I have purchased in Chennai over the years. I rubbed the little elephant till it was quite warm and breathed in its perfume.

Scanning the Google globe, I seek out markers in the conglomeration which is modern Chennai: the Marina and its broad boulevard along the ocean front – the scene of the 2004 Boxing Day tsunami tragedy. The Law Courts and the Port are easily visible too, places that are both part of my personal map. I scan south, find the Adyar River and the Theosophical Society on the Adyar's southern bank, its sprawling grounds and large trees a green oasis in the urban map of multiple greys. On then, along Lattice Bridge Road where I walked to find air, exercise and household necessities. I am excited as I approach the neighbourhood where we lived for over three years.

The bakery on the corner just where we used to turn into 1st Main Road Indira Nagar is not discernible. Is it still there? Four

The map

rupees for a small, frail, sweet loaf of 'modern bread' seemed an indulgence, but it was bread, and the only bread sold locally. Supposedly inspired by Australian know-how, it suffered in translation. I detour briefly from the map to seek out the bakery elsewhere on Google and discover it has multiplied itself into a chain of sixteen plate-glass fronted air-conditioned establishments across the city.

I guide my laptop to the rural areas outside the city. Once again, I am making the forty minute journey north beyond the city through the shabby roadside market town of Red Hills. Turn left here a little beyond the town and travel on a narrow, sharp-edged bitumen strip beside the dry river bed. Over many wet seasons, swollen waters have gouged deep ravines in the river's banks, threatening the ancient trees along the roadside and the huts clustered nearby.

The giant tamarind trees that were a legacy from generations many decades past, and whose careful planting shaded hot and dusty travellers, have been torn out to make way for a wider road for the trucks that now feed sprawling warehouses and acre-wide steel sheds. The Google image must be a few years old because the home built by my brother-in-law and his wife near this spot is not visible.

On my laptop, sand-coloured river beds snake through a landscape mosaic of velvety green, dark blood reds, rust, greys and fawn in tiny irregular swatches. Emerald crops of rice contrast with ripening saffron of the cereal ragi. I search for familiar villages and sprawling shallow lakes. My husband's village is there, and his childhood home, where the well waters are sweeter and softer than any other I have known. Adjacent to the family home is the local school, and behind that a lake. I tilt the view on the screen so that I am looking laterally towards the horizon. And, as I discover that the landscape is as flat as I remember, I am swamped again with the homesickness I felt twenty years ago for the undulating familiarity of my native Hunter Valley.

I scan further, and I am back in a dusty green bus listing drunkenly on its way to another village further north. I travelled this way often. Villagers crowd the bus – women on the left, men on the right, a mixed remnant jammed in the middle. Our fellow-travellers are returning from the city or from Red Hills, from meetings with bankers, lawyers, family or doctors; sellers of fish, of flowers, of vegetables; gatherers of household or business provisions. Many look weary, and we are all hot, grateful that while the bus moves, a breeze fans through the unglassed windows. There is cargo aboard, carried on in large sacks, woven bags or fluoro plastic baskets. The driver blasts the horn with random frequency as we pass pedestrians, cyclists, ponderous bullock carts with teetering loads of hay and an occasional car. The bus makes many shuddering stops along the way, and lurches off again, each time leaving a choking halo of diesel fumes.

We leave the bus at the shallow strip of houses and shops along the bus route which is Palavakkam village. We alight at a flimsy tea shop with its rough wooden counter. The steaming aroma of the milk being scalded in a large copper vessel for tea and coffee awakens comforting memories of childhood bedtimes a lifetime away in Australia. We need to walk about two kilometres east of the village along an unsealed road which is a map of many lives. Daily, women pad on toughened feet away from the village in search of firewood. They return late, having trekked for kilometres, bearing on their heads bundles of twigs and kindling. Young children tend goats or geese. When there is water in the tank which the road passes, old men and young boys will fish. When the lake is dry, much of its water evaporated by the fierce sun, villagers will use it as a cottage garden.

The land that in 1983 was red, flat and gravelly is now thick with trees. The well we dug is there and the solid brick training centre still stands. Each tree there was planted by hand, watered by hand, and protected by a hedge of thorn from the ravages of the passing goats.

Skimming the key pad of my laptop I swoop over places I have travelled. From this familiar detail, I move back to scan the great sub-continent in its entirety. From space, India is a pendant of marbled greens and browns suspended off the vast European continent

The map

which fits snugly like a cap on the skull of the globe. Tamil Nadu rests across the most southern part of India. The Bay of Bengal laps grey-blue waters against Tamil Nadu on the east. The Eastern Ghats rise up to the north of the state, and the Nilgiri, Anamalai and Palakkad Hills embrace the state from the west. Sri Lanka is a jewelled tear drop resting in the Palk Strait off the south Indian state of Tamil Nadu. The shallow waters between the two nations shine turquoise crystal.

Mountain ranges, rivers, highways, footpaths and flightpaths crisscross the surface of the map. It is a network of major cities and over 500,000 villages. But the subdued earth colours on my screen are a disguise. Underneath this disguise, the real map of India is a kaleidoscope: of music, movies, food, languages, dress, histories, politics, cultures and religions. The stories of this map are interwoven and layered upon each other; they collide, diverge and fuse into a fantasy of colour.

It is a map of a billion lives. In this context, my story is infinitesimal. I am reminded of a Tamil proverb that goes:

> What we have learnt is a handful of sand.
> What we have not learnt is as big as this world.[20]

'And how do you like India?' The question is put with a smile. The South Indian looks at me, head to one side, waiting on my answer; I sense that he expects me to reply with a large smile and a one-word 'Wonderful'. It is impossible for me to respond that way. Besides, the man is – like every other Indian I have met – so proud of his country that I like to tease him a little with my reply.

It is a question that I have been asked, and continue to be asked, many times. In attempting to answer the question honestly, I think first of my husband and the world into which he invited me; I think of

---

[20] Proverb quoted by Kala Ramesh, Director, World Haiku Festival, Bangalore, India 2008.

the warmth and companionship I found in friends and family; I think of the complexity of India's history, politics and cultures; I marvel at her wealth in talent and resources, and the enormity of the challenges that she faces year after year; I try to fathom the spirit of India in her resilience, diversity, contradictions and unpredictability; I weep with the pain of her people; I rail at her torturous bureaucracy and the obduracy of politics; I am confounded by the scale of everything in India.

Besides, India has become far more personal to me: it is the place to which I went as a bride and where I bore my first child; a vast land to which I travelled as a stranger; India has shaped my husband and who he is; it is the home of my family, my children's family and of friends; India invited me into the intimacy of its poverty and brokenness. I went to India as a blank sheet for those who met me: a person without a village, without a history, without a family. And I was accepted for who I was. In the few years of my time there, I lived through events that were traumatic both for me and for India. In many ways, I have never left India, even though I live in another country because the experience of living there has redefined who I am and how I see myself.

So, there is no one-word answer to the question, 'How do you like India?' I went to India expecting to find mystics, crowded streets and poverty. I found crowded streets and poverty, and much more. I found a country that startled my senses and shook my preconceptions. I did not find the meditative quiet mysticism I had conjured up from afar. Instead, I found mysticism, unexpectedly, by the side of the rutted street. One evening, I watched a woman as she emerged from the nearby slum. She carried a small child to a crude shrine fashioned from old bricks by the side of the street. Together they stood, silent silhouettes against the dusk. The clay lamps burning before the Ganesh figure reflected on their faces. Sandalwood incense rose in the windless night. On the woman's face was a weary tenderness. And the child's face glowed with wonder.

The map

This book is my attempt at a response to the question of how I like India. Through writing this, I have begun to understand a little bit more of what I was experiencing.

There was immense advantage living in India with a local, especially with one as large, as intelligent, energetic and networked as Benjamin, my personal *Googleji* – I had a ready-made interpreter, introduction agency, travel and tourist guide, and other advantages that came with the territory. If there was a disadvantage in this arrangement, it was that it was very easy for me to rely, both on his introductions and his interpretations. I didn't have the discomfort of queuing to buy my own ticket in the ladies compartment on a train to Mumbai, for example, but I didn't learn this skill either.

Through him, I was able to meet people from across a very wide spectrum. Consequently, I lived *in* India, not on the fringe. Over the years, I have needed to learn to distinguish between India and my husband. What is India? What is Benjamin? It has taken me years to distinguish the two. But he is *not* India, even if there were times when I thought he knew everyone of her one billion inhabitants. I have begun to sort out Benjamin the person from Benjamin the man from India. Often, however, he still leaves me guessing.

I have learnt that relationships need to be worked at. One might fall in love in the first instance, but life together is a process of choosing to be with the other, on his side. For this reason, I have no difficulty with arranged marriages – not that ours was one – but it is a system which brings to the seriousness of marriage strong support from the couple's families.

Saffron is the colour of mysticism, the colour worn by Buddhist monks and Hindu ascetics. It is the colour of the upper band of the Indian national flag, a colour added to the flag, almost at the last minute, to represent 'sacrifice' and 'salvation'. It is also the most expensive of spices. Tiny hairlike threads from the saffron crocus are used in lengths of barely a centimetre for special rice dishes. A few rich red saffron threads transform a large vessel of rice from white to warm yellow. So too my life in India: I touched such a small part of this large country and people. My whole life has been transformed.

So I have an answer now.

'Tell me, how did you like India?' The question is always put with a smile. The South Indian looks at me, shaking his head from side to side, waiting on my answer.

'It's like saffron', I say. I too am smiling. 'It has changed my life.'

Anne Benjamin is a Sydney-based writer and educator with roots in the Hunter Valley of NSW and strong links with South India.

Her writing includes tanka, tanka prose, poems and fiction published in journals and anthologies in Australia, Japan, UK, New Zealand, USA and Canada, including anthologies from the Montreal Poetry Prize (2011) and the ACU Literary Prize (2014).

She has directed two nationally-awarded curriculum projects and co-edited a monograph on education in 2008. She has published numerous academic papers on education, leadership and ministry.

In 2016, *Gemstones*, an anthology of tanka written in collaboration with eight other international poets was published by the UK-based Skylark Publications.

Anne is an experienced academic, teacher and education consultant. She has authored or co-authored nearly 40 significant reviews in Australia and internationally. For 16 years, she held senior administrative roles within education in Western Sydney, including university governance, involvement in NSW government education boards and committees, and for nine years was Executive Director of 75 schools in the Catholic Diocese of Parramatta in Western Sydney.

She has a number of new writing projects under way.

www.ingramcontent.com/pod-product-compliance
Lightning Source LLC
Chambersburg PA
CBHW031105080526
44587CB00011B/830